THE DISABLED HIKER'S GUIDE TO WESTERN WASHINGTON AND OREGON

HELP US KEEP THIS GUIDE UP TO DATE

Every effort has been made by the author and editors to make this guide as accurate and useful as possible. However, many things can change after a guide is published—trails are rerouted, regulations change, techniques evolve, facilities come under new management, etc.

We appreciate hearing from you concerning your experiences with this guide and how you feel it could be improved and kept up to date. While we may not be able to respond to all comments and suggestions, we'll take them to heart and we'll also make certain to share them with the author. Please send your comments and suggestions to editorial@falcon.com.

Thanks for your input, and happy trails!

THE DISABLED HIKER'S GUIDE TO WESTERN WASHINGTON AND OREGON

OUTDOOR ADVENTURES ACCESSIBLE BY
CAR, WHEELCHAIR, AND ON FOOT

Syren Nagakyrie

FALCONGUIDES

ESSEX, CONNECTICUT

For Jen
And all the hikes I wish we could take

FALCONGUIDES®

An Imprint of The Rowman & Littlefield Publishing Group, Inc.
4501 Forbes Blvd., Ste. 200
Lanham, MD 20706
www.rowman.com

Falcon and FalconGuides are registered trademarks and Make Adventure Your Story is a trademark of The Rowman & Littlefield Publishing Group, Inc.

Distributed by NATIONAL BOOK NETWORK

Copyright © 2022 Syren Nagakyrie

Photos by Syren Nagakyrie

Maps by Melissa Baker © The Rowman & Littlefield Publishing Group, Inc.

British Library Cataloguing in Publication Information available
Library of Congress Cataloging-in-Publication Data

Names: Nagakyrie, Syren, author.
Title: The disabled hiker's guide to Western Washington and Oregon :
   outdoor adventures accessible by car, wheelchair, and on foot / Syren Nagakyrie.
Description: Guilford, Connecticut : FalconGuides, [2022] | Identifiers: LCCN 2022009237 (print)
   | LCCN 2022009238 (ebook) | ISBN 9781493057856 (Paperback : acid-free paper) |
   ISBN 9781493057863 (ePub)
Subjects: LCSH: Hiking for people with disabilities—Washington (State),
   Western—Guidebooks. | Hiking for people with disabilities—Oregon—Guidebooks.
Classification: LCC GV199.56 N33 2022 (print) | LCC GV199.56 (ebook) |
   DDC 796.51087/3—dc23/eng/20220406
LC record available at https://lccn.loc.gov/2022009237
LC ebook record available at https://lccn.loc.gov/2022009238

∞™ The paper used in this publication meets the minimum requirements of American National Standard for Information Sciences—Permanence of Paper for Printed Library Materials, ANSI/NISO Z39.48-1992.

CONTENTS

THE HIKES

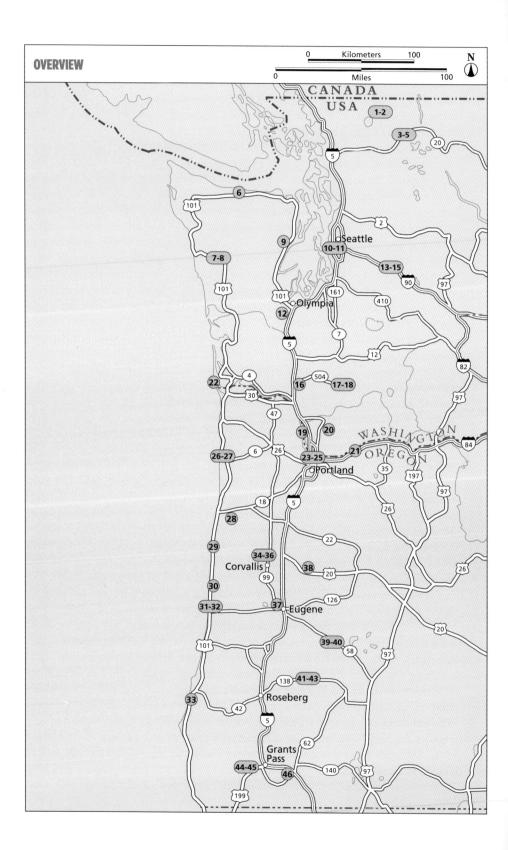

ACKNOWLEDGMENTS

Thank you to the Disabled Hikers community—this book exists because of and for you. I also have immense appreciation for our many partners who have committed to creating a more accessible outdoors. Deep gratitude to the Indigenous peoples of this region—thank you for sharing information with me to create the land acknowledgments in this book.

Thank you to my friends, patrons, and backers for your support and encouragement. This book was written under incredibly challenging circumstances and I couldn't have done it without you. Special thanks to Kali and Lupa, who helped me with the project when I needed it most. Thanks to my first readers and field testers for your feedback. And, of course, thank you to my family for believing in me.

MEET YOUR GUIDE

Syren Nagakyrie is the founder of Disabled Hikers, a disability-led organization building community, access, and justice in the outdoors. Syren has multiple disabilities and chronic illnesses and is neurodivergent. They have loved the outdoors since childhood, but a lack of information made access very difficult. Inspired by the beauty and diversity of the Pacific Northwest, Syren founded Disabled Hikers and began writing trail guides in 2018. They created a unique trail rating system called the Spoon Rating. Syren also leads group hikes and other events in the Pacific Northwest and beyond.

They believe that guidebook authors have a responsibility to give context on their ability, because ability influences the way we share information. Syren is primarily ambulatory with the use of a mobility aid, including a wheelchair periodically. They are generally able to hear, speak, and see clearly. A typical hike for Syren ranges from 1 to 3 miles, though they can do 4 to 6 miles followed by severe fatigue.

The information provided in this book is written as objectively as possible, and the author has tried to consider all types of disabilities and access needs. Given the incredible diversity of people with disabilities, the author recognizes that this information may be inadequate for some people.

You may contact the author through DisabledHikers.com.

BEFORE YOU HEAD OUT

This guide is designed to provide you with as much information as you may need to decide whether to attempt a trail. If you are someone who needs all of the information, read the entire chapter. If you just want a quick summary, then the opening overview, stats, and spoon rating should provide all you need. Below is an explanation of each section, what they mean, and how they were measured.

WHY GO?

This section provides a general description of the trail and highlights some of what you may experience. It also makes note of general trail design aspects to be aware of, such as traveling along a rocky cliff or making a water crossing.

THE RUNDOWN

The Spoon Rating System

The spoon rating is a system to identify how much effort a trail might take. The rating system is based in an understanding of Spoon Theory by Christine Miserandino (a metaphor for the energy rationing that many disabled and chronically ill people have to do). It offers a representation of how accessible a hike is and how much effort it may take with consideration for how replenishing the experience may be. You may think of it as a combination accessibility, difficulty, and quality rating.

Any one factor within a rating can shift without changing the overall rating. For example, a 5-mile-long trail with gentle elevation changes may be rated at 3 spoons, while a 3-mile-long trail with rocky terrain and steep grades may be rated at 5 spoons. Elevation, grade, trail surface, and location (front country vs. backcountry) have been generally weighed most heavily. Grades have been measured for trail lengths of 5 feet or more. In the rating system, a short grade is typically under 10 feet, a prolonged grade is over 30 feet.

Wheelchair accessibility has been determined based upon established accessibility guidelines, including the Architectural Barriers Act, Americans with Disabilities Act, and US Forest Service guidelines, as well as my personal experience. However, since the effort that wheelchair-accessible trails require can vary, and accessibility is influenced by the type of equipment used and the user's experience, it has been included as a factor in the rating system. Trails that meet all guidelines and would be accessible to most wheelchair users are listed in the Trail Finder as "ADA accessible" (a somewhat inaccurate term used for simplicity). For all other trails, "wheelchair accessible" means it is accessible to most wheelchair users with caution or assistance. "Wheelchair hikeable" means it may be accessible to experienced outdoor wheelchair users with adaptive equipment.

Since each person's ability and energy level is different and can change from day to day, I cannot tell you how difficult a trail might be for you—only you can decide that. The spoon rating, in combination with the thorough information provided in the guide, is meant to help you decide whether to attempt a trail, but it is not definitive. You may find trails that meet your particular needs in different ratings.

1 Spoon = 0–2 miles, level and even with grades under 8%, paved, very easy to navigate, probably wheelchair accessible

2 Spoons = 1–3 miles, short grades up to 12%, firm but unpaved surface with no obstacles, access takes a little planning, probably wheelchair hikeable

3 Spoons = 2–4 miles, generally gentle elevation changes with short grades up to 20%, firm surface with minimal obstacles, possibly wheelchair hikeable

4 Spoons = 3–5 miles, prolonged grades of 10–15%, elevation changes over 500 feet or longer than 0.5 mile, soft surface with obstacles, requires advance planning or basic trail map reading

5 Spoons = 5+ miles, prolonged grades of 15–20%, elevation changes 1,000 feet or longer than 1 mile, trail has many obstacles, requires extensive planning or navigation

Type

This gives the layout of the trail. There are generally two types in this book: an out-and-back or a loop.

An out-and-back trail starts and ends at the same point and returns on the same route you went out on; you hike the same route in both directions. Read the hike description with this in mind—it means that all inclines will be declines on the way back and you'll have to cross difficult sections twice, for example.

A loop trail starts and ends at the same point, but returns on a different route. It can use multiple trails to form a loop, but in this guide loops are typically single trails that roughly circle a particular feature, such as a lake. The description follows the entire loop and will give you the direction of travel. Some loops may be easier for you to travel in the opposite direction given; a note has been made if this seems likely.

A lollipop loop is a variation of a loop trail. It combines an out-and-back section with a loop. You start and end at the same point but will travel out on one trail, then connect with the loop trail. You finish the loop at the same point where you began, and then return on the same trail you came in on.

Distance

The distance is given for the entire length of the trail. For a loop, it represents the length of the entire hike start to finish. For an out-and-back, it represents the total hike from the start, to the recommended turnaround point, and back. Many trails in this book continue beyond the recommended turnaround point, so you may see different mileages given in different sources. Distance has been recorded using a GPS trail application, and compared with topographic maps, official trail listings, and other resources when available. However, recordings can be impacted by a number of factors, and sources may disagree on the mileage. In these cases, I have made a best estimate.

Elevation and Elevation Gain

The numbers given here represent the starting elevation above sea level, and the total elevation gained on the hike. If you have breathing difficulties, or you are used to only being near sea level, you may feel more shortness of breath at elevations above 3,000 feet due to slightly lower air pressure. Consult your doctor if you have concerns about being at higher elevations. With a few exceptions, most of the trails in this book are below 3,000 feet.

Many of the trails in this guide take rolling grades, and elevation gain seldom occurs at a steady rate.

Elevation has been recorded using a GPS trail application, and compared with trail listings, topographic maps, and other measurements when available.

Max Grade

The grade represents the steepness of a trail. Expressed as a percentage, it represents the amount of elevation gained over a length of trail, or rise over run. For example, a typical wheelchair ramp is a maximum 8.33% grade; a 15% grade is almost twice as steep as a typical wheelchair ramp.

The max grade listed is the steepest section of the trail that is longer than 5 feet. The length of a grade greatly affects the amount of effort it takes; for example, a 5% grade for 100 feet may feel more difficult than a 15% grade for 20 feet. However, even a short, steep grade may make a trail inaccessible. Only you can decide how steep of a trail is appropriate for you, and it may take some trial and error to figure it out.

Grades were measured using a handheld clinometer and compared with GPS recordings and topographic maps. It is impossible to record grades that are 100% accurate without technical computerized equipment, so in many cases I have averaged several measurements along a section of trail, or made a best estimate based upon measurements and personal experience.

Max Cross-Slope

The cross-slope is the steepness of a trail on the horizontal axis; i.e., the grade of the surface from the inside to the outside of a section of trail. A steep cross-slope requires more effort to hike, and may be difficult if you have problems with balance, sensory motor control, or a difference in length of limbs. A cross-slope steeper than 2% is considered not wheelchair accessible, though some wheelchair users may be able to navigate a 5% cross-slope, depending on the terrain and your equipment.

Typical Width

This is the width of the trail for the greatest distance. A trail that is narrower than 2 feet will allow people to travel single file, and passing will be difficult. A trail must be a minimum of 3 feet to be wheelchair accessible. A trail 4 feet or wider will be the most comfortable for passing or traveling as a group.

Typical Surface

This is the material of the trail that you will be traveling on for the greatest distance. It may be paved, compact gravel, or natural. Natural surface means it has been unimproved other than creating the trail. The surface will be a combination of dirt and other natural elements depending on the terrain, and will likely have roots, rocks, and wet or muddy sections.

Trail Users

Who will you share the trail with? I have tried to stick to hiker-only trails as much as possible, but there are some mixed-use trails in the book. This can include trail runners, mountain bikers, or horseback riders. These other users may be traveling much faster than you, so you should always be alert. On mixed-use trails, bikers yield to hikers and everyone yields to horseback riders. However, this etiquette is not always followed, and you may need to yield the trail regardless of other users.

A note on wheelchairs and Other Power-Driven Mobility Devices (OPDMD) on trails: Generally speaking, any device that is designed for use by someone with a mobility disability and is also suitable for indoor use is allowed on public trails, unless the land manager has conducted a formal assessment to prove that such devices pose a safety risk. This includes devices such as track chairs and other motorized wheelchairs. In some instances, OPDMD such as golf carts and segways, and self-powered devices such as handcycle bikes, may be allowed. More information about these rules is in the resource section.

Season/Schedule

This lists the time of year that the area is open. However, some trails may be too difficult or dangerous during certain seasons, so the best season to visit is provided. For areas with designated opening and closing hours, that schedule is provided. Schedules and seasons can change depending on the weather and other factors, so always confirm before heading out.

Water Availability

Water availability describes any reliable source of water. Surface water (i.e., from creeks, rivers, or lakes) should always be filtered with a water filtration device designed specifically for outdoor use. Water sources can vary greatly, and often dry up in the summer, so confirm with the land manager if you intend to rely on surface water for your hike. Details about the water source are provided in the description.

Special Notes

These are any special points to be aware of, particularly around access and terrain. For example, there may be a note about the number of stairs or a rocky cliff.

Amenities

This lists comfort stations that are available at the trailhead or along the trail, such as tables, benches, water fountains, and toilets. ADA accessible features will also be listed.

Dog-Friendly

This describes whether pets are allowed on the trail, and under which conditions (leashed or unleashed but under control at all times). I've also mentioned whether it is recommended to bring a pet—some trails technically allow them, but aren't suitable for a variety of reasons.

Service animals are allowed on all trails and recreation sites, inside buildings, and anywhere else their handler goes, even if pets are not allowed. Service animals are trained to perform one or more specific tasks related to a person's disability, and their access is protected by the ADA. Emotional support animals and therapy animals do not qualify as service animals.

Cell Phone Reception

This is provided so that you know whether or not you'll be "off grid." It is up to you whether you go outdoors to escape technology or need to stay connected for safety, comfort, or potential emergencies. Cell reception can vary depending on network and weather conditions, and even when it is available it can be spotty. You should always tell someone where you are going and have a plan in case of emergencies. You may want to consider a personal locator beacon or other GPS device.

Nearest Town

The nearest town or city where you will have access to basic services such as gas, restrooms, and food is provided. Medical services may not be available in small towns, and the hours of other services may be limited.

Land Manager

The land manager is the entity that is primarily responsible for the trail or recreation site. It is typically a national forest, national park, or state park. Contact information is provided so that you can inquire about current conditions, closures, fee requirements, etc.

Pass/Entry Fee

Passes or day-use fees are required at most national parks, developed national forest recreation sites, and all Washington state parks and state-managed developed recreation sites. Only a few Oregon state parks and recreation sites require fees. However, there are plenty of exceptions to this rule, so the type of pass or entry fee is listed for each hike. Always display the pass in your vehicle—do not carry it with you.

In general, two passes cover the vast majority of the hikes in this book: the America the Beautiful Interagency Pass and the Washington Discover Pass. If you have a permanent disability, you can receive a free lifetime America the Beautiful pass, called the Access Pass, which grants entry to all national parks, national monuments, and national forests, and offers a discount on camping and some other fees. More information is provided in the resources section.

The Washington Discover Pass is valid at all Washington state parks and all Washington Department of National Resources, Washington Department of Fish and Wildlife, and other state-managed lands. Washington state residents with a temporary or permanent disability, and disabled veterans with a 30% or greater service-connected disability rating, can receive a pass that grants free entry and discounts on camping and other services at state parks. A Discover Pass is still required for all other state-managed lands.

Many land managers in the region are moving towards implementing day-use permitting and reservations at popular sites. None of those sites are included in this book because it creates another barrier to access, but always verify pass requirements—the fines can be hefty.

Land Acknowledgment

Recognizing the Indigenous peoples of a place and their connection and stewardship with the land is an important practice. The land acknowledgment names the Tribe(s) whose traditional lands include the place where the hike is located. Native place names and other points of cultural significance are included when appropriate. This information has been provided or verified by the Tribe whenever possible. If information is not publicly available, then the land acknowledgement has been left out. More information about the Indigenous peoples of the region is included in the opening sections. I have made my best effort to ensure the accuracy of this information, but summarizing 10,000 years of Indigenous history and 500 years of settlement and colonization is a difficult task for a hiking guide. Please use this as a starting point for your own research.

Finding the Trailhead: Getting There

Detailed directions to the trailhead or for the scenic drive are provided from an easily located starting point, typically the nearest town. I've also provided a description of the roadway—whether it is a highway, two-lane paved road, or single-lane dirt road—and any things to be aware of such as potholes or hidden curves. All of the trailheads in this book can be reached by a standard passenger car (I got to all of them in a Prius); however, some may require careful driving on unimproved dirt roads. In wet or snowy weather, these roads may be impassable without a four-wheel-drive and/or high-clearance vehicle. Many roads through popular recreation areas are closed in winter or during the spring melt or periods of heavy rain. You can verify road closures on TripCheck.com.

The directions are as detailed and accurate as possible so that you can follow them using your car's odometer. However, odometer readings can vary among vehicles, so important landmarks and junctions are provided when available. Most of these trailheads can be easily located on smartphone map services, but they can be unreliable in remote areas and depend on good cell reception. You may be able to download the map area to your phone from the map service.

I've also included information on the parking area, including surface and the number of parking spots, especially designated accessible parking. Small parking areas at popular sites can fill quickly on weekends, though accessible parking is usually available if provided.

Public transit options are provided when available. With a little planning, many trailheads are accessible without a vehicle, and efforts are being made to enhance public transit services to trailheads.

Start

This is a short summary of the starting location for the hike.

The Hike

Every trail description is a step-by-step or roll-by-roll guide. Broken down to as little as every one-tenth mile, it should provide a tour of the entire trail from start to finish. Read it ahead of time to decide whether to attempt the trail, then bring it with you so you know what to expect up ahead. The descriptions focus less on providing information about the flora and fauna of a place—there are many guides already available that provide that information—but I have included unique and remarkable things to be attentive to, and some information about the ecosystem and other relevant natural features.

Many of the trails offer options that may be more or less accessible; for example, by changing the length, taking a side trip, or traveling in a different direction. Some trails may have an accessible portion. This information has been included in each description, and the trail will be listed in the Trail Finder under each applicable rating.

Detailed information is also provided for every scenic drive and viewpoint, with turn-by-turn directions, optional side trips, and information about accessibility. Because the guidelines for wheelchair accessible trails are so specific, those descriptions provide a little less detail but still cover directions, what you'll experience, and anything to be aware of.

Maps

Maps illustrating the specific route are included for each hike, and they are as accurate as possible. I have tried to avoid the need for purchasing multiple maps, so the trails in this book are all generally well marked and easy to follow, and detailed map reading or navigation should not be required.

Your smartphone should be an adequate GPS device for the trails in this book. Always download a map to use offline—never rely on having cell reception.

Additional maps and brochures are typically available for free at the respective land managers. Check at national park and state park entrance stations and national forest visitor centers. Even tourism visitor centers usually stock maps for nearby recreation areas.

Elevation Profiles

Elevation profiles are provided to give you a visual representation of the length and grade of elevation changes. You can view these as a graph, with points representing elevation points on the trail. However, they shouldn't be viewed as an exact replica of the steepness of the trail. For example, a 10% grade will look steeper on a shorter trail than a longer one.

Happy Creek Nature Trail

INTRODUCTION

Western Washington and Oregon offer an incredible diversity of ecosystems. Old-growth temperate rain forest, craggy mountain peaks, stunning beaches, active volcanoes, and fertile river valleys define the region, making the area one of the top recreation spots in the country. You can visit the ocean, the rain forest, and the mountains all in a single day.

Of course, this popularity has had an impact, and outdoor recreation has been experiencing a boom in the past several years. While land managers and outdoor enthusiasts scramble to figure out how to adapt to increased use, many communities get left behind, including Disabled communities. Improving access to outdoor recreation is often viewed as a way to (a) make the experience less authentic for outdoor enthusiasts, and (b) make it too easy for people to enjoy the outdoors, thus bringing in more people.

But improving accessibility benefits everyone. That includes access to information. While this book is written specifically for people who are disabled, chronically ill, or otherwise face access barriers to the outdoors, my hope is that non-disabled people will also recognize the importance of detailed, objective trail information. We all need information to decide whether or not to attempt a trail, and it should be easily available.

This book was written during the most challenging season in recent history—a pandemic, which closed many sites while also encouraging more people to get outdoors; record-breaking wildfires, which altered many places for the foreseeable future; and major snowstorms, which also left many areas with severe damage. For the first time, many people who typically do not have to think about access were faced with unclear information and questions about whether or not they would be able to access their favorite places. As more of these changes take place, the experience of non-disabled hikers is going to more closely resemble that of disabled hikers. It is the perfect time to think more about accessibility in the outdoors, and who better to learn about access from than Disabled people?

I've always loved nature, but it took a long time for me to feel comfortable doing outdoor recreation. A lack of information that met my needs, limited understanding and acceptance of disability in the outdoors, and not seeing any other disabled people represented in the community all contributed to feeling excluded from outdoor recreation. It just didn't feel like something that was meant for me. But nature has always offered a sense of belonging even when I felt excluded otherwise.

This book is designed to remove one of the barriers to experiencing the outdoors for people with disabilities: a lack of information written by disabled people for disabled people. I have attempted to include factors that are left out of other guides. Wheelchair accessibility has been expanded to include trails that meet standard accessibility guidelines and trails that may be hikeable for experienced hikers who use wheelchairs or have all terrain equipment. Not all wheelchairs, or wheelchair users, are the same! Information on foot hiking trails have also been expanded to include the broad variety of people who are ambulatory and may or may not use mobility aids. I've also included scenic drives and viewpoints for people who want or need to experience the outdoors from their vehicles. That is a valid and sometimes necessary way to get outdoors—especially on the days when you don't have the spoons for a hike! The overarching intent of this guide is to provide you with information so you can make your own decision about what you want to attempt.

The conditions under which this guide was written definitely impacted the places included in the book. There are areas that I could not include and popular sites that were inaccessible during this writing. Hopefully, future editions can include some of these locations. However, every location in this guide was selected for a reason—its beauty, opportunity to experience something unique, historical and cultural significance, or accessibility—and they each offer a significant "reward" to be worth the effort. I've tried to select a variety of hikes in every area to meet the needs of the most people. Unfortunately, as you may already know, there is a significant lack of trails that are suitable for disabled hikers in most areas—especially for people who are Blind, Autistic, or have other sensory or developmental disabilities. All of the hikes may not be accessible to you, but my hope is that something in this guide will offer you a new and meaningful experience.

With a little preparation, hiking opportunities abound year-round in the Pacific Northwest, given the variety of elevations and ecosystems. Summer is typically dry and warm, and wildfire season is becoming longer with more campfire bans, so you will need to plan ahead if you're camping. But the mountains burst into color with summer wildflowers, and extreme tides uncover tide pools on the coast. Winter can be wet and cold, and you will need to prepare for standing water and slippery conditions, but low-elevation hikes can offer an entirely different experience in the winter than the dry summers. The coast offers incredible storm watching (always from a safe distance!) at this time.

The shoulder seasons of spring and fall are really some of the best hiking in the area. Spring is typically muddy, but the creeks and waterfalls are usually at maximum flow, offering a glimpse of the astounding power of water in the Pacific Northwest. Fall usually brings the first rain showers in months, and the forest suddenly seems to come alive in a final burst of green before putting on an encore of fall colors.

I hope this guide helps you to get out there and enjoy this beautiful area. You belong outdoors.

TRAIL FINDER

SCENIC DRIVES AND VIEWPOINTS

8. Quinault Lakeshore Scenic Drive
14. Meadowbrook Farm
19. Ridgefield Wildlife Refuge Auto Tour
29. Yaquina Head Outstanding Natural Area
33. Coquille River Scenic Drive
36. Mary's Peak
41. The Waterfall Highway Scenic Drive

ADA ACCESSIBLE

1. Picture Lake
5. Happy Creek Nature Trail
11. Sqebeqsed Trail (partial)
12. McLane Creek Nature Trail (partial)
15. Gold Creek Pond
16. Silver Lake Wetland Haven Trail
19. Ridgefield Wildlife Refuge Auto Tour
20. Moulton Falls Regional Park (partial)
23. Marine Park
24. Bristlecone Pine Trail
26. Old Growth Cedar Preserve
27. Kilchis Point Reserve
29. Yaquina Head Outstanding Natural Area (partial)
30. Thor's Well and Spouting Horn (partial)
31. Sutton Creek Loop (partial)
32. Darlingtonia State Natural Site
35. Jackson-Frazier Wetland
37. Alton Baker Park

1 SPOON

1. Picture Lake
5. Happy Creek Nature Trail
12. McLane Creek Nature Trail
14. Meadowbrook Farm
15. Gold Creek Pond
16. Silver Lake Wetland Haven Trail

20. Moulton Falls Regional Park
23. Marine Park
24. Bristlecone Pine Trail
26. Old Growth Cedar Preserve
27. Kilchis Point Reserve
29. Yaquina Head Outstanding Natural Area
30. Thor's Well and Spouting Horn
32. Darlingtonia State Natural Site
35. Jackson-Frazier Wetland
37. Alton Baker Park

2 SPOONS
3. Trail of the Cedars
6. Marymere Falls
7. Quinault Loop
9. Big Creek Nature Trail
11. Sqebeqsed Trail
13. Cottonwood Loop
20. Moulton Falls Regional Park
25. Redwood Loop
31. Sutton Creek Loop
45. Limpy Creek Botanical Area

3 SPOONS
2. Bagley Lakes
4. Thunder Creek
10. Discovery Park Loop
18. June Lake
22. Coastal Forest Trail
34. Calloway Creek Loop
42. Wolf Creek Falls
46. East Applegate Ridge Trail

4 SPOONS
2. Bagley Lakes
7. Quinault Loop Trail
13. Cottonwood Loop
21. Pool of the Winds
28. Drift Creek Falls
36. Mary's Peak
39. Deception Creek
43. Toketee Falls

5 SPOONS

6. Marymere Falls
17. Devil's Point
38. McDowell Creek Falls
40. Larison Creek
44. Rainie Falls

PUBLIC TRANSIT ACCESSIBLE

6. Marymere Falls
10. Discovery Park Loop
11. Sqebeqsed Trail
13. Cottonwood Loop
14. Meadowbrook Farm
24. Bristlecone Pine Trail
25. Redwood Loop

MAP LEGEND

Municipal

≡(15)≡ Freeway/Interstate Highway

≡(62)≡ US Highway

≡(137)≡ State Road

≡(410)≡ County/Paved/Improved Road

= = = = Unpaved Road

├──•──┤ Railroad

───── Leader Line

Trails

------ Featured Trail

------ Trail or Fire Road

Water Features

Body of Water

Marsh/Swamp

River/Creek

Intermittent Stream

Spring

Waterfall

Land Management

National Park/Forest

State/County Park

National Monument/
Wilderness Area

Symbols

▬ Bench

⊃⊂ Bridge

■ Building/Point of Interest

▲ Campground

∩ Cave

•─• Gate

▬ Inn/Lodging

▲× Mountain/Peak/Elevation

P Parking

⊃⊂ Pass/Gap

Picnic Area

Ranger Station/Park Office

Restroom

Scenic View/Overlook

‖‖‖‖ Steps/Boardwalk

○ Towns/Cities

(21) Trailhead

? Visitor/Information Center

♿ Wheelchair Accessible

WASHINGTON NORTHERN CASCADES

The Northern Cascades is generally defined as the region around North Cascades National Park and Mount Baker. Perhaps most recognizable for craggy peaks and alpine lakes, it is home to an incredible diversity of rare plants, ancient cedars, mountain goats, pika, and more.

Life in this area was defined by the rivers and seasons. Indigenous peoples built permanent villages along the rivers, hunted and gathered in the meadows, and traded over the mountain passes. The mountains continue to be places of spiritual and cultural importance. This area is the homelands of Nuxwsá7aq (Nooksack), Sah-ku-me-hu (Sauk-Suiattle), and Upper Skagit, and Nlaka'pamux First Nation of present-day Canada. Neighboring Tribes also have a connection with this place, including Lhaq'temish, Lummi People.

Four different Salishan languages were spoken by the people. For example, Mount Baker has different names in each language. Nooksack call the top of the mountain Kweq' Smánit, and the high meadows Kwelshán, which means "shooting place." In Lummi the mountain is also known as Kwelshán, though the meaning is understood to be "place wounded by a shot." In the Halkomelem language, the mountain is Kwelxá:lxw. Speakers of Lushootseed call Mount Baker Teqwúbe7, meaning "snowcapped peak."

The Tribes of this area of present-day Washington State signed the 1855 Treaty of Point Elliot, which guaranteed their continued hunting, fishing, and gathering rights as well as the establishment of reservations. The treaty created a government-to-government relationship between the Tribes and the United States, but those treaty rights have been violated by the United States. Much of the land was taken without compensation, and the Nooksack and Sauk-Suiattle Tribes were not given reservations. Both Tribes later fought for and won federal recognition.

1 PICTURE LAKE

WHY GO?

This accessible loop offers incredible views of an alpine vista, with towering Mount Shuksan mirrored in the water. You are surrounded by wildflowers and wetland plants, and though the road is very nearby, it feels miles away. There are ample places to stop and take in the experience.

THE RUNDOWN

Spoon rating: 1 spoon. Wheelchair accessible, but there is no accessible parking.
Type: Loop
Distance: 0.5 mile
Elevation: 4,200 feet
Elevation gain: Under 10 feet
Max grade: 5%
Max cross-slope: 2%
Typical width: 3 feet
Typical surface: Pavement, boardwalk
Trail users: Hikers
Season/schedule: Open summer through fall

Water availability: None
Amenities: None. Nearest toilets are at Austin Pass Picnic Area or Heather Meadows Visitor Center.
Dog-friendly: Yes, on leash
Cell phone reception: None
Nearest town: Glacier
Land manager: Mt. Baker–Snoqualmie National Forest, (360) 854-2553
Pass/entry fee: Federal recreation pass

FINDING THE TRAILHEAD

Getting there: Travel the Mt. Baker Scenic Byway for 21 miles past Glacier. At the fork in the road, turn right. Parking is at gravel pullouts on both sides of the road, which may be difficult to navigate if it is busy. GPS: 48.86625, -121.67662

Start: There are several gravel pullouts around the lake. Begin on the northernmost side of the lake. The trailhead is located at a trail sign.

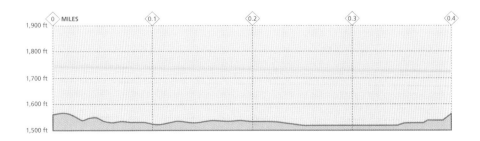

Viewing deck at the lake

THE HIKE

This 0.5-mile accessible loop path provides scenic views and interpretive signs for a little more information about the area. The gravel path begins on a very slight decline before it reaches pavement, then continues mostly level with a few bumps, rolls, and cracks, but they are all passable. The path rolls uphill on a less than 5% grade before coming to a fork; the paved trail continues on the left to an overlook of the lake. The overlook is made of lateral boards with benches on either side, providing a place to stop and take in views of the mountains and Picture Lake.

Once you finish here, return to the fork and continue straight ahead on the board-walk—it is slightly uneven with a 2% cross-slope. Return to pavement then continue on a slight incline to the left to another large paved overlook with a bench. There are two informational signs here talking about glacial sculpting that helped shape the Cascades. If it is sunny, there are incredible views of Mount Shuksan reflected in Picture Lake; if it's cloudy, you'll get to enjoy the more moody face of the mountains. There are lots of mountain hemlock, Pacific silver fir, and willow trees around the lake.

Beyond this overlook, the paved path continues with a few cracks in the pavement. You'll come to a few short rolls and a cracked and slightly raised section of pavement before taking a short, quick decline into a dip in the path—there may be some water here. Take a 2% incline for about 50 feet, then the trail forks left to a non-accessible

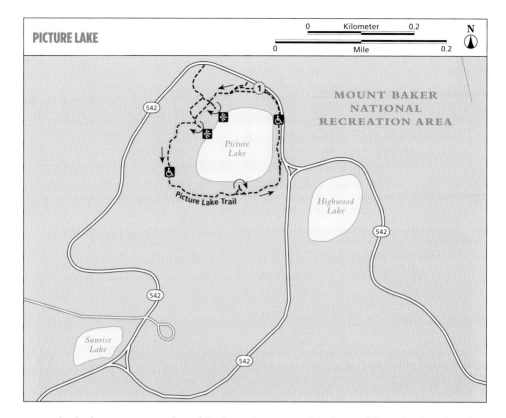

overlook; the pavement ends at this viewpoint onto a 6-inch step. There is a bench and a couple of steps down to the water before it loops back onto the trail. The accessible path continues on a slight decline until the end, where the pavement gets bumpier and uneven, descends slightly onto a short boardwalk with level and closely placed boards, then rises back up to the parking area that is a couple hundred feet down the road. There is a narrow dirt section for walking along the parking area; if the parking area is full, it is too narrow to travel in a wheelchair and you will have to return to your car on the shoulder of the road.

MILES AND DIRECTIONS

0.0 Start at the northern side of the lake, next to a trailhead sign.

0.1 Overlook on the left.

0.4 Arrive back at the road. Continue left to return to your car.

0.5 Arrive back at the trailhead.

2 **BAGLEY LAKES**

WHY GO?

This trail can be done as a loop or a slightly easier out-and-back. Whichever route you choose, the trail offers a lot for the effort—enjoy two alpine lakes, abundant wildflowers and berries, a small waterfall, incredible mountain views, and a neat stone bridge. Snow can linger on the trail into late July, forming unstable snow bridges that may appear solid but have actually melted out underneath. I recommend avoiding the trail in those conditions, for your own safety and to protect the sensitive landscape. Check trip reports or contact the Forest Service if you plan to visit early in the season.

THE RUNDOWN

Spoon rating: 3 spoons as an out-and-back, 4 spoons as a loop. The trail is short but there is a steep grade down to the lakes. It is narrow with several slick areas and steep drop-offs, and there are lots of rocks on the return loop. There is also no shade.
Type: Loop
Distance: 1.6 miles
Elevation: 4,200 feet
Elevation gain: 131 feet
Max grade: 25%
Max cross-slope: 8%
Typical width: 2 feet
Typical surface: Natural, rocks, boardwalk

Trail users: Hikers
Season/schedule: Open summer through fall, best late summer through fall
Water availability: Creek
Amenities: Vault toilet and picnic tables at visitor center, picnic area
Dog-friendly: Yes, on leash
Cell phone reception: None
Nearest town: Glacier
Land manager: Mt. Baker–Snoqualmie National Forest, (360) 854-2553
Pass/entry fee: Federal recreation pass

FINDING THE TRAILHEAD

Getting there: Travel the Mt. Baker Scenic Byway for 21 miles past Glacier. Just past the Mt. Baker Ski Area, turn right into a large paved parking lot with a sign for Bagley Lakes. There are no designated accessible parking spots in this lot. GPS: 48.86136, -121.68264
Start: The trail begins to the left of two accessible toilets at the south corner of the lot.

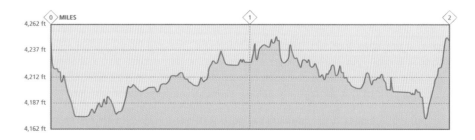

View of Table Mountain and Bagley Lake from the Chain Lakes Trail

THE HIKE

The most difficult portion of this trail is the first few hundred feet from the trailhead. Beginning at the trailhead you will immediately come to a signed fork—go right for the Bagley Lakes Trail, then immediately arrive at a set of steep, uneven, rocky stairs. Beyond the stairs, the trail surface is semi-firm crushed gravel, approximately 2 feet wide. Continue on a 20 to 25% decline, losing approximately 75 feet in elevation in about 300 feet, then curve sharply left and take in your first view of Lower Bagley Lake and Bagley Creek. Take a 1-foot-high step down and continue on loose gravel on a 5% decline, curving right. You'll cross rocks and boulders in the path and continue to a slightly wet area. There is a 6-inch-wide ditch to step across, then another set of stairs with steps rising 8 inches high.

At 0.1 mile arrive at a bridge—this is where the loop ends if you opt for that route. For now, go left to continue along Bagley Lakes. The trail narrows and becomes a soft, slightly muddy natural surface. Travel over a stream on a turnpike, then continue onto a moist rocky area and step up onto rocks. The trail then levels and evens out and crosses to a boardwalk as you travel along Lower Bagley Lake with views of Table Mountain ahead. There is a potentially muddy 50-foot-long incline on the other side of the boardwalk, then the trail narrows as you pass between rocks, over a small ditch, and step up onto a boulder. Come to another boardwalk; this one is uneven and partially collapsed in the center, so watch your step.

The trail widens again and continues mostly level as it curves slightly right, before narrowing and crossing between rocks and starting to roll slightly. There are a few footpaths leading down to the water on the right here. The trail continues ahead; it is pretty rutted with roots rising above the surface, so again watch your step. Curve right and take a 5% incline for approximately 50 feet before curving right again and enter some possible shade. Take four rock steps up, then take a slight step down onto rocks; the trail declines slightly for about 200 feet to a narrow, rocky, and moist area over a gap for water flow. You may want to pause here and enjoy the beautiful views of Table Mountain ahead of you, more mountains behind you, and the lakes below. Pass narrowly between rocks on a soft surface surrounded by berry bushes. Step down off of a rock, then continue onto a long boardwalk that curves left and right on uneven boards. Step off the boardwalk back onto a natural surface, and curve left and right, stepping over rocks.

At 0.5 mile you arrive at an area where a stream flows down the hillside. You have to cross on rocks, but the surface is well constructed. It is level and fairly even and was dry at the beginning of September, but it could be slick or a shallow water crossing earlier in the season. It is very pretty, though, with water trickling down the rocky hillside to the creek below. The trail then continues mostly level on natural surface before crossing another long, uneven boardwalk with a 1-foot step up. It ends onto pea gravel. Continue through the meadow above Bagley Creek with a boulder field on the right and Lower Bagley Lake behind you. Cross onto two more sets of uneven boardwalk; the second boardwalk has a rocky 6-inch step up and a rocky 4-inch step down. The trail then continues on compact gravel.

At 0.6 mile there's a place to get down to the creek—this might be a good water source (always use an appropriate filter!). Either way, it's a great place to take a break, enjoy the view up to Table Mountain, and notice the life that thrives in and around the creek. The trail continues level along the creek for a short distance and enters a boulder field. Take one step up, come to a wet area on a 5% incline, then continue stepping up onto several rocks as the trail gradually inclines while following rapids along the creek. Take one more 1-foot-high step up on a rock. The trail then continues level, with the creek flowing gently to your right and a meadow on your left.

At 0.8 mile you arrive at a signed junction with the Chain Lakes Trail. If you are doing this as an out-and-back, you can turn around here after taking as long as you want to enjoy the close-up views of Table Mountain and the creek valley. If you are continuing on the loop, go right and cross the bridge over the creek. Take four steep and uneven stone steps up onto boulders, cross the bridge, then take five steep stone steps up on the other side. The bridge is about 4 feet wide with no guardrails, and I felt it was a little dizzying.

Go right on the Chain Lakes Trail to continue the loop. Cross narrowly between boulders and continue on a 5% grade on the narrow path with loose gravel. Step up over a boulder, continuing on a gradual incline as you rise above the creek. Step over another boulder and come to a loose gravel 10% incline; step up over roots, then up onto boulders before the trail switchbacks left around more boulders. You are now higher above the creek, with views of the mountains back to the north. Take two steep steps up as the trail continues rocky and slightly muddy with lots of roots. Step down, then decline on boulders with a steep drop-off on the right and a cliff rising above you on the left.

The trail continues to roll over lots of boulders and loose rocks with a drop-off on the right, then declines on a scree-covered slope. Take a steep, narrow step down with roots

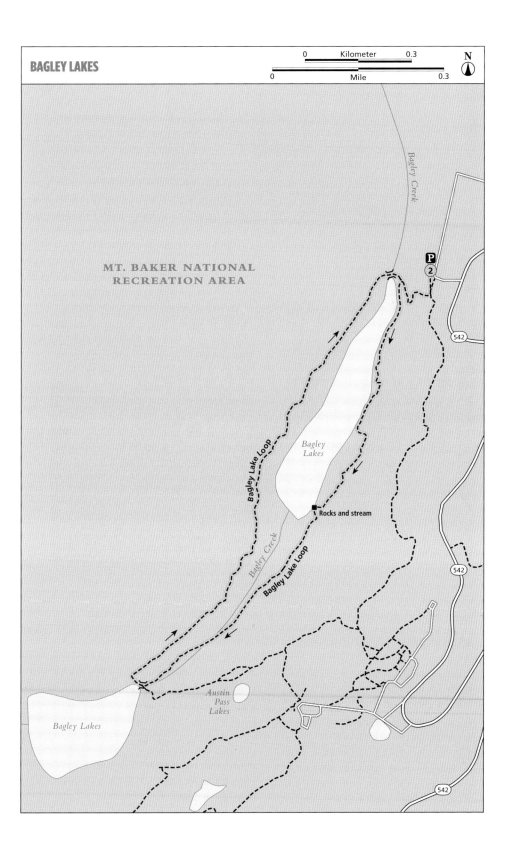

BAGLEY LAKES

MT. BAKER NATIONAL
RECREATION AREA

Bagley Creek

Bagley
Lakes

Bagley Creek

Rocks and stream

Bagley Lake Loop

Bagley Lake Loop

Bagley Lakes

Austin
Pass
Lakes

0   Kilometer   0.3

0   Mile   0.3

N

P
2

542

542

542

and boulders in the trail—it is tricky footing here, so be careful—then pass narrowly next to more boulders with roots in the trail, up a short incline with several root mats, and decline again onto more roots. The trail then levels out slightly on a soft surface with a view of the lake ahead. You then take a long decline on loose gravel with two steep steps down. Curve to the right and left, crossing narrowly between boulders with loose gravel.

At 1.1 miles take three steep steps down over boulders, pass around rocks at a wet area, and step across a small stream. Cross a rock field as the trail continues left around the hillside on lots of loose gravel. Step up onto a rocky area across another small stream, then take a 5% incline for about 50 feet and curve left. The trail levels out but crosses several uneven rocks with unstable footing. Take a slight step up onto rocks and then across a small ditch, traveling on rocks through a wet area covered in moss and wildflowers with cliffs towering above you.

At 1.2 miles the trail curves right and crosses on boulders, then takes a steep decline on boulders—it is slick and narrow here. Take seven steep stone steps, then continue level onto gravel before rising slightly. Curve to the left to two more small streams—these may be a wet crossing. The trail continues mostly level but narrows and becomes slightly rutted, curves to the right, then goes up over boulders. Rise on a 5% grade and cross narrowly between several boulders. The trail continues narrow and uneven among boulders and rocks and over roots.

At 1.4 miles you arrive at a small shady area under some trees with a place to step off the trail—a fallen log makes a nice place to sit before finishing the loop. Continue narrowly over roots and rocks as the trail curves to the right and descends on a 10% grade. Step up onto rocks and cross a small ditch, another boulder, then step up again onto roots and rocks passing narrowly next to a drop-off on the right. Step up onto a tall, steep boulder and then step down, then up over roots. Go past a tree with roots across the trail, then cross another ditch. The trail continues over roots and rocks with two trees pinching the trail that you have to step over steeply on a decline. You then arrive at the first bridge over the creek. Step down steeply over rocks and boulders onto the bridge—it is very steep and narrow with tricky footing. Cross the bridge, step up onto rocks on the other side, take a set of steep steps up, and then you are back at the original fork. Continue straight ahead, rising back to the parking area.

MILES AND DIRECTIONS

0.0   Start at the trailhead for Bagley Lakes.

0.1   Go left at the bridge.

0.5   Cross a rocky stream.

0.8   Junction with the Chain Lakes Trail. Go right for the loop.

1.1   The trail becomes very rocky, with a couple of small stream crossings.

1.5   Cross the bridge over Bagley Creek. Continue up the hill, then turn left to return to the trailhead.

1.6   Arrive back at the trailhead.

3 TRAIL OF THE CEDARS

WHY GO?

This short loop is a delightful oasis along the Skagit River and away from some of the crowds. You'll be in a beautiful mossy forest with ancient western redcedar, accompanied by the gentle sounds of the river. There is even a cool suspension bridge! It's a great place to feel like a kid for a little while, and I encourage you to take some time to enjoy it with all the senses available to you.

THE RUNDOWN

Spoon rating: 2 spoons for the entire loop. Wheelchair hikeable with caution. The first half of this loop along the river is level, compacted gravel with one narrow section that is a few feet long with a steep cross-slope. The second half ends with a 12 to 15% incline. You could do this as an out-and-back along the river to avoid the steep section at the end.

Type: Loop

Distance: 0.6 mile

Elevation: 515 feet

Elevation gain: 20 feet

Max grade: 15%

Max cross-slope: 5%

Typical width: 4 feet

Typical surface: Compact

Trail users: Hikers

Season/schedule: Year-round, but best in summer through fall. May be wet in winter/spring.

Water availability: Water fountains at visitor center

Amenities: None here, but water, picnic tables, and restrooms available at the visitor center nearby

Dog-friendly: Yes, on leash

Cell phone reception: Spotty

Nearest town: Marblemount

Land manager: North Cascades National Park Service Complex, (360) 854-7200

Pass/entry fee: None

Land acknowledgment: Upper Skagit and Sauk-Suiattle. The Sauk-Suiattle and Upper Skagit Indian Tribes have brought lawsuits against Seattle City Light's dam projects on the Skagit river, asserting that the projects harm endangered salmon and infringe on the rights of nature.

FINDING THE TRAILHEAD

Getting there: From Sedro-Woolley, travel approximately 55 miles on WA 20/North Cascades Highway to Newhalem. Turn right into the Newhalem Creek Campground, at the sign for the North Cascades visitor center. Cross a bridge, and turn left onto the first road through Loop C. Travel the paved road through the campground, then continue on the gravel road for a few miles until you reach the powerhouse. Park in the small gravel parking area or off of the loop. GPS: 48.66921, -121.24974

Start: Trailhead at the historic powerhouse

The narrow trail next to an old blowdown

THE HIKE

This trail actually begins in the Newhalem Creek Campground, which doesn't add anything except mileage to the hike, or at the suspension bridge over the Skagit River; neither option is wheelchair friendly. The most accessible way to reach this trail is to continue driving down the service road that leads through Loop C. Pass the trailhead for the Rock Shelter on the right (another worthwhile hike that you can find at DisabledHikers.com) and continue on the good gravel road until it ends at the powerhouse. Although this trail is on federal lands within the National Park Service Complex, it is courtesy of Seattle City Light, which owns and operates the historic powerhouse. The hydroelectric powerhouse currently provides emergency power to the larger Skagit River project. There are several interpretive signs providing historical information about the powerhouse, and you can look through its windows to see some of the equipment.

Pass the powerhouse and curve to the left on a 4-foot-wide compact gravel path, following a small creek. The trail then forks for the loop—continue to the left on level gravel. The trail curves slightly right and you come to the first of a number of interpretive plaques about the plants, animals, and ecology of the area. The trail continues level then takes an 8% incline for about 10 feet and curves to the left before leveling out again. You are surrounded by towering western redcedars, cottonwoods, and maples and will start to hear the river. Take a 5 to 8% decline for about 50 feet, then curve left next to a very big western redcedar; a sign informs you that it is 188 feet tall and 7 feet, 6 inches in diameter. The trail continues generally level.

At 0.1 mile there is a short path to an overlook with views across the Skagit River. An interpretive sign explains that the concrete barrier here prevents salmon from swimming

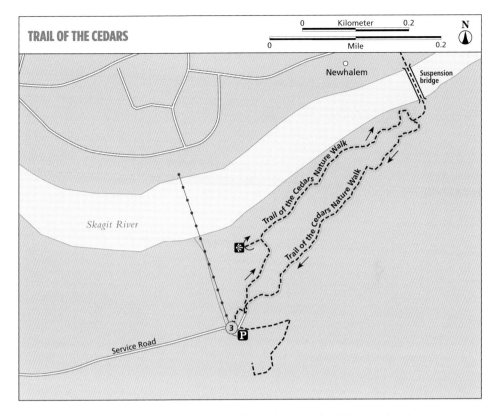

upstream to the powerhouse. The main trail continues to the right past the viewpoint on an 8% decline for 10 feet then levels out. Continue following the Skagit River through a lush Pacific Northwest forest, with ferns and salal carpeting the ground; another sign displays the range map of western redcedar. The trail rolls on a short 8% grade over a culverted stream as it travels in between lots of really big redcedars and vine maples. There are a couple of small, shallow roots in the trail but they are easy to bypass. A small footpath on the left leads to the rocky banks of the river.

At 0.2 mile the trail narrows to about 2½ feet as you pass an old blowdown on the right, curving right on a slightly steep incline and cross-slope where the ground was raised—wheelchair users may need assistance with this section. The trail curves left, passing a few more blowdowns. It gets a little brushy for a few feet, and the trail may be less than 3 feet wide depending on the growth. It then widens back out to 3 feet and

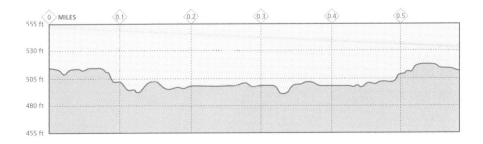

The suspension bridge over the Skagit River

continues level, curving a few times with views up the cliffs above the river. Another small footpath leads down to the river. Continue straight ahead, then pass a woodpecker tree. The trail curves left and right on a couple of slight rolls.

At 0.3 mile you reach the other side of the loop and the suspension bridge. There are a couple of views of the bridge from the trail, but to get to it you have to go left; take an 8 to 10% incline and a 4-inch step up. The bridge has a couple of slightly uneven boards with a 5% incline, but it is pretty sturdy and doesn't sway too much. It's a really incredible view up and down the river, and you can feel the wind and hear the water as it flows through the canyon.

To finish the loop, go right instead of left to the bridge. This path ends on a long incline, but if that is an issue you could go back the way you came. The path continues on wide, compact gravel with a slight incline, then passes some old burned stumps with signs about fire in the valley. Continue on a level grade and pass the "see-through tree"—an old tree with an opening in its trunk. Take a slight 2 to 5% incline for 50 feet, then come to a 12% incline for about 100 feet, increasing to 15% for the last 10 feet. It then decreases to 8% as it curves left and levels out as you curve right to return to the powerhouse.

MILES AND DIRECTIONS

0.0   Start at the powerhouse trailhead.

0.2   The trail narrows to 2½ feet.

0.3   The suspension bridge is on the left. Go right to finish the loop.

0.6   Arrive back at the trailhead.

4 THUNDER CREEK

WHY GO?

This stunning trail winds along the Thunder Arm of Diablo Lake then follows Thunder Creek through ancient forests of cedar and fir. There are rocky cliffs and boulders, berries, and perfect picnicking spots along the creek. The hike ends at a wooden bridge with views along the creek.

THE RUNDOWN

Spoon rating: 3 spoons. There are no prolonged steep grades or stairs, but in the wet months there may be a couple of shallow stream crossings. The biggest obstacles are rocks that regularly rise a couple of inches above the surface.
Type: Out-and-back
Distance: 2.8 miles
Elevation: 1,230 feet
Elevation gain: 95 feet
Max grade: 15%
Max cross-slope: 8%
Typical width: 2 feet
Typical surface: Natural, rocky

Trail users: Hikers, horseback riders
Season/schedule: Spring through fall
Water availability: Creek
Amenities: Flush toilets at parking lot
Dog-friendly: Yes, on leash
Cell phone reception: None
Nearest town: Marblemount
Land manager: Mt. Baker–Snoqualmie National Forest, Sedro-Woolley, WA 98284; (360) 854-2553
Pass/entry fee: Federal recreation pass
Land acknowledgment: Upper Skagit and Sauk Suiattle

FINDING THE TRAILHEAD

Getting there: From Sedro-Woolley, travel approximately 65 miles on WA 20/ North Cascades Highway to mile marker 130 at Diablo Lake. Turn into the south side of Colonial Creek Campground (on the right). There are three accessible parking spots in the large parking lot when you enter, along with flush toilets, and two accessible parking spots in the day-use area inside the campground. GPS: 48.68848, -121.09458
Start: At the far end of the loop inside Colonial Creek Campground

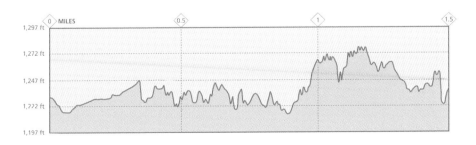

A rocky section of trail

THE HIKE

The trailhead is inside Colonial Creek Campground, at the far end of the main loop; you can either park in the large paved lot when you first enter and walk 0.3 mile through the campground to the trailhead, or drive through the campground to a small day-use parking area at the trailhead. The route here begins at the trailhead, so add 0.6 mile to the total distance if you start from the paved lot.

There is a large trail board with a map and information about the area at the trailhead. Starting out from the trailhead, you immediately pass the amphitheater on the left—continue on the Thunder Creek Trail with a sign pointing straight ahead. Another map on the right provides information about the wilderness. The trail begins on natural surface, level and 4 feet wide. You are already amongst large cedar and fir trees—pass next to one of each in the trail and then curve left. The trail inclines at 10%; step over an 8-inch-wide, 3-inch-tall root and then underneath a tree that has fallen across the trail—there is about 6 feet of clearance. The trail rolls a couple of times with a few rocks in the surface then takes a 15 to 20% incline for about 20 feet, levels out for a few feet, and then continues on a 10% incline. A small footpath leads off to the right; continue straight ahead on the 3- to 4-foot-wide path. The turquoise water you see below you is the Thunder Arm of Diablo Lake; this stunning color is due to the amount of glacial rock flour carried down by the creek. Just don't get too distracted, because there are several large rocks rising up to 6 inches above the trail and a sharp drop-off on the left.

Take a 10% decline weaving between some roots and rocks. At 0.1 mile on the trail you come to a sign for the Thunder Woods Nature Trail—this trail is no longer included in the park service trail list and is not maintained. Continue straight ahead on Thunder Creek with gentle rolling grades and lots of rocks, some of them rising 6 to 8 inches. You are moving deeper into ancient forest, with a rocky cliff above you and the water of Thunder Creek flowing into the lake below. Take a rocky 10% incline then decline for about 10 feet. The trail then rolls slightly a couple of times, continuing rocky and passing lots of old blowdowns and large cedars. Pass next to an old-growth Douglas fir, then curve right next to a patch of devil's club. Take a 12% incline, stepping up on some roots, then curve to the left on a 10% incline, stepping up over more rocks. The trail then levels out to a very rocky 100-foot-long section over a seasonal stream. There is more devil's club here and some loose rocks, but then the trail returns to firm natural surface. Take a 10% incline, stepping up on some rocks, and continue on a few gentle rolls with slight grades. You're now traveling through mossy, ancient forest above Thunder Creek.

At 0.5 mile on the trail, cross a small root mat and take a 5% incline with views up to the top of the mountains across the creek. You can start to hear the sound of rushing water. The trail narrows to about 2½ feet with a sharp drop-off to the left where the outer edge is eroded. Stepping over some rocks and a large root, pass a couple of old snags and then take a couple of short rolls on a slight incline, passing what looks like a small seasonal stream. Pass between an old cedar and fir, then take a 12% decline. The trail continues to roll a few times on slight grades then gets a little more wet and rocky with some eroded sections on the outer edge.

At 0.7 mile you pass a really cool, giant split boulder on the right with a couple of old-growth western redcedars. There's a footpath to the boulder. The rocky trail continues about 2 feet wide, passing through lots of thimbleberry. You then arrive at a grove of old-growth western redcedars, with another nice place to rest off the trail. The trail then declines at 8% and narrows to 1½ feet, passing through more thimbleberries, elders, and

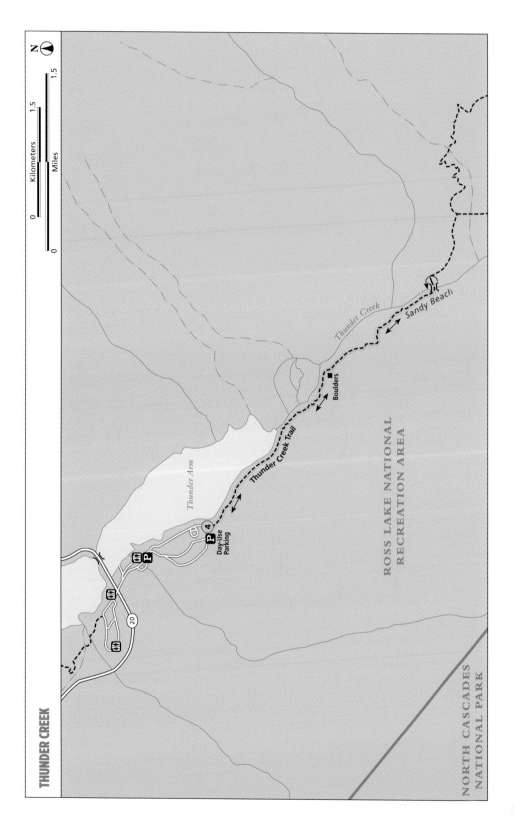

THUNDER CREEK

THUNDER ARM

Day-Use Parking

Thunder Creek Trail

Boulders

Thunder Creek

Sandy Beach

ROSS LAKE NATIONAL RECREATION AREA

NORTH CASCADES NATIONAL PARK

N

Kilometers
0   1.5   1.5

Miles
0   1.5

maples. The trail continues level with a few slightly wet areas, then at 0.8 mile you pass closely to the creek with a couple of spots to get down to the water. The creek flows very shallow here as it spreads out on its approach to the lake, and you are surrounded by plants along the bank. Take a 10 to 12% incline as the trail curves to the right and left for about 100 feet, increasing to 15% for the last 20 feet. The trail then levels out on gentle rolling grades, traveling above the creek and passing next to an old-growth Douglas fir with boulders under its roots. There are gorgeous views looking up to the mountains and the creek down below.

At 1.0 mile come to a 10% incline with a few eroded sections creating a sharp drop-off. The trail then narrows to about 1½ feet and curves left to cross a couple of rocky areas over seasonal streams. Take a couple of 10% inclines for a few feet, passing underneath old-growth western redcedars. At 1.1 miles the trail widens to 3 to 4 feet and passes under several massive and ancient cedars. Take an 8% incline for about 15 feet as the trail curves to the left then levels out. The trail continues rocky on slight grades, curving left and right. At 1.2 miles pass a large boulder on the right; the trail takes a very slight decline then passes another boulder on the right. A rocky cliff rises above you with the creek on the left. Continue passing lots of boulders as the trail continues level then narrows to about 1½ feet.

At 1.3 miles there is a footpath leading down a steep hill to the creek. The trail inclines at 10% for 50 feet, then you can see the bridge ahead of you. Take a 10% decline for about 30 feet, stepping down between some rocks, and arrive at the bridge at 1.4 miles. Step up about 3 inches onto the bridge; it is very sturdy with level, tightly placed boards. There is a beautiful view of the creek here, and it is a nice place to enjoy the scenery for a few minutes. If you want to get down to the water, just before the bridge there are two large rocks that you have to cross narrowly between. Take a short, fairly level footpath to a sandy area along the creek. This is a prime picnic spot, with some nice logs to sit on, but be aware that bears are often sighted in the area.

On the other side of the bridge, the Thunder Creek Trail continues to the left and immediately starts to gain elevation to two backcountry camps and then travels further into the wilderness. Continuing on the trail requires being prepared for a backcountry experience, so I recommend turning around at this point and enjoying your return trip.

MILES AND DIRECTIONS

0.0 Start at the trailhead inside the campground.

0.1 Pass a sign for the Thunder Woods Nature Trail.

0.7 Pass a large split boulder on the right.

1.3 A steep footpath on the left leads to the creek.

1.4 Reach the bridge across Thunder Creek. Turn around to return to the trailhead.

2.8 Arrive back at the trailhead.

5 HAPPY CREEK NATURE TRAIL

WHY GO?

This wheelchair-accessible boardwalk and gravel path through ancient North Cascades forest is definitely worth a visit, whether you are passing through the area or as a destination itself. The bubbling sounds of Happy Creek greet you on the path, and giant cedars and firs surround the boardwalk. There is no traction material on the boardwalk, so it may be slippery in the wet months.

THE RUNDOWN

Spoon rating: 1 spoon. Wheelchair accessible. There is less than a 1-inch rise onto the first boardwalk and a few slightly uneven boards.
Type: Loop
Distance: 0.3 mile
Elevation: 2,159 feet
Elevation gain: Under 40 feet
Max grade: 5%
Max cross-slope: 2%
Typical width: 4 feet
Typical surface: Boardwalk, compact gravel
Trail users: Hikers
Season/schedule: Late spring through fall, pending seasonal road closures
Water availability: None

Amenities: Accessible vault toilet, benches
Dog-friendly: Yes, on leash
Cell phone reception: No
Nearest town: Marblemount
Land manager: North Cascades National Park Service Complex, (360) 854-7200
Pass/entry fee: None
Land acknowledgment: The mountain pass that WA 20 now travels through was a popular trade route for Upper Skagit, Nlakapamux, Methow, Chelan, and others who continue their traditional relationships with the land.

FINDING THE TRAILHEAD

Getting there: From Sedro-Woolley, travel approximately 70 miles on WA 20 to mile marker 134.5. The trailhead is easy to miss; there is a partially hidden brown park service sign directly across from the parking area, so be prepared to turn as soon as you see the sign. The parking lot is a small paved loop with four diagonal spots and two accessible parking spots, but neither have access aisles. For van access, you could possibly use the right parking spot, which has enough space in front of the toilet, or there is a long parallel spot on the loop. GPS: 48.72857, -121.05596
Start: A small parking area off of WA 20

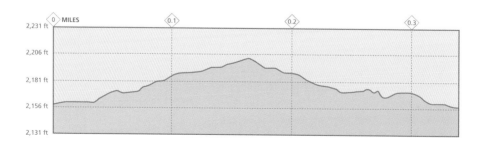

A creek-side rest spot

THE HIKE

A trail board and map at the parking area describes some of the plants and animals you may see along the way and explains the nature of this changing forest. There is also information about Indigenous peoples who traveled through this area—the Upper Skagit from the west, Nlakapamux from the north, Methow from the east, and Chelan from the south. These mountains continue to be crucial to Indigenous lifeways, including hunting, gathering, and ceremony. Take a moment to appreciate this place, and be mindful during your visit.

The boardwalk begins right at the parking area. There is a ½- to 1-inch rise onto the boardwalk, and it continues on a 5% incline with a level section at least every 20 feet. Some of the boards are a little uneven and raised about ¼ inch, but the boardwalk is generally level and sturdy with tightly placed boards. You then arrive at the beginning of the loop, with a gravel path on the right and a boardwalk straight ahead. This description continues straight ahead, traveling clockwise around the loop, but if you go right and continue counterclockwise, you will have a better view up the creek as you travel the loop.

Continuing straight ahead, the boardwalk continues on a 5% incline with level areas every few feet. You'll come to a small bench on the left, suitable for one person. At 0.1 mile you transition to a compact gravel path that is 5 feet wide. Take a 2 to 5% incline, curve right, then level out. Pass a bench that is just outside the trail on the left. Continue on a 2 to 5% incline with level sections at least every 30 feet. The trail curves right, inclines at 5%, and transfers back to boardwalk with a few slightly uneven boards. You then come to a big round viewing area at Happy Creek with two benches and plenty of

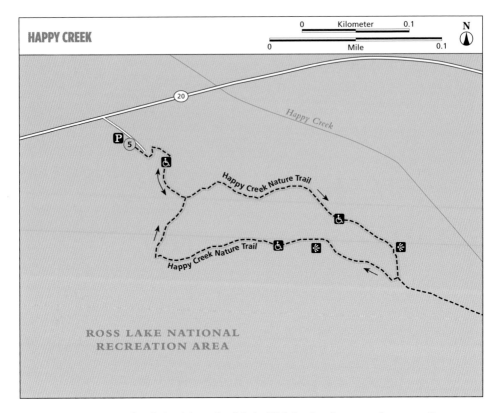

0 — Kilometer — 0.1

N

0 — Mile — 0.1

20

Happy Creek

P 5

Happy Creek Nature Trail

Happy Creek Nature Trail

ROSS LAKE NATIONAL RECREATION AREA

space to turn around and sit with a wheelchair. This is a lovely spot to hang out, listen to the rushing creek, and watch for wildlife. You can hardly tell that the highway is nearby. The Happy Creek Falls Trail leads off to your left from here—it is a narrow 1.2-mile trail that travels to a waterfall and old sawmill.

Continue on the boardwalk on a 2 to 5% decline with level areas every 30 feet. You're now traveling along Happy Creek, with lots of little waterfalls and pools along the way, passing underneath large western redcedars, Douglas firs, and vine maples. The board-walk does have a few uneven boards; none of them rise more than ¼ inch. At 0.2 mile there is a bench on the right with a large pullout and an overlook of the creek with ancient western redcedars. You may notice signs of squirrels who eat the seeds from the cones of the fir trees and leave piles of stripped scales on the boardwalk. At 0.3 mile reach another viewing area with two benches overlooking a little waterfall. Keep an eye out for mushrooms and coral root growing beyond the boardwalk. You then transfer onto level gravel and go left back onto the short boardwalk to return to the parking area.

MILES AND DIRECTIONS

0.0 Start at the boardwalk at the parking area.

0.15 Reach the first Happy Creek overlook.

0.2 Reach the second Happy Creek overlook.

0.3 Reach the third Happy Creek overlook. Return to the parking area.

OLYMPIC PENINSULA

The Olympic Peninsula, at the most northwestern point of Washington State, is surrounded by the Pacific Ocean on the west, the Strait of Juan de Fuca on the north, and Puget Sound on the east. It contains some of the last remaining old-growth temperate rain forest in the continental United States. The western side of the peninsula is defined by rain, with some areas receiving up to 200 inches per year. However, the northern and eastern sides of the peninsula are in a rain shadow created by the Olympic Mountains and receive an average of 17 inches of rain per year. This incredibly unique area is home to thirty-five endemic species.

Nine present-day Tribes have lived on the peninsula since time immemorial: Lower Elwha Klallam, Jamestown S'Klallam, and Port Gamble S'Klallam (S'Klallam is the anglicized version of *nəxʷsƛ̓áy̓əm̓*, meaning "the strong people") to the north; Makah, Quileute, Hoh, and Quinault to the west; and Twana/Skokomish and Squaxin Island to the east. Several distinct languages are spoken by the people: Klallam, Quinault, and Twana are Salishan languages spoken by S'Klallam, Quinault, and Skokomish, respectively. The Makah language is a Wakashan language. The Quileute language, spoken by Quileute and Hoh, is a Chimakuan language.

S'Klallam, Twana, Skokomish, and Chemakum signed the 1855 Treaty of Point No Point. The Treaty of Olympia, or the Quinault River Treaty, was made with Quinault, Queets, Quileute, and Hoh Tribes. The Treaty of Neah Bay was signed by Makah and Ozette. In exchange for ceding their lands, the Tribes received negligible compensation and a tiny fraction of their lands in reservation. The Tribes maintained their rights to hunt, fish, and gather in the usual and accustomed grounds. The people continue their stewardship of the land and engage in critical restoration work. The Quinault Indian Nation is highly respected for their advances in natural resources management and Native rights and self-determination. The Tribes are also major economic drivers in the community, operating many large businesses and employing thousands of people.

Typical trail with large Sitka spruce

6 MARYMERE FALLS

WHY GO?

Marymere Falls is a 90-foot waterfall in a beautiful old-growth forest with multiple creeks and a mossy ravine. It is located at Lake Crescent in Olympic National Park. The trail follows the lake before entering an old-growth forest and then climbing to an overlook of Marymere Falls. It is often referred to as an easy hike for all—I disagree with that assessment. The first section is wheelchair hikeable; it is a hard-packed gravel surface and generally level, but there are a couple of troublesome areas.

THE RUNDOWN

Spoon rating: 2 spoons for the first 0.5 mile, which is wheelchair hikeable and gains under 100 feet in elevation. The surface is mostly compact earth and gravel, but there are two areas of incline and uneven ground that may be difficult. 5 spoons for the complete hike to the falls, which gains an additional 250-plus feet in less than 0.5 mile. It is very steep and slippery in places, with over 120 stairs.

Type: Lollipop loop

Distance: 1 mile wheelchair hikeable, 1.7 miles total

Elevation: 600 feet

Elevation gain: 300 feet

Max grade: 12% on first 0.5 mile, 40% total (stairs)

Max cross-slope: 8%

Typical width: 2 feet

Typical surface: Compact gravel

Trail users: Hikers

Season/schedule: Year-round

Water availability: Water fountains, creek

Special notes: 45 stairs to falls, 76 stairs leaving falls

Amenities: Accessible restrooms, picnic tables, ranger station

Dog-friendly: Pets not allowed

Cell phone reception: Pretty good in the beginning, none near the falls

Nearest town: Port Angeles

Land manager: Olympic National Park, (360) 565-3130

Pass/entry fee: Federal recreation pass

Land acknowledgment: Ancestral lands of the S'Klallam. The Klallam name for Lake Crescent is čəłmət.

FINDING THE TRAILHEAD

Getting there: From Port Angeles, take US 101W to Lake Crescent. Turn at the ranger station sign located at mile 228. Turn right at the four-way stop and follow the road straight to the parking area. There are three accessible parking spots about halfway around the loop, near the restrooms, but no curb cuts; the parking spaces have a slightly lower lip to the sidewalk. GPS: 48.05808, -123.78914

Public transit: Take Clallam County Transit Route 14 from Port Angeles or Forks to Barnes Creek Road.

Start: Next to the historic Storm King Ranger Station

THE HIKE

The trailhead is marked by a small sign next to the ranger station, near the lake. It starts out level, over 3 feet wide, on compact gravel. In about 50 feet it declines on uneven ground with trees and a small drop-off to your left. There is lake access on the left. The trail levels out and curves to the right, entering a short tunnel under the roadway. It then rises at 10% for about 50 feet; the ground is uneven with loose gravel on one side and worn pavement on the other. The trail then levels out to a wide, compact gravel path. You have the road on one side with a narrow buffer of trees (you can hear road noise) and a hill on the other as you move deeper into the forest. There are a couple of fallen logs and stumps to rest on along the way, but no benches.

In about 0.25 mile the trail leaves the road and begins a very gradual incline. You will come to a sharper incline for approximately 25 feet and then a signed fork in the trail—continue straight. Continue on another slight incline. You will find yourself surrounded by old-growth trees and may be able to hear the creek.

The next eighth of a mile is a bit more difficult. The trail starts to roll slightly and then you come to another signed fork in the trail with a huge boulder on the left—continue straight. The trail slopes and rolls and there is a steep drop-off on the right. You will then come to an overlook on the creek—a gravel section on the right that juts off the trail, giving you a partially obstructed view of the creek. You are surrounded by huge trees. There isn't a good place to sit, but it is quite peaceful. This is the end of the "accessible" trail—turn around here if you are not continuing to the falls.

The trail to Marymere Falls starts out similarly to the rest. Continue past the overlook. The surface becomes more compact soil and gravel with rocks in the trail—watch your step. It rolls three times, with two inclines shorter than 20 feet, then comes to another fork. Head right down a steep 10-foot decline. Take a small rise in the trail, and then you will come to a giant old-growth cedar. Enjoy the tree, but be careful of the roots in the trail.

The trail then meets the creek with a nice place to get close to the water if you choose. There are no places to sit here, but it's a nice place to take a break. From here the trail curves left and meets a wide, sturdy footbridge over the creek with two steps on each side. Keep right after the bridge. The trail then becomes more rugged and narrow. The path curves along the creek with a dip in the trail and a sharp, eroded drop-off on one side before coming to a rough narrow footbridge with six steps. There are rails and the bridge is well supported.

Now the trail begins to climb steeply on many stairs. Take seventeen stairs to a steep switchback and then thirteen more stairs. The trail becomes a loop to see the falls—go left at the fork for the fewest stairs. You will be following the side of the cliff, with the creek below you and rails most of the way. Traverse a steep incline about 80 feet long and you'll catch your first glimpse of the waterfall. Take six stairs. The trail curves left and continues climbing. Take nine narrow, uneven stairs that curve around a tree—you may have to twist sideways a bit to pass. You are then at the overlook of the falls. It is a lovely, secluded amphitheater with the creek far below you, surrounded by forest with mountains rising on every horizon. There is no place sit, but there are rails to lean against and you could rest on the stairs.

You have two options: You can go back the way you came for fewer stairs, but if it's busy you run the risk of running into people and there isn't anywhere to step aside. Or you can complete the loop and get another view of the falls, but there are far more stairs and slippery areas.

The loop trail continues on a series of switchbacks: There are fifty-two steep, narrow, uneven steps with a high rise. You then come to the upper overlook; to access it you head

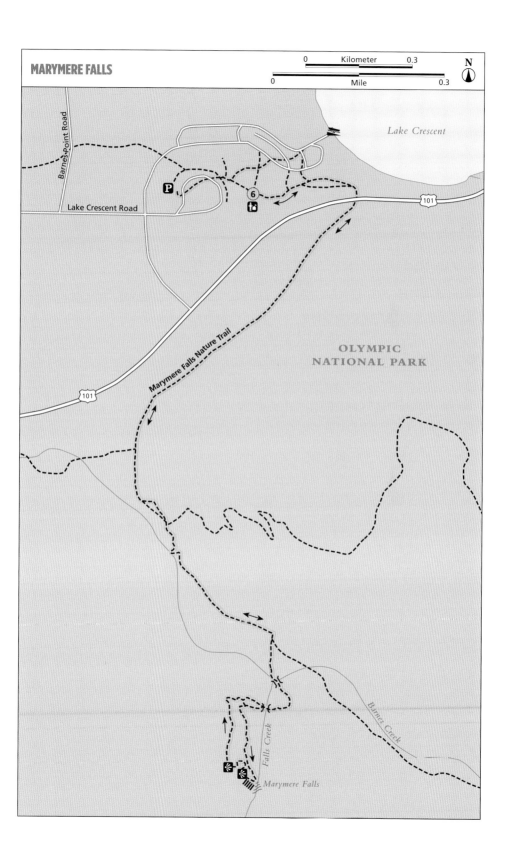

MARYMERE FALLS

0 Kilometer 0.3

0 Mile 0.3

N

Barnes Point Road

Lake Crescent

P

Lake Crescent Road

6

101

Marymere Falls Nature Trail

101

OLYMPIC
NATIONAL PARK

Falls Creek

Barnes Creek

Marymere Falls

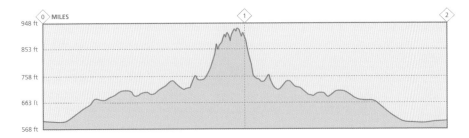

left up a slight hill. There is a bench here. To continue on the trail, go right. There is scree (loose gravel) on the trail as it starts descending steeply without any rails. Watch for rocks and a couple of wooden barriers set into the trail. The trail then narrows as you cross roots and take seven stairs. Pause here a moment and take in views of the surrounding mountains. Continue on a steep switchback with seventeen stairs. You'll then be back at the beginning of the loop—continue straight and retrace your way back.

MILES AND DIRECTIONS

0.0   Begin at the trailhead next to the Storm King Ranger Station.

0.1   Take the tunnel under the road.

0.5   Arrive at the end of wheelchair-hikeable portion.

0.8   Beginning of the loop. Go left for the shortest route to the falls.

0.9   End of the loop. Return on the main trail.

1.7   Arrive back at the trailhead.

7 QUINAULT LOOP TRAIL

WHY GO?

The Quinault Lake Recreation Area provides a number of possible loops and a variety of things to see, including waterfalls, old-growth rain forest, and one of the largest Sitka spruce trees in the world. On this loop, you'll pass through rain forest, travel along a roaring creek to an old-growth western redcedar bog, and end with a couple of waterfalls and a stroll along the lake. I was actually inspired to create Disabled Hikers here!

THE RUNDOWN

Spoon rating: 4 spoons. There is minimal elevation gain overall, but there are two short steep sections, two sections with difficult obstacles, and a few trail intersections that require navigating. The first 0.25 mile is wheelchair hikeable.
Type: Loop
Distance: 4.4 miles
Elevation: 240 feet
Elevation gain: 350 feet
Max grade: 25%
Max cross-slope: 8%
Typical width: 2 feet
Typical surface: Gravel, natural, boardwalk
Trail users: Hikers
Season/schedule: Year-round
Water availability: None
Amenities: Flush toilets, trash cans, benches, picnic tables—not wheelchair accessible

Dog-friendly: Yes, on leash
Cell phone reception: Spotty to nonexistent
Nearest town: Quinault
Land manager: Olympic National Forest, Pacific Ranger District, (360) 288-2525
Pass/entry fee: Federal recreation pass
Land acknowledgment: This is Quinault country. Quinault is the anglicized version of kʷínayɬ, the name of a village at the mouth of the Quinault River. There were 55 permanent village sites along the Quinault and Queets Rivers, and seasonal villages around Lake Quinault.

FINDING THE TRAILHEAD

Getting there: Lake Quinault is 40 miles north of Aberdeen on US 101. Turn right onto South Shore Road and travel 1 mile to the signed trailhead on the right. There is a large paved parking area with one accessible parking spot. GPS: 47.45985, -123.86206
Start: Paved parking area at the Quinault Rain Forest Nature Trail trailhead

THE HIKE

Start to the left of the information board and pay station that is on the left side of the parking area as you drive in. The path begins on somewhat loose compact gravel on a 3 to 5% incline. It is generally 3 feet wide, with a couple of roots pinching the trail. You immediately come to a fork—continue straight ahead on the Rain Forest Nature Trail. Interpretive signs along the way explain what makes the Olympic Peninsula rain forest

A view of Quinault Lake

so unique; the signs are approximately 3 feet tall and angled, but placed a few feet off the trail. Continue on a 3 to 5% incline as the trail curves slightly left and right then narrows to about 2 feet with swordferns encroaching on both sides for a few feet before widening to 3 feet. Curve very sharply right on a 3% incline, then curve sharply left continuing on a steady 3% incline. You then reach a large Douglas fir encircled by a platform. This is the end of the most accessible portion and is the easiest place to turn around. Unfortunately, the platform is not accessible. You can take several wood steps up or continue on the gravel path to the right, curve left, and take one 6-inch step up onto a very uneven and broken ramp that leads to the platform.

Continuing past the tree, the trail is generally level and 3 feet wide with a compact gravel surface. There are lots of Douglas firs and devil's club lining the trail. Cross a couple of rocks and one root in the middle of the trail rising about 1 ½ inches above the surface. At 0.1 mile arrive at another intersection with the Lakeshore Trail on your left. You'll end the loop here, but for now continue straight ahead on the Rain Forest Nature Trail, following the wooden fencing on the left as you travel along the hillside with Willaby Creek below. The trail narrows to 2 feet as a rocky cliff rises above you—it is narrow here, but take a moment to appreciate the feel of the many varieties of moss on the rock. The trail then curves right at another interpretive sign about water in the rain forest and continues generally 2 feet wide. Pass another sign about old-growth trees, then come to an 8% incline with lots of rocks in the trail for about 5 feet. Curve left next to an old blowdown and pass narrowly between rocks before arriving at a bench overlooking the creek at 0.2 mile. This is a good place to turn around for the easiest hike.

The trail curves sharply left and continues over some roots and rocks rising up to 4 inches. Take a 5% incline for 10 feet increasing to 12 to 15% for a total of approximately 100 feet. Step up over roots rising 3 to 4 inches and come to a set of eroded roots across the trail, acting as steps rising 6 to 8 inches. Arrive at a bench as the trail levels out for a few feet then continues on a 10% incline for another 30 feet, levels out, and passes narrowly next to a moss-covered Douglas fir with some roots pinching the trail. The trail levels out on a 5% incline then increases to 10% for 30 feet. You then pass an interpretive sign about the importance of standing dead trees—known as snags—and have the opportunity to experience them up close as you pass several giant, old standing snags. Continue on a slight incline under 5% and soon pass an old nurse stump on the right with the roots of a hemlock tree snaking around it. You can also get a peek at a small waterfall in the creek down below to your left. Step over a couple of roots rising about 3 inches and then pass next to wooden fencing on the left with a bench on the right.

At 0.3 mile come to an intersection. The Rain Forest Nature Trail loops to the right and returns to the parking area—this path is generally level and easy, but I have not traveled it in a long time. The Quinault Loop Trail continues straight ahead. There is a large wooden trail board here, which usually has a map on it. Continue on a slight decline and travel between several large Sitka spruces, stepping around lots of small roots crossing the surface. Pass an old log and then come to lots of small rocks and step down four times on eroded roots that rise about 4 inches. Take a 10% decline for about 50 feet—you can start to hear the creek again off to the left. Continue on an 8% decline, stepping over lots of roots rising no more than 3 inches.

At 0.4 mile the trail narrows to about 2 feet and gets pretty brushy; curve right and left a few times, continue level, and then take a slight incline as it curves to the left. Continue passing narrowly between ferns and brush, crossing over a few small root mats and lots of rocks rising no more than 2 inches. The trail gets a little more brushy as it comes to a 10% incline pinched by trees. Step up on a series of rocks and roots next to a large Sitka spruce. Take five steps up, each 4 inches tall, and pass several large western redcedars. Continue on a 12% incline to a 20% incline for about 30 feet on slightly loose gravel and sand, decreasing to approximately 15%. Pass a blown-down tree and root ball as the trail levels out briefly and then descends at 10%, passes another large blowdown, and comes to a very steep section. Take a 25-foot-long 25% incline, stepping up on rocks. The trail then levels out to a slight incline and passes a large western redcedar on the left and a Sitka spruce on the right. Take a slight decline, curve right, and then enter a really nice grove of old-growth Sitka spruce with lots of devil's club. Pass over a series of roots rising a couple inches, then take a 10% incline and step up over lots of roots rising several inches as you pass between very large Sitka spruces. There are nice places to sit by a tree and take a break here.

Continue on a 5% incline, curve to the right, and at 0.7 mile you pass a closed trail on the right. Continue towards the left on the 3 foot wide compact gravel trail, then come to what appears to be another fork in the trail—on the left is an overlook of the creek and a waterfall when the water level is high. Continue past a couple of large western redcedars arching over the creek and at 0.8 mile come to a bridge over Willaby Creek. There's about a ¾-inch step up onto the bridge, which is made of tightly placed natural wood boards with railings on both sides. There is an old rough bench on the other side of the bridge. This is a really nice place to take a break, surrounded by the sound of water and lush green trees—I often enjoy a snack here before continuing on. But if you feel like turning back, this is the last place before you are too far around the loop. After this point, you will continue on a gentle, steady incline to a few steep sections through a not particularly interesting area until you reach the cedar bog in approximately 0.5 mile. Beyond the bog the trail gets a little more rugged, but you will pass many huge trees and a couple of waterfalls.

Continuing on, the trail curves to the left on a 10% incline on slightly loose gravel for about 200 feet as you rise above the opposite side of the creek. Pass a large Douglas fir as you take a 5% incline and curve to the right, continuing on a 3 to 5% incline on a loose gravel surface. The highlight of this section are the many salmonberries, thimbleberries, and huckleberries along the trail, but otherwise it is a bit unremarkable. It levels out on a pea gravel surface before narrowing to 1½ feet wide at 0.9 mile and passes through a very brushy and exposed section. The trail is lined with self-heal, geranium, and other common wildflowers.

At 1.0 mile you start to pass a few large Sitka spruces and western redcedars and the trail surface becomes deep pea gravel with a few small rocks. Continue on a long, gradual incline for a few hundred feet. Step over a couple of small metal culverts with some loose rocks. At 1.2 miles there's a small downed log on the left side that you can sit on. The trail continues about 1½ feet wide and brushy; as it starts approaching the woods again, there are nice views of the surrounding hillsides—on a foggy day you can watch the mist cling to and dance around the trees. At 1.3 miles there is another trail board on the right with a decommissioned trail behind it. Continue on the wide gravel trail to the left. There may be some mosquitoes and flying insects here as you are nearing the bog, but they have never been overwhelming. Pay attention for the sound of owls that nest in the area.

At 1.4 miles pass narrowly to the left of a root mat and a blowdown, then step down steeply about a foot from roots and cross over an area that is typically muddy during the wet months. You then arrive at the cedar bog. This section travels through old-growth western redcedars on boardwalks. Step up 2 inches onto the first boardwalk made of even boards with 1- to 2-inch gaps. You'll pass several old blowdowns with giant root balls, large skunk cabbage, and other wetland plants. At 1.5 miles there are two benches set off to the side on the boardwalk in an open and exposed area surrounded by western redcedars. The boardwalk continues for about 100 feet and then reenters the shady forest. There are a couple of very large trees here.

Continue on level compact gravel for about 100 feet and then arrive at another boardwalk. This boardwalk is about 100 feet long and ends onto gravel, then there is another boardwalk. There is another bench in the shade here, and it is a nice place to take a break—there are several large redcedars and a lush green understory. Take some time to appreciate how the light filters through the trees and reflects on the green plants, or how the fog settles in the trees if it's a cloudy day. When you're ready, continue on the boardwalk for about 150 feet, then step down about 4 inches onto hard-packed gravel. The trail curves to the left then declines slightly for 20 feet before arriving at another boardwalk with a 2-inch step up. This 100-foot-long boardwalk is a little uneven with a slight cross-slope and a 3-inch rise on either side. Continue on pea gravel and natural surface, generally level, with a couple of roots rising 3 to 4 inches above the surface as you pass a large Sitka spruce.

At 1.8 miles you pass over an area that is muddy during the winter—there is a log placed in the center of the trail—and then pass between an old blowdown on a slight rise and fall. You may notice the sound of the creek again. Take an 8% decline and watch out for logs protruding into the middle of the trail as you pass a couple of old blowdowns on the right. The trail continues narrow and brushy on a rocky gravel surface. At 1.9 miles the trail curves right and crosses a short footbridge with a 2-inch step down on the other side, then continues on a rocky surface through a brushy corridor. There are a couple of large roots across the trail, then you'll pass several blowdowns and a large rock in the trail. Take a slight decline and curve to the left, then you can hear the sound of flowing water. Take a slight incline with a few roots and rocks and then cross several large rocks.

At 2.0 miles reach an intersection with a trail board. There is usually a well-marked map here. The trail to the left is the most direct route back to the lodge. You'll pass some large western redcedars, but otherwise it's kind of unremarkable and there are a couple of steep sections. This loop continues to the right; it is approximately 0.25 mile longer to the road and then you have to walk farther either along the road or the lake to get back to your car, but it is more level, and you'll pass a couple of creeks and beautiful waterfalls with nice bridges. I think it's worth it. So, continuing to the right, cross over a couple of small rocks and then approach a bridge over Falls Creek. The creek typically rushes through a shallow canyon, though the water flow varies slightly; it's a nice place to lean against the bridge and take in the sounds and sights. On the other side, take a 5% incline and then switch back left on an 8% incline, increasing to 12% for the last few feet. As you approach a large spruce, you have to step up over and around several of its roots—two of them are about a foot tall. The trail continues on gravel surface on an approximately 5% incline. Curve to the right and continue on an 8% incline for about 20 feet before leveling out. Step down on a root and take a slight decline. The trail continues generally level to slightly rolling for approximately 0.1 mile with the sounds of flowing water getting louder.

At 2.2 miles you reach Cascade Falls. A sturdy, well-constructed bridge travels very closely over the creek. You can view a few small cascades above the falls and see the top of the falls from the bridge, but the full view may be partially obstructed depending on plant growth. On the other side of the bridge the trail curves left to a troublesome area that is about 50 feet long in total. The trail surface is exposed rock with a 25% decline; step down carefully on the uneven rocks for about 20 feet, then continue on a 10% decline and step down on some roots. The outer edge of the trail is then eroded for a few feet next to a wooden barrier, where people have gone off-trail down to the creek. It is narrow and uneven with a steep cross-slope and a drop-off on the left, so be careful. The trail then continues evenly on a slight decline for about 50 feet then levels out. Watch out for a couple of roots protruding into the trail rising about 3 inches. You are surrounded by a forest of tall trees as you travel high above Falls Creek. You then cross over a small culverted stream with a short drop-off on the left. The trail continues level but narrow and brushy as you pass next to an old-growth Sitka spruce and step around its roots.

At 2.3 miles take a 10% incline as the sound of flowing water gets louder to your left. Step over a couple of eroded roots rising a couple inches and then be very careful as you continue next to a wooden barrier on the left—the trail has eroded significantly for a couple feet where people have created a social trail down to the creek. The level area is only about 6 inches wide with a steep drop-off on the left, but you can cross it in a step or two.

You'll continue on a level gravel trail, then at 2.5 miles approach a couple of very large Sitka spruces on the left, followed by an old-growth western redcedar on the left. Cross a short footbridge over a stream with lots of thimbleberries and devil's club. The trail then forks at another information board with a map. If you go straight ahead up the hill, it's 2 miles to Gatton Creek Campground and the road. Continue left on the level trail, and as you approach Falls Creek again, take a 5% decline for about 20 feet, switch back to the left, and continue on a 5% decline on slightly loose pea gravel. You'll see, and possibly smell, the new bridge across Falls Creek as you curve to the right and pass underneath a huge, mossy bigleaf maple. This is a nice, cool, shady spot where I generally take a long break. There are a couple of cut logs to sit on before the bridge and an old unstable bench on the other side. There isn't good access to the creek, but you can sit very close to it. The trail continues generally level on compact pea gravel then rises 10% for 15 feet and passes several large Sitka spruces. It then continues level and even, passing an old blowdown on the left and some exposed roots on the right. Incline again at 10% for 50 feet next to western redcedars and Sitka spruces, curve left on a 12% incline, and enter a hemlock forest.

The trail continues level briefly then curves right on an 8% incline, curves left, and continues on a 5% incline. You are traveling through a dense, dark forest of hemlock trees that can feel a little spooky under the right conditions, with lots of fallen logs and roots growing at odd angles in the forest. The trail curves right on an 8% decline, passes a large Douglas fir, then switchbacks left on a 10% decline for 30 feet. It then levels out and continues straight on level and even compact gravel. At 2.9 miles step down on a couple roots, then up on a 6-inch root, and take a slight decline as the trail curves left with views of the hillside across the lake. Curve to the right and the trail gets rocky and pretty rutted, with an old blowdown arching on the left side. Continue on a loose, rocky 8% decline for a few feet. Step down from a culvert onto loose rocks and curve left on a slight decline then right as you cross a short footbridge, then curve left and right.

At 3.1 miles you cross a 30-foot-long footbridge lined with horsetail as you approach the road. The bridge puts you out right onto the shoulder of the road, so be alert for cars. Cross the road to the small parking area on the other side. The ranger station will be on your left. The shortest route back to the Rain Forest Nature Trail trailhead is to walk about 0.25 mile along the road, but there is not much of a shoulder and people tend not to obey the 25 mph speed limit. If you choose to continue on the loop trail, you'll pass through the resort, follow the shore of Quinault Lake, and then ascend briefly along a creek and a waterfall, but there is one section that is difficult to navigate with steep steps and the lakeshore may be covered with large pieces of driftwood in the winter.

To continue the loop, follow the path at the edge of the parking area as it swings down to Falls Creek. There is a little waterfall under the bridge with a large bigleaf maple. You can sometimes see fish in the creek here. Continue straight ahead and then curve left, following the shore of the lake and signs indicating this is a National Recreation Trail. You'll enter the resort grounds, and might want to take a break at one of the chairs or benches. There are a few very large coastal redwoods, which are rare to see here. Continue on the path through the grassy area and pick up the gravel path along the lake. You'll pass several interpretive signs with Indigenous history, art, and legends of the area.

At 3.3 miles the trail forks; continue to the right. The trail narrows slightly and switchbacks to the left before leveling out again. You then closely follow the lakeshore, with private cabins above you on the left and some private docks on the right. At 3.5 miles pass another interpretive sign on the right with a large Sitka spruce growing from an old nurse log. Curve right and step over a couple of small roots. Come to a fork in the trail with a trail board and map. The trail to the left leads you to the Lake Lane trailhead; straight ahead leads to Willaby Campground and the Nature Trail. The Lake Lane trailhead leads back to the road; it is easier, though you have to walk on the road for 0.1 mile and cross the street and a bridge.

To finish this loop, continue straight ahead and step up onto a footbridge over a stream. The trail narrows and becomes brushy; take a slight incline then curve left, and enjoy some nice, clear views of the lake. Step across several rocks and log rounds on an uneven surface. At 3.7 miles take a slight incline and step up to a short footbridge. Curve left at

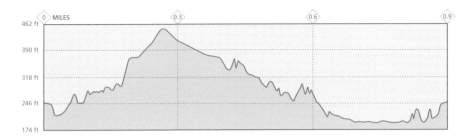

another interpretive sign and continue to follow the lake for 0.1 mile. You then curve left to cross a rocky outcropping with a slight incline. Pass next to a very large western redcedar and cross another bridge over a stream with a small waterfall—this is a tranquil spot to pause for a moment. The trail curves right and left then takes a 10% incline for 30 feet with the lake below you on the right. It then gets pretty rocky for a few feet and at 3.9 miles comes to a very eroded section of trail, very narrow with a sharp drop-off on the right. The trail rolls a few times with roots and rocks in the surface and an eroded outer edge, passing many western redcedars.

At 4.0 miles you enter the campground. Step up onto the paved campground road and follow it towards the right, passing several campsites and following signs for the Rain Forest Nature Trail. You'll pass the campground bathrooms on the left. Continue straight past the campground sitemap and take an 8% decline. At 4.1 miles there is a sign for the day-use picnic area straight ahead. Go towards the left and you'll see a good map for the trail system. There are icons indicating accessible trails, though they are appropriately labeled as moderate/difficult. Continue left on the gravel and natural surface trail with views of the creek on the right.

It is generally level and even until you reach an old stone and concrete bridge over Willaby Creek at 4.2 miles. It's a really nice spot, with the creek rushing below you and a couple of small waterfalls. There's an old log on the left that you can sit on and take a break, which I recommend because next you have to climb up to the road that you can see above you. The trail continues on an 8 to 10% incline as it curves to the left, then gets rocky and curves to the right, stepping up about 8 inches onto roots and rocks and then crossing on rocks as you pass underneath the road. This is a neat view under the bridge as it spans the creek. Continue on an incline, stepping up on roots, and then come to the most difficult section: a set of steep eroded stairs with eroded sections on both sides where people have tried to bypass them. The first two steps you can pass on the right, but the last one is really eroded and narrow with a 2-foot-tall step up you can pass on the side. Then take one step up rising about 10 inches followed by two short steps, and then you reconnect with the Rain Forest Nature Trail. Go right to return to the parking area.

MILES AND DIRECTIONS

- **0.0** Start to the left of the information board on the south side of the parking area.
- **0.1** The Lake Shore Trail forks to the left. Continue straight.
- **0.3** The Rain Forest Nature Trail forks to the right. Continue straight.
- **0.7** Continue left past a closed trail.

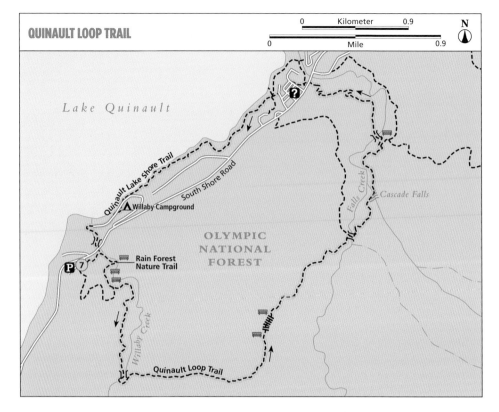

0   Kilometer   0.9

0   Mile   0.9

N

Lake Quinault

Quinault Lake Shore Trail

South Shore Road

▲Willaby Campground

Falls Creek

Cascade Falls

OLYMPIC
NATIONAL
FOREST

Rain Forest
Nature Trail

P 7

Willaby Creek

Quinault Loop Trail

0.8   Cross a bridge over Willaby Creek.

1.3   Continue straight past a decommissioned trail and a trail board.

1.45 Enter the cedar bog. Continue on boardwalk.

2.0   Reach a trail intersection. Go right and cross the bridge over Falls Creek.

2.2   Cross the bridge over Cascade Falls.

2.3   Reach a 2-foot-long section of eroded trail with a 6-inch-wide level area and steep drop-off.

2.5   Reach a trail intersection. Go left.

2.7   Cross the bridge over Falls Creek.

3.1   Cross South Shore Road and follow the trail down to Falls Creek.

3.3   The trail forks. Go right.

3.5   Pass the Lake Lane trailhead. Continue straight.

4.0   Enter Willaby Campground. Follow the road to the right.

4.1   Go left before the day-use area. Pick up the trail at a large trail information sign.

4.2   Cross a bridge over Willaby Creek and continue under South Shore Road.

4.3   Go right on the Nature Trail to return to the parking area.

4.4   Arrive back at the parking area.

8 QUINAULT LAKESHORE SCENIC DRIVE

WHY GO?

This scenic drive takes you on a tour around Lake Quinault and up the Quinault River valley through the rain forest. You'll pass two easily accessible waterfalls and a variety of environments, from open meadows to old-growth western redcedar and Sitka spruce, and end at giant bigleaf maples. There is a lot to experience here regardless of the season, but the waterfalls are strongest from October to May, and the fall colors can be spectacular. The road is mainly gravel and dirt, a wide single lane with pullouts, and has a couple of steep sections and hidden curves. It can be dusty and washboarded in the summer and wet in the winter with occasional closures, so be sure to call ahead.

THE RUNDOWN

Type: Scenic drive
Distance: 26 miles
Elevation: 300 feet
Typical width and surface: Two-lane pavement and wide singletrack dirt road. Drivable in a standard passenger car, not advised for large vehicles or RVs.
Season/schedule: Year-round, pending winter closures
Amenities: There is a gas station and food service in Quinault. Ranger stations are located at the beginning of both the South Shore and North Shore Roads.
Dog-friendly: Pets allowed on all roads and in parking areas. Allowed on leash on trails in Olympic National Forest (south side of the lake); not allowed on trails in Olympic National Park (north side of the lake).
Cell phone reception: None
Nearest town: Quinault
Land manager: Olympic National Forest, (360) 288-2525; Olympic National Park, (360) 565-3130
Pass/entry fee: None required for the drive
Land acknowledgment: Quinault. Kexnaxx'el (meaning "the people," referring to the Quinault) fish for sockeye from the shores of Lake Quinault and conduct canoe races, both important cultural traditions.

FINDING THE TRAILHEAD

Getting there: Lake Quinault is 40 miles north of Aberdeen on US 101. To begin this loop, start at South Shore Road, just south of Amanda Park. GPS: 47.45985, -123.86206
Start: South Shore Road at the Rain Forest Nature Trail trailhead

Typical trail with large Sitka spruce

THE HIKE

For the quickest access to the waterfalls, start the loop on South Shore Road in Quinault. Set your odometer at the Rain Forest Nature Trail trailhead and travel the paved two-lane road through Quinault. At approximately 2.0 miles, just past the Salmon House and Rain Forest Resort Village, there will be a large gravel parking area on the right. This is the trailhead for the "World's Largest Sitka Spruce." Cross the street to take a very nice short and level walk to the tree.

Continue through the small town of Norwood, passing through a valley with mountain views all around you. At 5.0 miles you arrive at a small bridge next to Merriman Falls. There are gravel pullouts on both sides with room for four cars total—if this is full, there are two more pullouts a little farther down the road. You can view the waterfall from the road, or you can walk behind the barrier and take a short, rocky path to the base of the falls. This is a really fun place to get out and enjoy the sound of the falls and the rushing mist on your skin.

At 6.5 miles the pavement ends and the road turns to a wide one-lane dirt road with turnouts. Unfortunately there is no sign warning you that the pavement ends, so go slowly and be alert—you'll see a sign that says you're entering Jefferson County. The condition of this road really varies depending on the weather and when it is graded, but it is generally moderately washboarded and bumpy. The speed limit is 25 mph, but 15 mph is the fastest I go in a small passenger car.

At 9.8 miles you cross a bridge over a creek while traveling through a really beautiful forest of Sitka spruce and western redcedar, with some bigleaf maples arching gracefully along the way. At 10.4 miles the forest opens up along the river with views into the mountains. Then at 10.7 miles you arrive at Bunch Falls. This is the largest waterfall in the Quinault area and is highly photographed. There are a couple of pullouts on both sides of the bridge. It is a nice place to pull over for a break to enjoy the waterfall and the river. There are a couple of small waterfalls along the road as well.

After Bunch Falls, you cross into Olympic National Park. The Quinault River continues on your left, with beautiful views of the surrounding mountains. The road is now gravel and goes past several large western redcedars, then starts to climb a little and curve a few times. You'll see a bridge ahead of you. At 11.6 miles the road forks. Straight ahead takes you 6 miles to the Graves Creek Ranger Station and Campground. To continue on the loop drive, turn left to cross the bridge. You are now on North Shore Road. The road changes to pavement for 1 mile as you pass through meadow. There are often elk and deer here, so be on the lookout. At 12.7 miles you reenter a nice, mossy green forest and then immediately hit gravel again—there is no warning here either, so go slowly. This road is a narrow one lane with pullouts but continues on gravel rather than dirt. You are traveling through a really pretty, mossy forest dominated by bigleaf maples.

At 13.3 miles the road inclines steeply, with a couple of pullouts. This section is very bumpy and has potholes as it passes among lots of big western redcedars. The steep grade ends at 13.5 miles as you curve right and then curve left and right on another steep grade; there's a sharp drop-off on the left. It is single lane with no pullouts then levels out with a pullout on the left. The road curves a couple of times and starts to decline. At 13.9 miles a little road goes uphill to the right; you continue straight and take the sharp right curve, then curve left, passing through old-growth trees. The road continues level, passing through mossy forest with a fern-covered floor. At 14.6 miles the road curves right and left and there are a lot of potholes here. The road widens slightly.

QUINAULT LAKESHORE SCENIC DRIVE

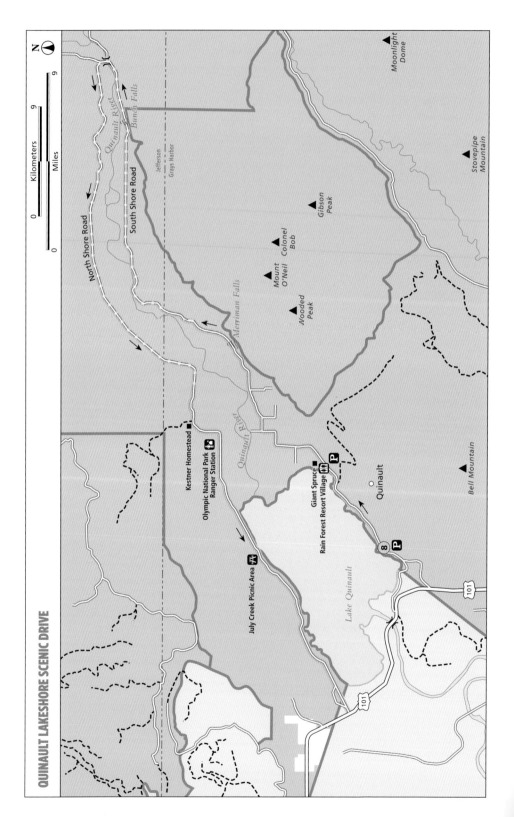

North Shore Road

South Shore Road

Quinault River

Bunch Falls

Jefferson

Grays Harbor

Kestner Homestead

Olympic National Park Ranger Station

July Creek Picnic Area

Merriman Falls

Quinault River

Giant Spruce

Rain Forest Resort Village

Quinault

Lake Quinault

Mount O'Neil

Colonel Bob

Gibson Peak

Nooded Peak

Stovepipe Mountain

Moonlight Dome

Bell Mountain

101

8

N

Miles

Kilometers

0   9

0   9

At 15.8 miles cross a paved bridge over Big Creek, returning to a gravel road. At 16.2 miles the road curves to the right and passes old-growth cedars then narrows to single lane again. Take a long left curve and then a short right curve. A wetland area is down below you on the left, with lots of large redcedars as the road continues to follow the hillside along the river. At 16.8 miles take a slight rise and there's a large pullout on the left with nice views of the mountains and trees. Descend slightly as you drop back into a mossy bigleaf maple forest.

At 18.0 miles the road returns to pavement with a 25 mph speed limit. At 19.1 miles you come to a stop and a single-lane wooden bridge that leads over Falls Creek. At 19.7 miles you pass the Kestner Homestead on the right; access to the homestead is from the ranger station at mile 20.2. There are restrooms and a visitor center as well as a couple of accessible trails—check out the Olympic National Park accessibility page for trail information. At mile 22.4 you come to the July Creek Picnic Area. This is a nice stop along the north shore of Lake Quinault. At 26 miles you return to US 101—go right to head north or left for south.

9 BIG CREEK NATURE TRAIL

WHY GO?

The accessible portion of the Upper Big Creek Loop Trail, sometimes referred to as the Big Creek Nature Trail, is truly a gem. It offers a rare opportunity to travel through mature second-growth rain forest, surrounded by towering mossy trees, the sounds of flowing water, and a little bit of solitude while still close to amenities and other people.

THE RUNDOWN

Spoon rating: 2 spoons. Wheelchair hikeable—there are five grades of 8 to 10% up to 50 feet long, with one grade approaching 15% for a few feet. There is one set of roots rising 2 inches above the surface that can be navigated with care. The Mount Rose Trail Crew plans to improve these sections.
Type: Out-and-back
Distance: 0.6 mile
Elevation: 980 feet
Elevation gain: 40 feet
Max grade: 15%
Max cross-slope: 2%
Typical width: 3 feet
Typical surface: Hard-packed, firm pea gravel
Trail users: Hikers
Season/schedule: Year-round
Water availability: In campground spring through fall

Amenities: Accessible toilets, accessible parking, picnic tables, benches
Dog-friendly: Yes, on leash
Cell phone reception: Spotty
Nearest town: Hoodsport
Land manager: Olympic National Forest, Hood Canal District, (360) 765-2200
Pass/entry fee: Federal recreation pass. You can park at the pullouts along the road and enter without a pass.
Land acknowledgment: Sqʷuqʷóbəš (Twana/Skokomish), "People of the River," whose traditional territory included the entire Hood Canal drainage basin in western Washington.

FINDING THE TRAILHEAD

Getting there: From Hoodsport, take US 101 to WA 119 and turn left (west). This two-lane paved road has sections of curves with speed limits of 25 to 45 mph through residential and forest areas. The road comes to a T-intersection with FR 24; turn left and then immediately right into the campground. There is one ADA accessible spot in a paved parking area in front of the gate, with four total spots. Additional parking is available along FR 24 in pullouts. There are two parking spots, including one accessible spot, at the restrooms nearest the trailhead. GPS: 47.49608, -123.21346
Start: Inside Big Creek Campground

THE HIKE

The gate to the campground is closed during the winter, but visitors may still access the trails. A footpath near the gate leads into the campground, but you may prefer to take the

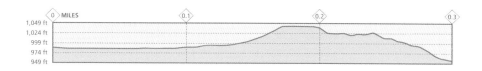

road in. There is a paved 4-foot-wide path around the gate. It is approximately 0.25 mile from the gate to the trailhead, all on a steady incline of approximately 5%.

The road into the campground is paved, turning to gravel after passing the camp-ground host site. Curve left past a broad gravel parking area with a fee station and restrooms. At the fork continue straight, following signs towards the north loop. Watch out for some loose gravel and potholes. Crest a hill past site 42 and look for the rest-rooms on the left with one accessible parking spot and one gravel parking spot. Park here if you drive in.

The trail starts behind the restrooms. Follow the wide, loose gravel path to the left behind the restrooms, as it immediately curves left to an 8 to 10% incline for approxi-mately 50 feet. Turn right at the T where the trail meets with another path, then take another 6 to 8% incline for 20 feet. You then come to a fork with a sign pointing to the Upper Big Creek Loop Trail, Big Creek Campground Trail, and Mount Elinor Con-nector Trail. Continue straight on the Upper Big Creek Loop Trail, heading towards the bridge. There is a short decline of 8 to 10% for 50 feet, then a very slight rise for 5 feet to the bridge. It is level going onto the bridge. There are a couple of boards on the other side with a 2-inch rise, but you can navigate around them easily. The bridge is a marvelous construction over rushing Big Creek; it's very sturdy with parallel boards and wood slat barriers on either side. The barriers somewhat block the view from sit-ting height.

On the other side of the bridge, the trail surface is hard-packed pea gravel, a very firm surface to travel on, and is 3 feet wide. The trail declines slightly then curves left. You will almost immediately come to a couple of roots rising about 2 inches above the surface. The trail crew plans to cover these, but they can be bypassed with very careful maneuvering. Traveling amongst towering mossy trees, the trail declines at 8 to 10% for approximately 50 feet as it curves to the right. It levels out with a pullout area on the left then curves sharply right again on a decline of 5%. The trail then levels out and passes between tall western redcedars before curving left and onto a small bridge over a seasonal water flow. The surface onto the bridge is level. On the other side of the bridge, the trail curves to the left on a 5% grade, continues level, then curves right between old-growth cedars. Curve left and right again then come to a 20-foot-long 10% decline, getting steeper near the bottom at 15% for a few feet. The trail continues to curve a few times amongst old-growth cedar and tall mossy maples in a gorgeous rain forest setting.

At 0.2 mile come to a small log bench on the right that blocks the old trail. You will continue on a level, hard-packed gravel trail that was recently built by the Mount Rose Trail Crew. Travel on a slightly crowned turnpike with a large fallen log on the left and a small ditch on the right then onto another level footbridge. The trail curves left around a western redcedar, then right and left around a hill with an 8 to 10% grade for 20 feet. It then continues level as you travel parallel to the creek before coming to a fork; the

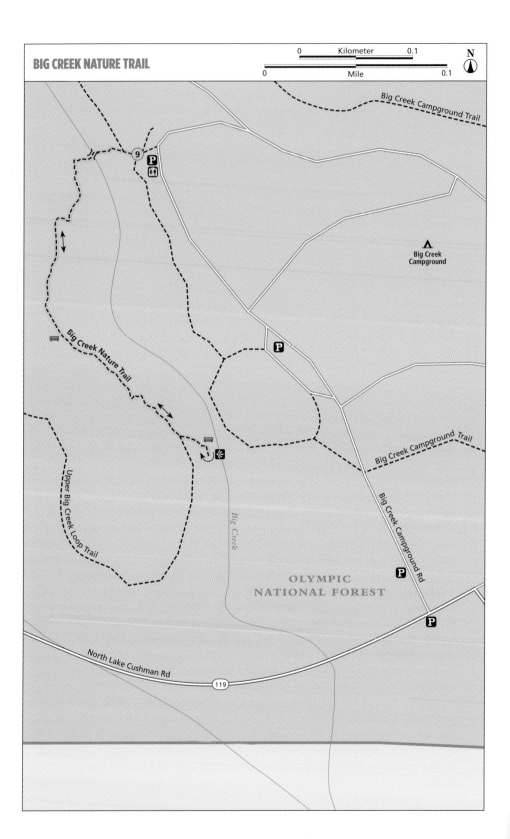

BIG CREEK NATURE TRAIL

Big Creek Campground Trail

9

Big Creek
Campground

Big Creek Nature Trail

Big Creek Campground Trail

Upper Big Creek Loop Trail

Big Creek

Big Creek Campground Rd

OLYMPIC
NATIONAL FOREST

North Lake Cushman Rd

119

upper loop trail continues right. To continue on the accessible trail, go left on a slight decline for 5 feet. You'll arrive at a beautiful resting spot next to the creek with a bench. The bench sits 16 inches above the ground and has an angled backrest with no armrests. There isn't a lot of space to turn around with a wheelchair, but you could back out slightly and turn around. This is the end of the accessible portion of the trail; turn back the way you came to return to the trailhead.

MILES AND DIRECTIONS

0.0   Start at the trailhead behind the restrooms. Turn right at the intersection, then go straight across the bridge.

0.3   Reach a bench overlooking Big Creek. Turn around here.

0.6   Arrive back at the trailhead.

PUGET SOUND

Puget Sound is the large inlet south of the Strait of Juan de Fuca, part of the larger body of water known as the Salish Sea. It is a complex environment with multiple waterways, islands, and peninsulas, representing one of the largest estuarine systems in the region. Puget Sound supports crucial environments for hundreds of species of fish, mammals, birds, and marine plants.

It is also the most densely populated area of Washington State, including the major cities of Everett, Seattle, Tacoma, and Olympia. But long before Europeans settled the area, it was the homeland of many Indigenous peoples. Duwamish, Suquamish, Nisqually, Puyallup, Snoqualmie, Snohomish, and many more have lived here since the beginning of human existence in the region. The area is rich and complex in history. The hikes represented in this section are in the ancestral lands of Dxʷdəwʔabš (Duwamish—meaning "people of the inside") and Qʷayʼáyiłq (Upper Chehalis).

Duwamish were the first to sign the 1855 Treaty of Point Elliot. However, settlers petitioned against the creation of a reservation and none has been created. The United States has yet to honor its obligation to the Duwamish Tribe, who have been fighting for federal recognition since 1978, and it is currently under appeal. Duwamish speak Lushootseed and are the host Tribe for Seattle. They operate nonprofit Tribal service programs and the Duwamish Longhouse and Cultural Center, as well as Real Rent Duwamish.

The Upper and Lower Chehalis lived along the Chehalis River and occupied much of the Chehalis River basin. The Chehalis languages are Quinault languages. The people rejected the treaties' unfair conditions and never ceded their lands to the US government. However, land was set aside for a reservation in 1864, and the Confederated Tribes of the Chehalis Reservation was federally recognized in 1939. The Tribe operates a number of successful businesses in southwest Washington.

10 DISCOVERY PARK LOOP TRAIL

WHY GO?

This loop trail circumnavigates Discovery Park and passes through forest and meadows, and along the edge of Magnolia Bluff above Puget Sound. In addition to typical ADA parking, the park offers a shuttle and parking passes to drive down to the beach for those who may not be able to access it otherwise. The park is a great place for a weekday hike close to the city or a weekend hangout if you don't mind the crowds. I highly recommend a visit to Daybreak Star Cultural Center, a major hub for Native American cultural activities and home to an art gallery. The center was founded in 1970 following a nonviolent occupation of the land by Indigenous activists after the military base was declared surplus by the US Department of Defense.

THE RUNDOWN

Spoon rating: 3 spoons. The park has a network of well-signed trails, but you should have a map or app with you. There are a lot of ups and downs on this loop, but none of the grades are very long and there are no other major obstacles. It is a mix of shade and exposed areas and offers a lot of variety and incredible views.
Type: Loop
Distance: 3.2 miles
Elevation: 213 feet
Elevation gain: 266 feet
Max grade: 20%
Max cross-slope: 10%
Typical width: 3 feet
Typical surface: Dirt, gravel, sand
Trail users: Hikers, trail runners
Season/schedule: Open year-round, 4 a.m. to 11:30 p.m.

Water availability: Water fountains
Special notes: Few benches and several narrow places where it may be difficult to allow someone to pass
Amenities: Restrooms, picnic tables
Dog-friendly: Yes, on leash
Cell phone reception: Yes
Nearest town: Seattle
Land manager: Seattle City Parks, (206) 684-4075
Pass/entry fee: None
Land acknowledgment: Duwamish. Long before its military use, the West Point of Discovery Park was named PKa'dz Eltue, meaning "thrust far out." This was a popular gathering spot for Duwamish and other Tribes.

FINDING THE TRAILHEAD

Getting there: Discovery Park is in the Magnolia neighborhood, south of Ballard and northwest of downtown Seattle. From W. Emerson Street, south of the Ballard Bridge, cross the railroad and turn right on Gilman Avenue W. Continue on this road all the way into the park. Turn left into the second driveway for the East Parking Lot at the visitor center. GPS: 47.6583, -122.406
Public transit: Metro Route 33 stops nearest to the visitor center on W. Government Way, and Metro Route 24 stops on W. Emerson Street near the parking lot at mile 2.5 on this loop.
Start: Parking area at the visitor center. The trailhead is located at the southwestern corner of the parking area, right as you drive in.

View of Puget Sound from Magnolia Bluff

THE HIKE

There is an information board with a map of the park and sometimes trail brochures, but you can download an app for Discovery Park. The trail starts next to a metal pole with green directional signs—these signs are placed at regular intervals on the trail and they are fairly easy to follow. Take five wooden steps down and continue on a 4-foot-wide, hard compact gravel trail. Immediately come to an 8% incline on loose dirt and gravel for about 100 feet, then come to an intersection at the start of the loop. Continue to the right, following signs for the Daybreak Star Center and the North Bluff. Continue on a slight incline, then level out and travel through a 40-foot-long tunnel under the road. Take another 8% incline on loose gravel and dirt for 50 feet, level out for a couple hundred feet, then take a slight decline as you travel through a brushy forest along the road into the park. There are bigleaf maples, cedars, and lots of stinging nettle along the side of the trail, so be careful with your hands and ankles. The surface continues on dirt and gravel, 2 to 3 feet wide and generally level.

At 0.2 mile take a slight roll next to two very large bigleaf maples and cross over a couple of roots rising 2 to 3 inches. Take a 10% decline with an 8% cross-slope for 15 feet, then a 10% incline for about 100 feet. The trail surface varies from slightly rocky to fresh compact gravel to dirt. At 0.4 mile there's a bench on a concrete platform on the left with a 6-inch step up. Continue on the wide dirt and gravel trail to another sign for the Discovery Park Loop Trail—continue straight ahead. The trail descends at 10% with a rut down the center as you approach the road—there is a crosswalk but be careful of cars and bicycles.

Across the road you continue through the forest on an 8-foot-wide gravel trail. The trail remains level for a few hundred feet and then inclines at 8% underneath some red alders and maples and curves to the right. A small hill rises to your left and a ravine on your right as you travel along the northern side of the park. Continue on a 3 to 5% incline for 200 feet, then the trail levels out briefly and curves to the left on an 8% incline. Pass under a large bigleaf maple that arches over the trail; the surface gets a little more rocky and narrows to 4 feet. Take a slight decline, passing through more bigleaf maples and lots of salmonberries, curve right, and then take a slight incline.

At 0.8 mile pass next to a large Douglas fir and underneath some western redcedars—the red-cedars' branches arch elegantly over the trail. The trail surface is mostly dirt with some small roots and an eroded outer edge. Continue level to a steep 15% decline for 10 feet then continue on a generally 10% decline, traveling above a ravine on the right. Take a short 10% incline with a sharp drop-off on the right and an uneven surface. Continue on a slight incline and at 0.9 mile take a 12% incline on a rocky surface, then cross a bike and pedestrian roadway. Continue straight, following signs for the Loop Trail. Take a 10% incline for about 10 feet and continue to a level, hard compact surface. Curve left on an 8% incline, then cross over several low roots on a 12 to 15% incline, curve right, and continue on a 10 to 15% incline for about 75 feet.

At 1.1 miles take a 10% decline and cross another pedestrian roadway. Continue straight ahead on the gravel path. The trail continues generally level for a bit and then comes to three steps down and an 8% decline on dirt and loose gravel to two more steps. Curve to the right and at 1.2 miles arrive at a grassy area with a fork in the trail—continue towards the left. You then cross another roadway and the trail forks—follow the sign for the Loop Trail, continuing on the gravel path towards the left. (The right trail leads downhill to North Beach and then steeply back uphill to reconnect with the Loop Trail.) Continue on a 5% incline for a couple hundred feet, passing a large bigleaf maple. Take a 10% incline then come to a paved section with a signed fork—continue to the right. Continue on the paved surface, passing underneath cottonwood trees, and at 1.3 miles meet up with the main road in the park. There are lots of cracks and potholes in the pavement as you travel parallel to the road; some cracks rise 6 inches and are 6 inches wide, and the surface is very uneven.

Cross the road at 1.4 miles, being very careful about cars and bicycles. Pick up the Loop Trail across the road (there is a porta-potty here if you need it) and continue on level compact gravel through an open area until 1.5 miles, when the trail curves to the left and becomes loose gravel on a 5% incline for a couple hundred feet. You then reenter a shady forest, traveling on a 10 to 15% cross-slope on slightly uneven ground. Then come to a 10 to 15% incline for about 100 feet, passing underneath many large maples. At 1.6 miles the canopy starts to open and you get glimpses of water through the trees.

At 1.7 miles you arrive at a large overlook of Puget Sound with a picnic table and a couple of benches in the shade. You can see Bainbridge Island and the Olympic Mountains to the west and the Cascade Range to the east, with sweeping views of the coastline. It is a really nice place to take a break, though it can be busy here. The Loop Trail continues straight past the picnic table and back into the forest. The trail becomes mostly dirt and continues on a slight decline, then levels out along a steep ravine on the right. The surface then becomes more sandy, inclines slightly, and levels out. At 1.8 miles there's a viewpoint on the right with a large maple and a bit of an overlook along the coastline—this is the last good shade for about 0.4 mile. Past the overlook, continue on a sandy trail

Typical trail view

across an open, grassy and sandy bluff with more incredible views of the sea—there are several overlooks and benches along the bluff. Follow the trail towards the left, continuing on some 2- to 3-inch-deep sand, then come to another trail sign at a trash can. Continue straight ahead for the Loop Trail. The trail surface then becomes a combination of compact gravel and sand and continues through an open area along the bluffs.

At 2.1 miles there is a fork on the right that leads to restrooms and a water fountain (if it's turned on). At 2.2 miles the trail moves back into the forest and takes a 5 to 8% incline then inclines at 12 to 15% for 50 feet, passing underneath a large arching maple, and continues on a gradual incline for about 100 feet and then levels out. You then come to another signed intersection—continue straight, curving right up the hill on a 10% grade for about 100 feet. At 2.4 miles go past a set of stairs that lead to W. Emerson Street and continue to the left. Take a 20% incline on dirt for about 75 feet, then cross a road and continue straight ahead. Take a 10% incline on loose gravel and sand, then the trail levels out. Pass an open area on the left with a couple of very large bigleaf maples. Continue straight ahead and at 2.5 miles the trail meets up with the road—continue towards the parking area (there are porta-potties here), then cross the road and pass another trail sign indicating you are 0.6 mile from the visitor center. Continue towards the right on a level, gravel and sand trail with W. Emerson Road on your right. Pass underneath a very large madrone and continue through a shaded forest.

At 2.7 miles you come to another fork—go left and continue on a 3-foot-wide path. You're back in the secondary forest near the developed areas of the park, and passing through lots of stinging nettle and maples. Pass another sign and continue straight ahead. You then come to another fork—continue towards the left on a generally level, sandy trail. Take a slight incline as the trail curves left. Pass around a root in the trail and watch out for

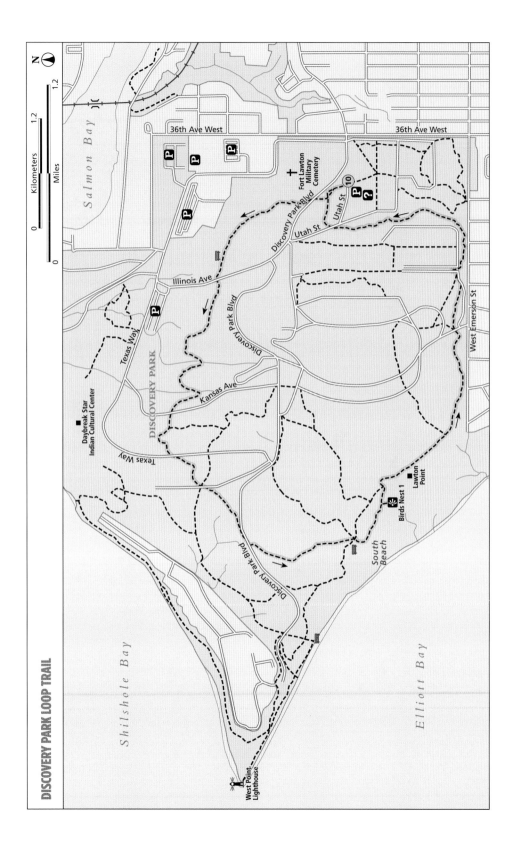

DISCOVERY PARK LOOP TRAIL

N

Kilometers
0   1.2   1.2

Miles
0   1.2

Salmon Bay

36th Ave West

36th Ave West

Fort Lawton
Military
Cemetery

Utah St

Utah St

10

Discovery Park Blvd

Illinois Ave

Texas Way

DISCOVERY PARK

DISCOVERY PARK

Daybreak Star
Indian Cultural Center

Texas Way

Kansas Ave

Discovery Park Blvd

West Emerson St

Lawton
Point

Birds Nest 1

South Beach

Discovery Park Blvd

Shilshole Bay

West Point
Lighthouse

Elliott Bay

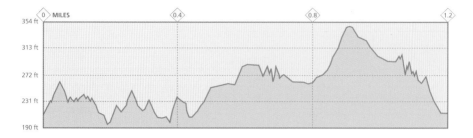

a couple of holes. The trail continues at a 10% cross-slope for about 30 feet. You're up on a hill with the road down below you. At 2.8 miles step down on a set of roots at about a 15% decline, passing next to a bigleaf maple in the center of the trail. Continue on a slight decline, curving left and right, passing many large maples, then take a 5% incline. Take a sandy 12% decline with a couple of roots rising a few inches above the surface.

At 3.0 mile arrive at a paved roadway. You can either turn right and follow the road to return to the visitor center in 0.1 mile or go left and follow the Loop Trail to continue to the visitor center in 0.2 mile. I continued on the Loop Trail, crossing the road and taking the trail towards the left. Continue on a sandy gravel trail that is 2 to 3 feet wide. Curve right on a slight incline, then take a 10% incline for about 50 feet to another fork in the trail. Continue straight ahead for the Loop Trail. Take a 10% decline with a root in the center of the trail, then curve to the right on a 20% decline for about 30 feet with one root rising about 4 inches across the trail. Continue on a 15% decline, curve to the left, and at 3.1 miles return to the start of the loop. Go right to return to the visitor center parking area.

MILES AND DIRECTIONS

0.0 Start at the trailhead next to the information board.

0.05 Arrive at the beginning of the loop. Go right and pass through a short tunnel under Discovery Park Boulevard.

0.4 Cross Illinois Avenue.

0.9 Cross a paved bicycle and pedestrian roadway, then continue straight at the fork.

1.1 Cross a paved bicycle and pedestrian roadway.

1.2 Go left at the fork, following signs for the Loop Trail.

1.4 Cross Discovery Park Boulevard.

1.7 Reach an overlook of Puget Sound.

2.1 The trail forks. Restrooms and a water fountain are to the right. The Loop Trail continues straight.

2.4 Go past the stairs to W. Emerson Street and cross the paved bicycle roadway.

2.5 Pass a parking area and cross Wisconsin Street. Arrive at a trail sign. Follow the Loop Trail to the right.

2.7 The trail forks. Go left.

3.0 Cross the road and pick up the Loop Trail towards the left.

3.1 Reach the end of the loop. Go right to return to the parking area.

3.2 Arrive back at the parking area.

11 SQEBEQSED TRAIL

WHY GO?

Seward Park on the Bailey Peninsula is home to one of the last old-growth forests in Seattle and a rare western prairie with Washington State's only native oak tree. It is truly a magical oasis in the city. The Washington Audubon Society has a center here where you can find a lot of information about the birds in the park. Friends of Seward Park also provides bird and plant checklists on its website.

THE RUNDOWN

Spoon rating: 2 spoons, wheelchair hikeable. Firm, compact surface and very short gentle grades until the final 0.1 mile. The only obstacles are two short boardwalks without railings and a few roots.
Type: Out-and-back
Distance: 2.2 miles
Elevation: 115 feet
Elevation gain: 59 feet
Max grade: 12%
Max cross-slope: 5%
Typical width: 6 feet
Typical surface: Compact gravel
Trail users: Hikers
Season/schedule: Open 6 a.m. to 10 p.m. year-round

Water availability: Water fountains
Amenities: Restrooms, benches, picnic tables
Dog-friendly: Yes, on leash
Cell phone reception: Yes
Nearest town: Seattle
Land manager: Seattle City Parks, (206) 684-4075
Pass/entry fee: None
Land acknowledgment: Duwamish refer to the peninsula as skEba'kst, meaning "nose," and the marshland as cka'lapsEb, meaning "neck." These were important hunting and fishing grounds, and the people gathered cattails to build summer houses.

FINDING THE TRAILHEAD

Getting there: From downtown Seattle, take I-90 to exit 3—Rainier Avenue South. Turn right and continue for 3 miles. Turn left at S. Orcas Street and continue into the park on Seward Park Road. Go past the Audubon Center and some street-side parking, and take the first right into a one-way parking lot (if you miss it, just continue around the loop past the amphitheater). Park here and cross the road to the trailhead. GPS: 47.55179, -122.25388
Public transit: Metro route 50 stops at Seward Park.
Start: Trailhead across the street from the parking area

THE HIKE

The Sqebeqsed Trail (pronounced skuh–BUHK-suhd) is named for how Duwamish refer to the peninsula. It is a Lushootseed word that translates as "the noses." This trail

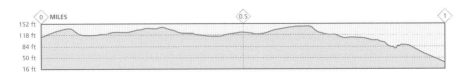

Old western redcedar and vine maples along the trail

is an old service road that runs the length of the peninsula through old-growth forest before descending to North Beach. Several trails branch off from it, but just stick to the wide gravel path and you can't get lost. From the trailhead, go left on a gravel path, then curve right next to a large western redcedar. Continue on a 5% incline to a gravel hump over a tree root with an 8% grade on either side. Take a 10% decline for about 10 feet, decreasing to 5% and then crossing on a turnpike. Continue on a level gravel path, passing huge western redcedars. At 0.1 mile come to a boardwalk with a 1½-inch rise on either side and tightly placed but somewhat uneven boards with no barriers and a 10-inch drop off the edge. Transfer to gravel and then come to another boardwalk; this one has no barriers and a 5% cross-slope with a 2-inch rise on the opposite side. Next is a short metal boardwalk with a ½- to 1-inch rise on either side.

Take a 5% incline, then continue straight past the fork at 0.2 mile. There are several exposed roots here that may catch your toes and be difficult to navigate with a wheelchair. Continue on a 6-foot-wide compact gravel path with a 3 to 5% incline. You are traveling beneath towering cedars and maples, surrounded by lush forest. At 0.4 mile you come to another intersection with a low basalt column trail sign—continue straight ahead. The wide gravel path continues generally level until 0.5 mile. Take a 5 to 8% incline for about 50 feet, level out, then continue on a 3% incline. At 0.7 mile come to a 5 to 8% incline for 30 feet with a bench on the right. The trail levels out then takes a slight decline; the surface gets a little rocky here, with some large gravel. Continue straight ahead on a 5% decline. You'll start to get views of the water through the trees.

At 0.9 mile the trail begins on a gradual decline with grades of 3 to 5%. At 1.0 mile come to an 8% decline for about 20 feet. You are approaching the beach and may start to hear the sounds of watercraft and people recreating. Continue on a 5% decline, increasing

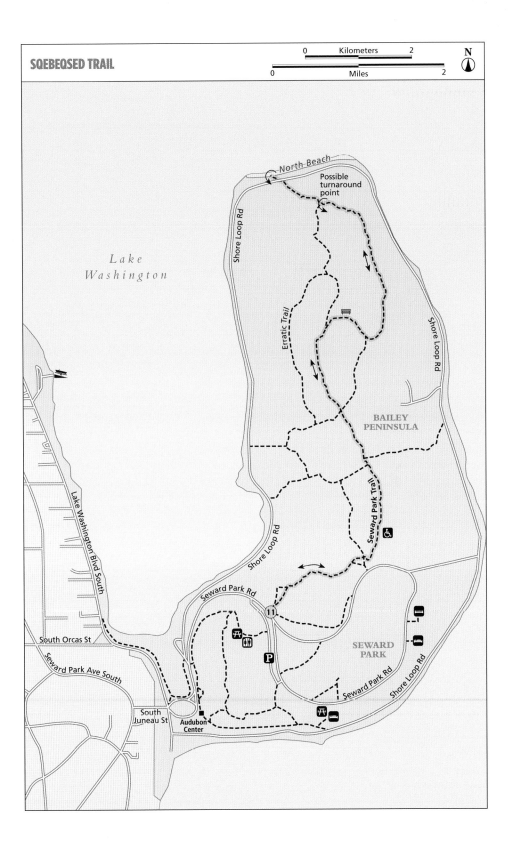

Lake
Washington

North Beach

Possible
turnaround
point

Shore Loop Rd

Erratic Trail

Shore Loop Rd

BAILEY
PENINSULA

Seward Park Trail

Shore Loop Rd

Seward Park Rd

11

SEWARD
PARK

Lake Washington Blvd South

South Orcas St

Seward Park Ave South

Seward Park Rd

Shore Loop Rd

South
Juneau St

Audubon
Center

Slightly uneven boardwalk near the beginning of the trail

to 12% for a few feet as the trail ends at the beach. You can cross the perimeter trail and hang out on the sand or one of the benches. There are great views of Seattle and Lake Washington. You can either go back on the Sqebeqsed Trail or take the Perimeter Trail, but that requires walking back on the road and up a steep hill to return to the parking area.

There are many additional trails within Seward Park, with varying degrees of accessibility. The Fairy Loop trail, described at the trail board at the parking area, consists of trail portions that have been modified to be somewhat accessible. The loop does not meet ADA accessibility standards, but you may find it to be wheelchair hikeable—it is a 0.35-mile loop with a maximum grade of 9% and cross-slope of 3%. The Perimeter Loop is a 3-mile, generally level paved roadway that circles the peninsula. It is a very popular wheelchair-friendly trail.

MILES AND DIRECTIONS

0.0   Start at the trailhead across the street from the parking area.

0.2   Continue on the wide gravel trail past the fork.

0.4   Continue on the wide gravel trail past the fork.

0.9   The trail starts to descend to North Beach.

1.1   Reach North Beach. Turn around or take the paved Perimeter Trail.

2.2   Arrive back at the trailhead.

12 MCLANE CREEK NATURE TRAIL

WHY GO?

The McLane Creek Trail in Capitol State Forest offers a beautiful sanctuary just 30 minutes from downtown Olympia. This nature trail travels through wetland and forest and follows a pond and a creek where visitors may see beavers, salmon, yellow pond lilies, and a myriad of other plants and wildlife. It is a 1.5-mile bisected loop trail, with options for a 0.6-mile loop and a 1.1-mile loop. The first portion is wheelchair accessible; the entire trail is mostly level, and there are many benches along the way. The trail is undergoing improvements, so the surface and design may change from what is described in this writing.

THE RUNDOWN

Spoon rating: 1 spoon for the 0.6-mile loop, wheelchair accessible for 0.25 mile on boardwalk and compact gravel. 1.5 spoons for the 1.1-mile loop—there are a few stairs, tree roots, and a couple of forks in the trail to navigate.
Type: Bisected loop
Distance: 0.6 mile or 1.1 miles
Elevation: 125 feet
Elevation gain: Less than 50 feet
Max grade: 15%
Max cross-slope: 5%
Typical width: 3 feet
Typical surface: Boardwalk, compact gravel, natural
Trail users: Hikers
Season/schedule: Open 8:30 a.m. to 8:30 p.m. year-round

Water availability: None
Amenities: Vault toilet, picnic tables
Dog-friendly: Yes, on leash
Cell phone reception: Yes, generally pretty good but GPS can be spotty
Nearest town: Olympia
Land manager: Washington State Department of Natural Resources, (360) 825-1631
Pass/entry fee: Washington Discover Pass
Land acknowledgment: Unceded territory of the Chehalis. Upper Chehalis (Qʷayáyiłq) or Tsihalis people (People of the Sands) had a large village (skwah-YAI'lh-hahbch) at the head of Eld Inlet at Mud Bay.

FINDING THE TRAILHEAD

Getting there: McLane Creek is on the east side of Capitol State Forest, less than 30 minutes from Olympia. Take US 101 towards Shelton, to Delphi Road. Delphi Road is a two-lane, paved semi-rural road. Continue for approximately 3 miles. The entrance to the park is slightly hidden, but there are signs for McLane Creek; look for a clear-cut area. Follow the one-lane paved forest road a short distance until it ends at the main parking area. There is paved and gravel parking for approximately twenty cars, with one accessible parking space. GPS 47.00072, -123.00328
Start: Next to the picnic shelter

THE HIKE

The trail starts near the picnic shelter. The wheelchair-accessible path is to the left, closer to the parking area. The walking path starts closer to the shelter; it is narrow but level, and brings you to an additional viewing platform before connecting with the accessible path. The accessible path is wide, crushed gravel and follows the edge of the parking area before passing the accessible toilet and curving to the right. It continues on then comes to an accessible viewing platform over the pond made of lateral wood boards with a bench at the end. The boardwalk continues to the left for 100 feet along the pond before transitioning to gravel and coming to a new composite-material boardwalk with an 8% gravel incline on either side. The trail then becomes compact gravel and passes narrowly between two trees before coming to the fork for the bisected loop. There is a bench here.

The right fork is the Old Railroad Grade Trail, which bisects the loop. It is primarily a boardwalk along the pond and is not wheelchair accessible, but offers up-close views of wildlife. The fork straight ahead continues on the outer loop. Continue on a boardwalk with no rise, covered in slip-resistant tread. There is a pullout area with a bench and an interpretive sign before the boardwalk curves to the left and continues 100 yards to another pullout with benches. The trail then forks again. To the left is a large viewing platform over the creek where you can see salmon in the spawning season. Travel on a short boardwalk covered in lateral metal slats over wood (they provide traction but are raised slightly, so watch your wheels/step) that then drops about 1 ½ inches to a compact gravel surface. There is a bench in this lovely grove of western redcedars. Continue a few feet on natural surface to the ramp to the viewing platform. It is lined with benches, so you can enjoy some time here.

Head back to the fork and continue the loop to the left. The boardwalk continues about 100 feet to a pullout with a bench. This is the end of the boardwalk; wheelchair users may want to turn around here, though the trail may be wheelchair hikeable for another 0.25 mile or so, depending on conditions. After the boardwalk, the trail widens and becomes compact gravel and natural surface, with some areas where trail-building material is exposed that may present a trip hazard, so be careful. The trail continues to follow the creek then curves to the right; a short path on the left leads to another viewing platform and bench at the creek beneath western redcedar. There is a 2-inch rise to the platform, and the boards are a bit uneven.

Continue on the trail among western redcedar, Douglas fir, devil's club, and other iconic PNW plants. Come to a short bridge with a 1-inch rise over a seasonal water flow. The trail then becomes natural surface and there are some muddy areas, a couple of dips, and a few low roots. Pass several remarkable tree stumps as the trail widens with a couple of larger roots in the middle—they are easy to navigate around. Come to another bridge with a 2-inch rise and 1-inch gap between the boards. The trail narrows again to 3 feet and there are several 2- to 3-inch roots in the path. There is another bridge with a 2-inch rise before the trail rolls slightly and comes to a short, narrow boardwalk and another path on the left. This path leads about 100 feet to a viewing bridge over the creek. The path is narrow and winds among the trees, with exposed trail material and roots and benches along the way. A set of seven stairs leads to a composite-material bridge that ends at a bench (it does not continue across the creek). It is a nice spot to sit under the trees with the creek flowing underneath.

Back at the main trail, continue left to a narrow boardwalk covered in slip-resistant tread. In about 200 feet there is a pullout with no bench, then the boardwalk ends at an intersection. To the right is the opposite end of the Old Railroad Grade Trail that bisects the loop—take this trail for the 0.6-mile loop. A set of seven stairs lead up to a board-walk that follows the pond. There is a sudden hump, then the boardwalk travels a short distance to a viewing platform with benches. The platform has a 2-inch rise and some

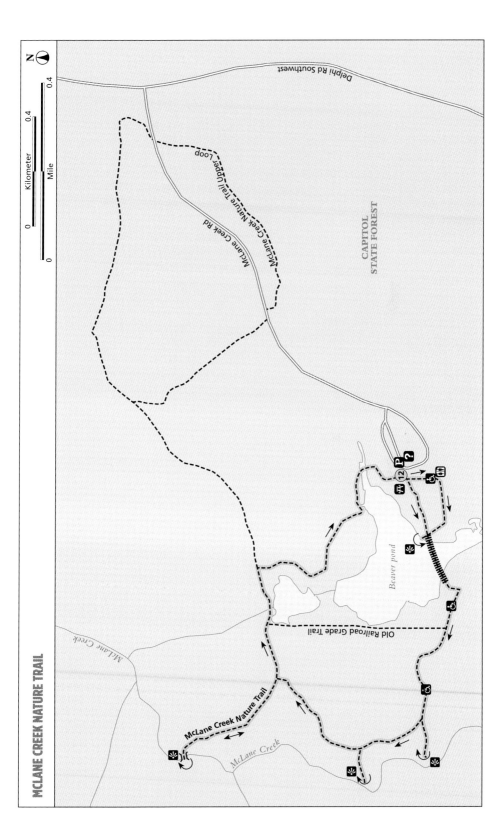

MCLANE CREEK NATURE TRAIL

McLane Creek

McLane Creek

McLane Creek Nature Trail

Old Railroad Grade Trail

Beaver pond

McLane Creek Rd

McLane Creek Nature Trail Upper Loop

CAPITOL STATE FOREST

Delphi Rd Southwest

N

0   0.4
Kilometer
0   0.4
Mile

unstable boards. The path then becomes compact gravel and rocks for 50 feet; there is a 6-inch root in the trail here. You reach another boardwalk with a pullout before ending at the first intersection you encountered on the trail. Go left to the parking area.

The fork straight ahead continues the 1.1-mile loop (and meets the Forestry Trail, a longer 3-spoon hike). You'll follow the shores of the beaver ponds, with many opportunities to stop and look or listen for birds and wildlife. Take two 6-inch steps to a bridge and then a slight decline to a gravel trail. The trail dips and then forks; continue to the right on a 15% decline for 10 feet. The trail narrows and rolls then curves to the left. There are several areas of mud and roots as the trail curves to the left, following the border of the forest around the pond. The path curves slightly to the right then comes to a short, 8% cross-slope. There is then a short path on the right to a viewing platform with two tall steps, overlooking the pond.

The trail continues to the left and becomes gravel with a couple of roots. There is a bench just before it curves again with a steep cross-slope. You then come to a bridge over the pond with two steps on either side. The trail rises on slightly loose gravel before it ends at the parking area and the shelter.

MILES AND DIRECTIONS

0.0 Start at the trailhead next to the picnic shelter.

0.3 Arrive at a viewing deck at the creek. This is the end of the accessible portion.

0.35 The path on the left leads to a viewing deck.

0.4 The path on the left leads to a viewing bridge over the creek.

0.5 Reach a trail intersection. Go right on the Old Railroad Grade Trail for the 0.6-mile loop or straight for the 1.1-mile loop (described below).

0.6 The trail forks. The Forestry Trail is to the left. Stay right on the nature trail, following the beaver ponds.

1.1 Arrive back at the picnic shelter.

WASHINGTON CENTRAL CASCADES

The Central Cascades are often defined by their proximity to the Seattle metro area and encompass the region around US 2 and I-90, and north of Mount Rainier. The mountains in this part of the Cascade Range are very different from the north but no less striking, and there are numerous alpine lakes. The biological diversity has been heavily impacted by development, but there are still martens, marmots, bobcats, bears, elk, and other animals in the wilderness areas. Mossy rain forests cover the west side of the slopes.

This area encompasses the ancestral lands of sdukʷalbixʷ (Snoqualmie), Skykomish, and Snohomish people. The Tribes signed the Treaty of Point Elliot, and in exchange the US government recognized their sovereignty as nations and promised to respect their reserved rights to their ancestral homelands. However, these rights have not been respected, and in 2019 the Snoqualmie Tribe sued the State of Washington for the protection of their federally recognized treaty rights. The case is currently in the Court of Appeals.

The Snoqualmie Tribe operates several successful businesses in the area. They also recently launched the Snoqualmie Ancestral Lands Movement, an initiative to raise awareness about the significance of these lands and provide information to help protect, respect, and restore Snoqualmie ancestral lands.

Snoqualmie Falls

13 COTTONWOOD LOOP

WHY GO?

Tolt-MacDonald Park, located at the confluence of the Tolt and Sno-qualmie Rivers, is truly a special place where you can feel like you are in the backcountry, with cell service and a campground, all less than 30 miles from Seattle. The park provides access to hundreds of miles of trails, but this loop offers some of the best of the park. It is particularly spectacular in the fall when the maples change color and the salmon return to the river.

THE RUNDOWN

Spoon rating: 4 spoons for the entire loop, 2 spoons for the river side. The forest section is a gently rolling ascent until the end, where it descends 100 feet in 0.1 mile on a very rooted and sandy surface. The river section has a firm, level surface with no obstacles.
Type: Loop
Distance: 2.7 miles
Elevation: 70 feet
Elevation gain: 150 feet
Max grade: 40%
Max cross-slope: 10%
Typical width: 3 feet
Typical surface: Natural
Trail users: Hikers, mountain bikers
Season/schedule: Year-round, gate is open dawn to dusk September through April, dawn to 10 p.m. May through Labor Day

Water availability: Campground
Special notes: No benches on the trail
Amenities: Vault toilet, picnic tables
Dog-friendly: Yes, on leash
Cell phone reception: Excellent
Nearest town: Carnation
Land manager: King County Parks, (206) 477-4527
Pass/entry fee: None
Land acknowledgment: Ancestors of the Snoqualmie Tribe occupied many permanent villages along the banks of the Snoqualmie and Tolt Rivers. The Snoqualmie continue their stewardship and connection with this land through many restoration projects.

FINDING THE TRAILHEAD

Getting there: Tolt-MacDonald Park is located at the south end of Carnation, Washington. Turn onto NE 40th Street from WA 203, and follow it for 0.3 mile into the park. There is a large parking area on the left before the gate, with two van-accessible parking spots. GPS: 47.64409, -121.92218
Public transit: Snoqualmie Valley Transportation bus route 629 stops at NE 40th Street and WA 203.
Start: The day-use parking lot. The trailhead is located on the other side of the suspension bridge.

THE HIKE

From the day-use parking area, head left on the road towards the campground. Go past the smaller campground parking area and veer left to the information and registration board. Go right and take the suspension bridge. The bridge is at a 15% incline on slightly

The 500-foot suspension bridge

unsteady, narrow boards with a 1½-inch gap; there is a 1-foot-wide section in the center of tightly placed boards. It levels out over the Snoqualmie River, but the bridge does sway a little bit and I found the gaps in the boards to be a little disorientating. The bridge declines at 15% on the other side. You then arrive at the backcountry campground and the beginning of the trail system. Note: This description starts the loop in the forest—it puts the steep grade on a descent. If you would prefer to take the grade on the way up, or if you only want to travel the river section, go to the right past the dumpsters and start on the wide sand and gravel path.

Continue straight past the dumpsters on the gravel path and you'll see an information board with a trail map. From the trail sign go right on compact gravel. Pass more campsites, then the trail transitions to a natural surface and you'll see a sign for the Cottonwood Loop. Continue straight ahead. The surface becomes slightly rocky as you cross a couple of small streams. Pass under several very large western redcedars. There is a slightly muddy area where two small streams flow down into the fern-covered ravine below you. Take an 8% incline, then step over another small stream. There are several signs cautioning you about bears in the area. Take a short 10% decline then incline as you pass over another little stream. There's a big hill rising above you on the left filled with mossy bigleaf maple, devil's club, and other native plants providing shade. Take a 10% incline for about 15 feet, then the trail rolls up and down a few more times. Take a 10% incline for about 8 feet, then pass over some roots across the trail; there is a 5% cross-slope for about 30 feet. The trail continues generally level then crosses another 8% cross-slope.

At 0.7 mile you come to an intersection with the Willow Walk leading off to the right. This is a shortcut to the other side of the Cottonwood Loop—if you want a shorter, easier loop, this is a nice option. To continue on the full loop, continue straight. Take a

A section of the riverside trail under the cottonwoods

rocky 5% incline with a slight cross-slope and then a 10% incline for about 8 feet. The trail levels out and continues pretty rocky, through a really beautiful mossy old-growth forest. After you cross over a culverted stream, pay attention for a wide, 6-inch-tall root across the width of the trail. At 0.8 mile the trail starts to roll again on slight grades and gets a little uneven, then comes to an 8% incline for about 100 feet. Level out briefly then take a 10% incline for 10 feet, and then a rolling 5 to 10% incline for 50 feet. The trail drops down slightly, passing under a large western redcedar, and then takes a 15% incline for 8 feet. Continue on a gradual decline, curving left on slightly uneven hard-packed natural surface. Cross over a small stream, declining then inclining slightly on either side. Step over a 4-inch-high root and then over a culverted stream. The trail continues generally rolling and uneven with some low roots and rocks in the surface.

At 1.0 mile take a 10% incline, stepping up on some low roots and passing a large western redcedar stump on the left. Cross over a few more roots rising up to 6 inches, then take a 15% decline for 15 feet then a 10% incline for 15 feet. Continue on a slightly loose rocky surface and take a 12 to 15% incline for about 20 feet. Curve to the right under a large maple, then take another 12% decline. Step down about 6 inches from a large cut-out log. There are views of the wetland down below on the right. Take a slight decline with a large root down the center of the trail, then a 5% incline as the trail curves right underneath large western redcedars and bigleaf maples. The trail continues level to slightly rolling.

At 1.1 miles you begin the steep descent back to the valley floor. The trail switchbacks right on a 20% decline, passing over more roots. Continue on a 15% decline, increasing to 25% as the trail switchbacks left. You then take a 200-foot-long steep decline with grades

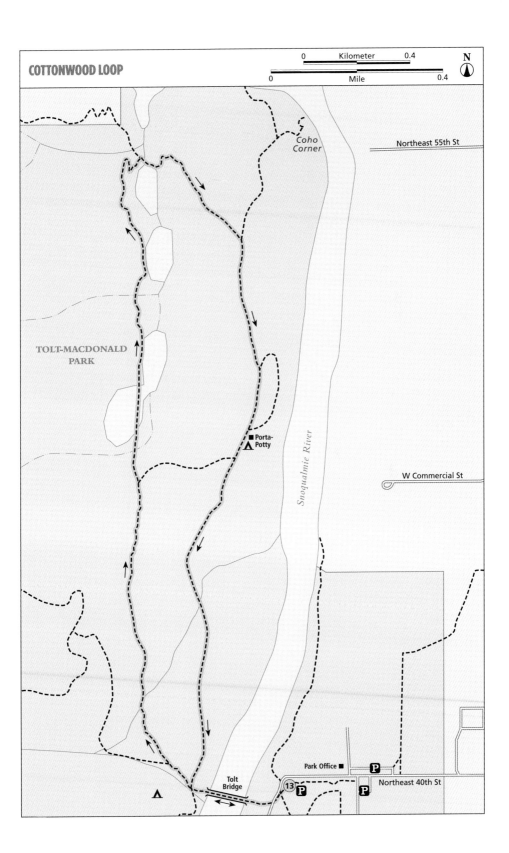

COTTONWOOD LOOP

0   Kilometer   0.4

0   Mile   0.4

N

Northeast 55th St

Coho
Corner

TOLT-MACDONALD
PARK

Snoqualmie River

■ Porta-
▲ Potty

W Commercial St

Park Office ■   P

Tolt
Bridge

13   P

Northeast 40th St

P

▲

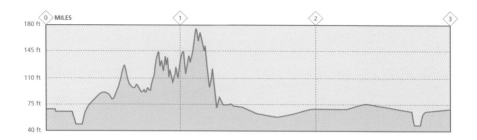

up to 40%, stepping down on roots and loose dirt. The trail is pretty eroded and very slippery, with not much to hold on to and lots of roots to catch your toes on—I managed without a trekking pole, but it was very difficult. At the bottom of the hill, go right to continue on the Cottonwood Loop. Continue on level, hard-packed river silt, traveling beneath large cottonwoods, maples, and cedars.

At 1.3 miles come to an intersection. To the left is Coho Corner—this level path leads 0.2 mile one-way to the Snoqualmie River. There are places to get down to the water on gravel bars and beautiful views of the surrounding hills. It is definitely worth the extra 0.4 mile round-trip. To continue on the Cottonwood Loop, however, go straight at the intersection. Continue on this slightly rocky old service road that is being reclaimed by nature. At 1.5 miles, or 1.9 if you went to Coho Corner, a path veers off to the left. Continue straight on the gravel road through open grassland. You'll pass a group shelter and campsite on the left (there are porta-potties here), then the intersection with the Willow Walk Trail. Continue straight ahead on slightly loose gravel.

At 1.7/2.1 miles you reenter a shady wooded area. The road starts getting rockier, alternating with sections of sand and gravel—it feels more like walking on a riverbed than a road. At 2.1/2.5 miles you reach the end of the loop—cross the bridge to your left to return to the parking area.

MILES AND DIRECTIONS

0.0   Start at the day-use parking area.

0.2   Cross the suspension bridge.

0.3   Reach the beginning of the loop. Go right at the trail board to start in the forest.

0.7   The Willow Walk Trail leads to the right for a shorter loop. Continue straight.

1.1   Begin a very steep decline with roots and loose dirt.

1.3   Reach a trail intersection. The path on the left leads to Coho Corner at the river. Continue straight ahead on the loop trail.

1.5   Continue straight at a fork, then pass a group shelter

2.1   Reach the end of the loop. Go left to cross the bridge and return to the parking area.

2.7   Arrive back at the parking area.

14 MEADOWBROOK FARM

WHY GO?

Meadowbrook Farm, once the largest Snoqualmie prairie where sdukʷalbixʷ tended camas and other traditional foods, is a scenic open space with expansive views of Mount Si and the Cascade Mountains. You can walk historic travel routes across the prairie, watch for wildlife, and enjoy an art installation honoring a Snoqualmie elder.

THE RUNDOWN

Spoon rating: 1 spoon. Partially wheelchair-accessible trails and picnic areas.
Type: Scenic viewpoint, out-and-back
Distance: 0.6 mile
Elevation: 420 feet
Elevation gain: None
Max grade: 8%
Max cross-slope: 2%
Typical width: 4 feet
Typical surface: Paved, gravel, grass
Trail users: Hikers, bicyclers, dog walkers, model plane fliers, picnickers, special events
Season/schedule: Year-round
Water availability: None

Amenities: Restrooms located inside of the interpretive center, which may be closed or reserved for special events
Dog-friendly: Yes, on leash or otherwise controlled
Cell phone reception: Excellent
Nearest town: North Bend or Snoqualmie
Land manager: Meadowbrook Farm Preservation Association, (425) 831-1900
Pass/entry fee: None
Land acknowledgment: This place is named baqʷab in the Snoqualmie Lushootseed language and is known as the birthplace of sdukʷalbixʷ.

FINDING THE TRAILHEAD

Getting there: From I-90 in Snoqualmie/North Bend, take exit 27 and turn onto SE North Bend Way. Turn left onto Meadowbrook Way SE then right onto WA 202E/Railroad Avenue. Make a left onto NW 14th Street then an immediate left onto Boalch Avenue NW. Meadowbrook is 0.3 mile on the left. The large paved parking area has two van-accessible parking spots. GPS: 47.50867, -121.79898
Public transit: King County Metro Route 208 stops at Boalch Avenue NW and NW 14th Street.
Start: Paved parking area surrounded by prairie

THE HIKE

Meadowbrook Farm is a beautiful place to pause and enjoy some time outdoors. You are surrounded by vast fields with Mount Si, known as qʼəlpcʼ to the Snoqualmie Tribe, rising above the land. There are several picnic tables right at the edge of the paved parking area, with a few more sprinkled through the fields. There are several trails here, including a paved trail that travels the length of the farm to Centennial Park. Although this trail is listed as wheelchair accessible, there are several large cracks and boardwalks with a high rise. Many of the other trails are not fully developed or end suddenly onto grassy footpaths that may be a challenge.

The Marie Louie art installation

The view of Mount Si from the parking area

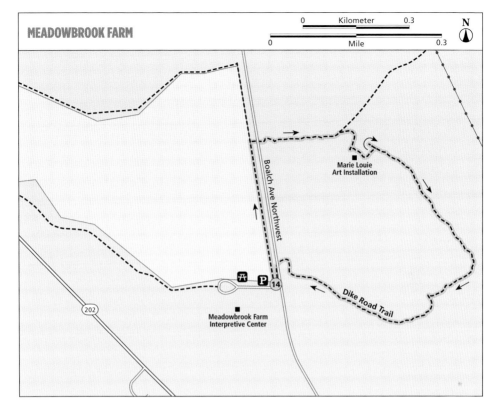

But I do recommend the short path to the Marie Louie art installation. From the main parking area, take the paved path for 0.2 mile along the road to a dirt parking area. Cross the road and take a paved 8% decline for 10 feet. Follow an old gravel roadbed for 0.1 mile, then emerge onto a meadow. A picnic table sits under an old cherry tree, and painted cedar poles form a semicircle around the meadow. This installation honors Xa-cha-blu, a Snoqualmie elder and medicine woman. The poles mark the position of the rising sun at various seasonal points of the year; interpretive signs explain their meaning and Lushootseed names. This is known as a "watching place," and you are invited to take some time to consider the turning of the year while appreciating this ancient place.

Return the way you came, or you can continue through the meadow on a faint footpath. The path gets very rocky, and the grass may be too high to notice the rocks. But it is a lovely path through forest and meadow that ends across the road from the main parking area.

MILES AND DIRECTIONS

0.0   Start at the main parking area. Continue on the paved path along the road.

0.2   Cross the road. Continue on an old grassy gravel road.

0.3   Reach the art installation. Turn around here.

0.6   Arrive back at the parking area.

15 GOLD CREEK POND

WHY GO?

This partially wheelchair-accessible trail loops around Gold Creek Pond, with spectacular views of the Gold Creek valley and Chikamin Peak. There is a picnic area on the shore of the pond with two accessible picnic tables and grills. It feels very remote, but you are not far from Snoqualmie Pass and I-90.

THE RUNDOWN

Spoon rating: 1 spoon. Wheelchair accessible for the first 0.6 mile. The other half of the trail has sections of cracked pavement and several boardwalks in various states of disrepair, but may be wheelchair hikeable. Benches are placed at overlooks around the loop.
Type: Loop
Distance: 1.4 miles
Elevation: 2,540 feet
Elevation gain: 40 feet
Max grade: 8%
Max cross-slope: 10%
Typical width: 4 feet
Typical surface: Paved
Trail users: Hikers

Season/schedule: Spring through fall
Water availability: None
Amenities: Vault toilets, picnic tables, benches
Dog-friendly: Yes, on leash
Cell phone reception: No
Nearest town: Snoqualmie Pass
Land manager: Mt. Baker–Snoqualmie National Forest, Snoqualmie District, 902 SE North Bend Way, Building 1, North Bend, WA 98045; (425) 888-1421
Pass/entry fee: Federal recreation pass
Land acknowledgment: Kittitas, Yakima, Snoqualmie

FINDING THE TRAILHEAD

Getting there: Take exit 54 from I-90 East, turn north, and pass under the interstate. Turn right onto FR 4832, a two-lane paved road, and travel 1 mile. Turn left onto Gold Creek Road—there is a sign for Gold Creek Pond. This is an unimproved gravel forest road, and it can be very bumpy. Turn left in 0.3 mile onto the paved road for the parking area. It is a large, paved parking lot with room for over thirty cars. There are two accessible parking spots (only one is van accessible) at the trailhead. GPS: 47.39674, -121.37911

Start: The paved trail begins behind the information board at the parking area.

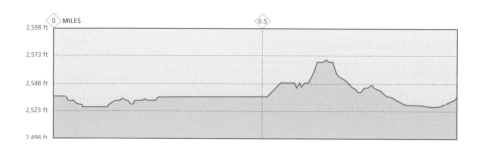

Footbridge over Gold Creek Pond

THE HIKE

The paved trail begins behind the information board. You immediately come to a 5% cross-slope for approximately 4 feet, then the trail levels out and continues on maximum 5% grades. Watch out for a large, 6-inch-deep pothole on the left; there is only about 2½ feet of level space to go around it. At 0.1 mile you arrive at a sign marking the beginning of the loop. To continue on the accessible portion to the picnic area, go straight ahead, taking the loop clockwise. You'll continue on maximum 3 to 5% grades with a couple of small cracks in the trail surface. There are beautiful views of Gold Creek and the surrounding mountains.

At 0.2 mile there are several cracks that rise 1 to 4 inches and run lengthwise down the center of the trail. There is 2 to 3 feet of clearance on either side and they can be navigated, but some wheelchair users may need assistance. Just beyond these cracks, a paved path leads to an accessible picnic table and the shore of the pond.

Continuing past the picnic area, the trail leads past more picnic tables and continues on a 5% incline for up to 100 feet. Another set of cracks run across the trail, rising up to 3 inches with an 8 to 10% threshold. These may also be navigated with care. The trail continues into the forest above the lake on short grades up to 5%, passing several overlooks with interpretive signs and stunning views of the mountains. Stay attentive to birds and other wildlife.

At 0.6 mile there is a large dip across the trail—it is 2 feet long with 1 foot of clearance on the left. Just beyond this is another overlook with a large viewing area overlooking the pond. Wheelchair users may want to turn around here. There are several bridges and boardwalks beyond this point with rises above 1 inch and steep cross-slopes,

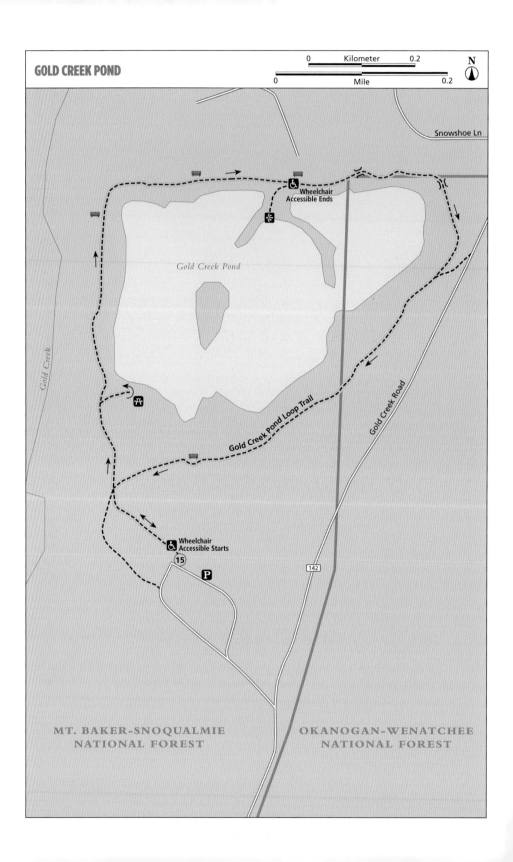

GOLD CREEK POND

Gold Creek Pond

Gold Creek

Snowshoe Ln

Gold Creek Road

Gold Creek Pond Loop Trail

Wheelchair
Accessible Ends

Wheelchair
Accessible Starts

15

142

0   Kilometer   0.2

0   Mile   0.2

N

MT. BAKER-SNOQUALMIE
NATIONAL FOREST

OKANOGAN-WENATCHEE
NATIONAL FOREST

and the trail becomes brushy, rocky, and uneven.

At 0.7 mile you arrive at the first bridge with a 1-inch rise onto uneven boards. Some of the boards have additional ¼-inch plywood nailed across them. The paved trail surface then becomes pretty rough, and you take an 8% incline for 50 feet to an old rock slide with loose gravel on the trail. Continue on lots of dips and rolls with maximum 8% grades as the trail gets brushy through ferns and berries.

At 0.9 mile cross another bridge, take an 8% decline for a few feet, then arrive at a very brushy boardwalk with a 10% cross-slope. The boardwalk levels out at a wide circle after about 50 feet, then continues on alternating 10% cross-slopes for another 50 feet. Continue on a cracked and uneven paved surface, then cross a short level boardwalk. Curve right and pass the start of the Gold Creek Trail on your left. Continue on the paved trail, crossing two more boardwalks. The trail continues on a general incline with rolling 3 to 5% grades.

Cracks in the pavement next to the picnic area

At 1.0 mile cross several large cracks—one is 6 inches high and at a steep slope. The trail continues on a general decline; the surface is uneven and bumpy with lots of dips and holes. At 1.3 miles you end the loop. Go left to return to the parking area.

MILES AND DIRECTIONS

0.0   Start on the paved trail behind the information board in the parking area.

0.1   Reach the beginning of the loop. Go left to do the loop clockwise.

0.2   Pass the picnic area.

0.6   Reach the end of the most accessible portion.

1.3   Close the loop. Go left to return to the parking area.

1.4   Arrive back at the parking area.

MOUNT ST. HELENS

Mount St. Helens is the youngest of the Cascade volcanoes and is, of course, most famous for the 1980 eruption that created a 1- to 2-mile-wide crater and reduced the mountain's height by 1,300 feet. The eruption devastated the north side of the mountain, which is now very different from the typical dense forest of the region—it is marked by burned snags, lahars and volcanic rock, and wildflower meadows. The south side maintains its original forests. This was not the last eruption of the volcano, and it remains active. You can often see smoke rising from the crater.

Mount St. Helens is Lawetlat'la (meaning "smoker") to Cowlitz and Loowit to Klickitat. Many of the Tribes in the region have their own names for the mountain. However, it holds significant meaning in Cowlitz creation stories, and the mountain is a powerful spiritual place and entity. In 2013, it was listed as a Traditional Cultural Property of the Cowlitz Indian Tribe and the Yakama Nation.

16 SILVER LAKE WETLAND HAVEN TRAIL

WHY GO?

Silver Lake was created 2,500 years ago following an eruption of the volcano now known as Mount St. Helens. The lake is an incredible wetland, providing sanctuary to numerous plants, migrating water-fowl, and people. The trail provides an up-close experience of this fantastic ecosystem, with stunning views of the mountain along the way. The Mount St. Helens visitor center, run by Washington State Parks, is also worth a visit, though they do charge an entrance fee. Seaquest State Park is across the street, accessed by a tunnel under Spirit Lake Highway.

THE RUNDOWN

Spoon rating: 1 spoon. Wheelchair accessible with caution. The trail is primarily level boardwalk and gravel, but there are several dips and rolls, and the last two boardwalks have a 1½- to 2-inch rise. There is an 8 to 10% cross-slope at a curve, and the return path is pinched by a couple of roots rising 2 to 3 inches with a 2-foot width.
Type: Loop
Distance: 0.8 mile
Elevation: 500 feet
Elevation gain: None
Max grade: 8%
Max cross-slope: 10%
Typical width: 3 feet
Typical surface: Boardwalk, gravel
Trail users: Hikers

Season/schedule: Open 8 a.m. to dusk year-round
Water availability: Water fountains
Amenities: Restrooms, benches, picnic tables, visitor center with snack booth
Dog-friendly: Yes, on leash
Cell phone reception: Yes, but spotty
Nearest town: Castle Rock
Land manager: Washington State Parks, (360) 274-8633
Pass/entry fee: Washington Discover pass. Additional entry fee is required for the exhibits at the visitor center; a discount is available if you have a state parks disability pass.
Land acknowledgment: Unceded land of the Cowlitz People

FINDING THE TRAILHEAD

Getting there: The visitor center is located just 5 miles off of I-5 on Spirit Lake Highway/WA 504. It is a two-lane paved highway that travels all the way up to the mountain. To access the trailhead, turn right at the visitor center and park in the looped parking area. Go towards the visitor center and then turn left behind a low brick wall with a bench. GPS: 46.2948, -122.82211
Start: At the visitor center

THE HIKE

The Silver Lake Wetland Haven Trail begins at the Mount St. Helens visitor center in Seaquest State Park. There are four van-accessible parking spots in the large paved park-ing area and gendered restrooms with a push-button entrance and one accessible stall.

View across the wetlands to Mount St. Helens

The trail begins to the left of a bench at an overlook in front of the visitor center. There is a view of Loowit from the overlook. It begins paved and 3 feet wide, switchbacks sharply right for 6 feet, then curves left, and there are some benches here and a sign for the wetland haven. Transfer to slightly loose gravel about ¾-inch deep on an 8 to 10% decline for 15 feet. The trail continues on a turnpike then curves right to a 5% decline and a slight cross-slope for about 30 feet before leveling out. The trail then forks to form the loop—go straight to take the loop counterclockwise.

Continue on compact gravel and sand to a brick-paved circular area. There is an interpretive sign about the events that created Silver Lake, with a view across the wetlands to the mountain. The trail then continues on slightly loose gravel and sand rising at 5 to 8% with a couple of dips in the surface for 30 feet, levels out slightly, then continues inclining at 5 to 8% with a couple of slight rolls. Arrive at a cracked and uneven paved section with two picnic tables; neither of them are wheelchair accessible. There are a couple of cracks rising 2 inches above the surface and a 5% cross-slope, but they can be navigated carefully. There is also a nicely framed view across the wetlands.

The trail continues back onto gravel and sand, with an exposed plastic trail surface mat as you transition to gravel—be careful you don't catch a toe or wheel on it. The trail then curves left and passes another path that leads down from the visitor center on the right. Continue curving to the left, and then the boardwalk is directly in front of you. It is an even transfer onto the boardwalk from the gravel, and the boards are laterally placed with no more than a ½-inch gap in between. You are traveling through cattails and other aquatic plants, with views of the mountain to the left. Come to a bench on the left and an interpretive sign about the habitat and the many plants that grow here. The boardwalk curves right and left. Pay attention to birds and dragonflies; there are usually not too many mosquitoes.

At 0.2 mile the boardwalk curves to the left and ends onto compact gravel. There is a 1½-inch high lip from the edge of the boardwalk. The trail then continues on sandy gravel. There's another interpretive sign about the wetland community and the plants and animals here. The trail dips and rolls unevenly several times with grades under 2% and a couple of cross-slopes of 2 to 5%. It's fairly exposed here as you travel between low trees and grasses with benches along the way to sit and appreciate the views of the mountain and the sounds of the wetland.

At 0.4 mile come to an interpretive sign about the birds that are found here, then the trail starts to curve left. There's an interpretive sign about the people who have been at Silver Lake, beginning with the Cowlitz. There is a little place where you can get down at the water level, but this curve might be difficult—the level section is about 2 feet wide, and the outer edge is at an 8 to 10% cross-slope for about 15 feet. It then returns to the boardwalk with a 1½-inch rise. There are some really pretty yellow and white pond lilies and other aquatic plants on the lake here along with a bench.

At 0.5 mile the trail transfers back on to gravel with a ½-inch high lip from the edge of the boardwalk. There are a couple of roots on the inner edge of the trail; it is still 2 to 3 feet wide around them, but you may need to navigate carefully because they protrude a couple of feet into the trail. Continue on a slightly crowned gravel turnpike with a couple of dips in the surface. At 0.6 mile there is a little path that leads up to the parking area on the right—you'll continue straight ahead to continue the loop. You're now traveling through a bit of forest with Douglas fir, horsetail, and salal. Come to an 8% incline for 8 feet, then continue level on a slight cross-slope. The trail passes between some trees, still generally 4 feet wide, but watch out for some protruding roots.

At 0.7 mile you come to another path on the right that leads a bit steeply back to the parking area, or you can continue straight ahead. Continuing straight, pass fairly narrowly between two Douglas firs; it's about 2½ feet wide between two roots that pinch the trail—one root rises less than 2 inches above the surface. There's then a root that rises about 3 inches above the surface in the middle of the trail—I caught my toe on it. The trail then continues 2 to 3 feet wide, crossing between trees, and comes to an 8% incline for 20 feet and reconnects at the beginning of the loop. Continue to the right to return to the visitor center.

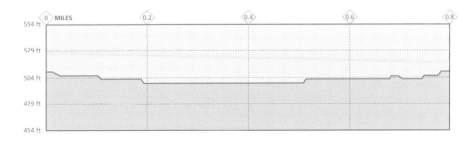

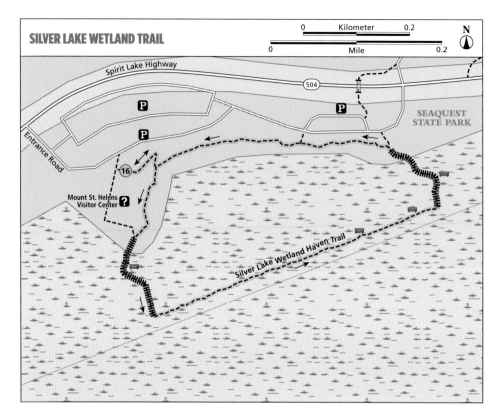

MILES AND DIRECTIONS

0.0 Start at the visitor center, going left next to a bench at the overlook.

0.2 The boardwalk ends onto compact gravel, with a 1½-inch rise.

0.45 There is a narrow curve with a 8 to 10% cross-slope. Transfer back onto a boardwalk with a 1½-inch rise.

0.5 The boardwalk ends onto compact gravel.

0.6 Continue straight past a steep footpath to the parking lot.

0.7 Continue straight past a steep footpath to the parking lot.

0.75 You reach the end of the loop. Go right.

0.8 Arrive back at the visitor center.

17 DEVIL'S POINT

WHY GO?

This section of the Boundary Trail leads from Johnston Ridge Observatory to Harry's Ridge, but the climb to that peak gains over 700 feet in 1.5 miles. Instead, we're going to Devil's Point, an overlook that provides almost the same views with much less elevation gain. You'll travel through an otherworldly environment with constant views of Mount St. Helens and be rewarded with views of Mount Adams, Spirit Lake, and the mountain's blast crater.

THE RUNDOWN

Spoon rating: 5 spoons. Long decline and incline each direction, with rolling terrain and narrow, rocky traverses. There are a couple of benches, but absolutely no shade or water.
Type: Out-and-back
Distance: 6 miles
Elevation: 4,200 feet
Elevation gain: 417 feet
Max grade: 25%
Max cross-slope: 15%
Typical width: 2 feet
Typical surface: Dirt, gravel, rock
Trail users: Hikers
Season/schedule: Summer and fall
Water availability: Fountains at the observatory, none on the trail
Special notes: No shade or water on the trail

Amenities: Flush toilets and water at the observatory, portable toilets in the parking lot. A food truck serves coffee and basic food like burgers during summer.
Dog-friendly: No pets allowed
Cell phone reception: None
Nearest town: Castle Rock
Land manager: Gifford Pinchot National Forest, Mount St. Helens National Volcanic Monument, (360) 449-7800
Pass/entry fee: None, except to enter exhibits at the observatory
Land acknowledgment: Unceded land of the Cowlitz People, who help manage the sacred peaks with the Yakama Nation and Forest Service

FINDING THE TRAILHEAD

Getting there: From Castle Rock, head east on Spirit Lake Highway/WA 504 for 52 miles until it ends. Park in the large paved parking area at Johnston Ridge. There are eight accessible parking spots, and a drop-off zone at the path up to the observatory. GPS: 46.27643, -122.21704
Start: At the Johnston Ridge Observatory

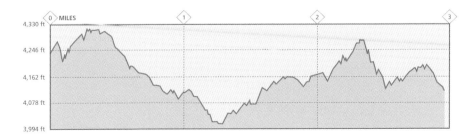

Descending towards Devil's Point with view of Spirit Lake

THE HIKE

There are two options to start this trail: at the Johnston Ridge Observatory or at the Boundary Trail #1 trailhead at the northern corner of the parking lot. If you start at the Boundary Trail, you'll shave about 0.5 mile from the total distance and bypass a lot of the crowd. If you start at the observatory, you'll immediately have iconic views of the mountain.

This description begins at the observatory. Follow the sidewalk south along the parking area and then continue uphill on a paved path at a 5 to 8% incline for 0.1 mile. There are benches along the way, and wildflowers line the edge of the trail. You then reach a level paved viewing area with an incredible view of Loowit. Note: The observatory is on your right—the building is wheelchair accessible; wheelchairs are available to borrow, and there are audio description units for the exhibits. The amphitheater is on the other side of the observatory, which offers views directly into the blast crater.

Go left from the viewpoint on the Eruption Trail, which leads up the hill. It is paved and 4 feet wide, but there are steady 8% grades, two places with a 10% cross-slope, and several cracks and potholes. There are viewpoints with benches and interpretive signs along the way. At 0.5 mile there is a memorial sign for those who lost their lives in the May 18, 1980, eruption. You then reach the intersection with the Boundary Ridge Trail #1. The paved trail to the left returns to the parking lot. You will go right, past a trail sign for the Boundary Trail—it is 2.2 miles to Devil's Point. Continue on a 4-foot-wide dirt and gravel trail bordered by rocks—please remain on-trail to protect the sensitive habitat.

The trail continues on a general 10% decline for the next 0.5 mile, taking several rolling inclines and declines up to 100 feet long on grades up to 15%, interspersed with level areas. You are surrounded by wildflowers, with views of the valley and surrounding hills.

Typical trail view with Loowit in the background

At 0.9 mile the trail curves sharply left at a bench overlooking the mountain. Continue on a gradual decline, then take a 20% incline as you round the edge of a small hill. Pass another bench at 1.0 mile.

At 1.2 miles you reach a large viewing area with a map, interpretive signs, and a bench. The trail then curves sharply left with some loose gravel and descends at 15% for about 10 feet. Continue on a 10% decline as the trail narrows and gets rutted. Switchback left and right a couple of times, traveling down the hillside with lots of wildflowers. The trail is 1½ feet wide, with some large rocks and a little uneven. Curve right around a hill with a slight decline, then incline as you curve to the left again and approach a rocky hill. Take a 15% incline for about 15 feet, level out, then take another 15% incline for about 10 feet and pass next to a large boulder on the right. Continue on a 12% incline for approximately 200 feet through a narrow corridor surrounded by low, brushy alder trees, then come to a 20% incline for 75 feet.

At 1.4 miles the trail levels out and there are some boulders to sit on. You're at approximately the lowest point on the trail and may (or may not) want to look back from here to realize how much of a gradual descent you've been on; you lost 270 feet in the last 0.8 mile. The trail starts to feel like you're on another planet—you are surrounded by lava rock and giant boulders that were tossed like jacks from the mountain in the eruption. You have a climb ahead of you too, gaining 260 feet in the next mile. Continue on rolling grades of 10 to 20% for 0.1 mile, with a few short inclines up to 25%. The trail then levels out and travels through another corridor of low, brushy alder trees; this is your last opportunity to possibly find some shade, so enjoy it if you can.

At 1.6 miles the trail opens up on the other side of the talus hill. Continue inclining at about 20% for 400 feet. The trail levels out slightly with rolling grades up to 10% and

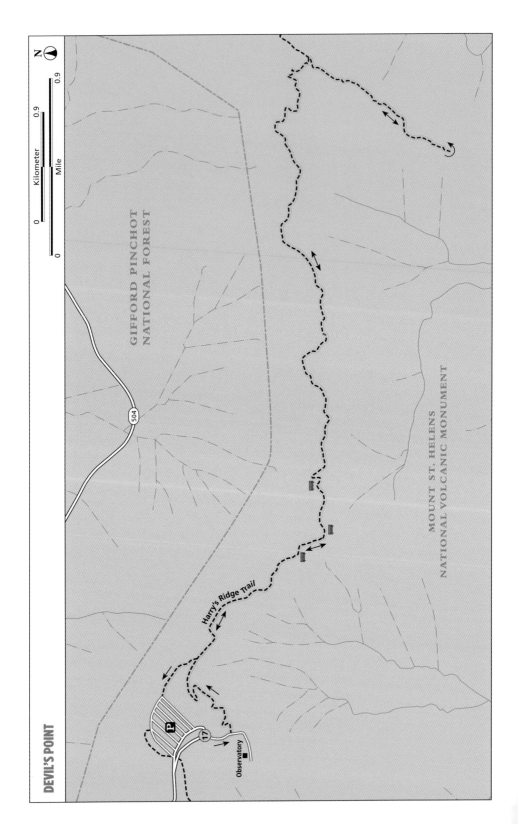

DEVIL'S POINT

GIFFORD PINCHOT
NATIONAL FOREST

MOUNT ST. HELENS
NATIONAL VOLCANIC MONUMENT

Harry's Ridge Trail

504

Observatory

P

N

Kilometer
0   0.9   0.9

Mile
0   0.9

a few short inclines up to 20%, continuing along the talus hills for the next 0.4 mile. At 2.0 miles the trail curves slightly right and approaches a hill covered in wildflowers with another view of Loowit. This is a wide, sandy spot where the trail gets a little lost—just continue straight across the sand and the trail becomes obvious again on the other side. The final mile of the trail gets pretty sketchy, with lots of rocks and with some steep grades. Take a 20% incline as you start rising up the hill, then continue on a long 15% incline with an uneven surface, steep cross-slope, and sharp drop-off on the left.

At 2.2 miles there are several large rocks and boulders to step across, and it is pretty uneven. The trail continues on a generally steady incline, curving left and right on a narrow traverse. At 2.3 miles you get the first view of Spirit Lake and start a general descent for the next 0.2 mile. Take a 20% incline on pretty loose, deep gravel and sand on a narrow traverse. Continue on a general 10 to 15% decline with awesome views of the surrounding hills. At 2.4 miles the trail curves sharply left and right at the top of a hill and comes to a steep descent with very loose gravel. Harry's Ridge rises ahead of you, with the trail continuing below.

At 2.5 miles you reach a signed intersection with Harry's Ridge and Devil's Point. Go right for Devil's Point. The trail is level and narrow on a gentle traverse. There are lots of wildflowers and low-growing trees. Step between two large boulders, then take a 10% incline for about 50 feet. The trail narrows with a bit of a drop-off on the left. You then come to a couple of places where it looks like the trail ends, but keep going—the views only get better. The trail rolls a couple of times as you continue out onto the point.

At 2.9 miles you emerge at a gorgeous wildflower-covered hillside. You can continue slightly downhill for another 0.1 mile to the end of the point, marked by a circle of rocks. Spirit Lake lies behind you in the east, with a view of the floating logjam. Mount Adams (Pahto or Klickitat to the Cowlitz) rises farther to the east, always bowing to Loowit, who looms large in front of you. It feels like you could reach out and touch the mountain. There is an excellent view of the blast zone, and you may see smoke rising from the still-active volcano. The observatory sits across the ridgeline to the right.

Take as much time here as you like, and rest up for the trip back. If you started the hike at the observatory, I recommend going right at the last intersection when you return to the paved trail—this will take you on a relatively gentle decline back to the parking area on the Boundary Ridge Trail #1.

MILES AND DIRECTIONS

- **0.0** Start on the path at the observatory.
- **0.1** Reach the viewing area at the observatory. Go left on the Eruption Trail.
- **0.5** Go right at the intersection with the Boundary Ridge Trail #1.
- **1.2** A large viewing area with a bench is on the left.
- **2.0** Continue straight across a wide, sandy area.
- **2.3** First view of Spirit Lake and start of a long decline.
- **2.5** Go right at the intersection of Harry's Ridge and Devil's Point.
- **2.9** Reach Devil's Point and the end of the trail. Turn around here, and take the Boundary Ridge Trail #1 at the last intersection.
- **6.0** Arrive at the parking area.

18 JUNE LAKE

WHY GO?

This often-overlooked trail takes a steady, gentle incline to a lake formed by a 2,000-year-old lava flow. A waterfall plunges from the basalt cliff above the lake. Peekaboo views of the south side of Mount St. Helens may surprise you on a clear day, and a variety of plants, berries, and wildflowers line the trail. It is a perfect place for a picnic or a backcountry camping trip.

THE RUNDOWN

Spoon rating: 3 spoons. A gentle incline that averages at 5%, with sections of 10 to 20% for up to 100 feet. A few roots and rocks to navigate. Partially shaded. Few easy places to sit.
Type: Out-and-back
Distance: 3 miles
Elevation: 2,730 feet
Elevation gain: 449 feet
Max grade: 25%
Max cross-slope: 10%
Typical width: 3 feet
Typical surface: Dirt, sand, rocks
Trail users: Hikers, mountain bikers

Season/schedule: Spring through fall
Water availability: Creek
Amenities: None
Dog-friendly: Yes, on leash
Cell phone reception: None
Nearest town: Cougar
Land manager: Mount St. Helens National Volcanic Monument, Administrative Headquarters, (360) 449-7800
Pass/entry fee: None
Land acknowledgment: Unceded land of the Cowlitz people

FINDING THE TRAILHEAD

Getting there: From Cougar, head northeast on WA 503 Spur. After 6.6 miles, turn left onto FR 83. This is a paved, two-lane forest road, but there are lots of potholes and long sections with big dips, so drive carefully. Continue 6.9 miles, then take a left at the sign for June Lake. The parking lot has room for about eight cars in the paved section, and a few spots where you can pull off onto gravel. There is no accessible parking. GPS: 46.13724, -122.15684
Start: Trailhead at the end of a small parking area

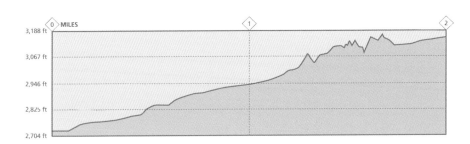

The waterfall at June Lake

THE HIKE

The trailhead is located at the end of the parking area, behind two large boulders. There is a small brown sign for June Lake Ski Trail No. 216B—this is the June Lake Trail. A trail board provides a map of the volcanic monument and an elevation profile for the trail.

Start on a wide, rocky path with a few roots crossing the trail. Loowit peeks above the trees, and a tributary of Swift Creek rushes below you on the left. Pass to the right of some large boulders on an 8% incline. The trail continues generally level with some unsteady footing on loose gravel and large rocks. At 0.1 mile step up over a couple of roots and logs in the trail, then around large boulders rising 3 to 6 inches above the surface, followed by a couple more roots and logs. The best view of the mountain is around this point, as the trail curves right, widens, and becomes dirt. Continue on a gentle incline of grades under 10%. At 0.2 mile there's a small footpath on the left next to a very large boulder that leads down to the creek and a view of a little waterfall.

At 0.3 mile the trail starts to climb a little more steeply. Take a 10% incline for about 50 feet, stepping over roots and rocks. The trail levels out and curves slightly left and right. Continue on a generally 5 to 8% incline. Step up over three logs with a 10-inch rise. Continue on loose gravel as the incline increases to 12% with a washed-out rut down the center of the trail. Step up on another log with a 10-inch rise. Continue on a generally 12% incline, step up on a log, then curve slightly left with a steep cross-slope. There are lots of boulders in the trail, but they can be navigated easily. At 0.45 mile the trail levels out briefly and curves left and narrows to about 2 feet with a steep cross-slope and a drop-off on the left. It then rises on a 10% grade for about 10 feet. The trail then rolls slightly and takes a rocky 15% incline for about 10 feet.

View of Mount St. Helens from the trail

At 0.5 mile you come to a 15% incline with large root mats; it's easiest to pass along the inside of the trail. Then come to a 10% incline on loose rocks, stepping up over roots across the trail. Continue on generally 5 to 10% inclines and an uneven surface with roots and rocks. The trail curves sharply left on an 8% incline then declines on a 5% grade with a 5% cross-slope. It levels out and then inclines on three logs with a 6- to 10-inch rise. The trail curves slightly right on a slightly washed-out trail to more wood steps; take six steps that rise up to 6 inches with a long landing in between. Continue on a washed-out, rocky incline with loose rocks and unstable footing. Step up over a couple of roots, continuing on a 5 to 8% incline, and come to a couple more log steps on a 10 to 12% incline—the last log has a 1-foot rise. Pass over lots of root mats, some rising 4 to 6 inches above the surface. Peekaboo views of the mountain lead you on.

At 0.75 mile the trail levels out slightly, with a view of the mountain and the sound of the rushing creek down below. The trail returns to a natural dirt surface and continues on a general 2 to 5% incline. The trail is pretty wide here, but washed out down the center with lots of loose rocks and eroded roots along the outer edge. It then narrows to about 3 feet as you continue traveling through second-growth forest—old mossy logs rest on the side of the trail, which may provide a place for you to rest as well. At 0.9 mile the trail starts a generally steeper incline to the lake, rising and falling but gaining 150 feet in about 0.3 mile. The surface is pretty uneven, with lots of rocks and eroded sections. The next 0.1 mile inclines at 10 to 20%—take a 12% incline as the trail curves left, increasing to a 15 to 20% incline for about 300 feet. Continue on loose rocks with roots in the trail.

At 1.0 mile the trail declines slightly before coming to another 10 to 15% incline for about 100 feet, then levels out for 10 feet before inclining again at 18 to 20% for about

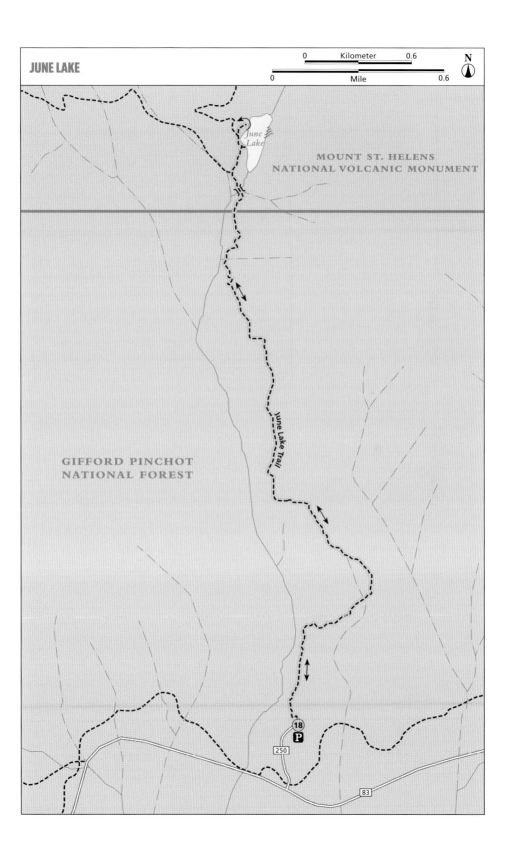

MOUNT ST. HELENS
NATIONAL VOLCANIC MONUMENT

June Lake

June Lake Trail

GIFFORD PINCHOT
NATIONAL FOREST

18
P
250

83

N

Kilometer
0   0.6
Mile
0   0.6

100 feet. The trail is deeply rutted down the center. Continue on a gentle incline, then come to a 20% incline for 20 feet, step over a log, and then take a very narrow, deeply rutted incline for 50 feet. It is pretty uneven, unstable footing with eroded roots, and the incline increases to 25% for the last 10 feet.

At 1.1 miles reach the top of the steep section; there's a large log on the left that you can sit on. Take another 12% incline for about 30 feet, then the trail levels out slightly with a view looking straight up to the mountain across a lava flow. Continue on a generally 5 to 8% incline. The trail narrows to about 3 feet and curves slightly right, passing lots of wildflowers, then curves left and right on 10 to 12% inclines. The trail curves left again, continuing on a general 5 to 8% incline, and then curves slightly right on a 10% decline. You may hear the creek rushing down below on the left, and there are more views of the mountain and lava flow.

Continue on a 5 to 10% decline, then curve right on an 8% incline. The trail then levels out for a few feet before coming to a steep decline with lots of eroded roots to step down on. It is about a 15% decline, stepping down up to 10 inches. You then come to a level, slightly muddy section with a large stream on the left. The trail widens out on sand and gravel and continues level for about 100 feet. You then come to a very eroded incline, with roots crossing diagonally across the trail. It is about a 20% grade, and you have to step up narrowly on and in between roots that rise up to 8 inches, or you can take one steep step up of about 1 foot onto a large root.

At 1.4 miles you arrive at a sturdy bridge over the creek. There is a bit of a steep, short path down to the creek, but it is the easiest place to get water. Step up about 1 foot onto the bridge, and then step down a couple of inches on the other side; watch out for a metal ring sticking out of the surface of the trail on the other side, along with a couple of rocks. Pass narrowly between two boulders, stepping up about 6 inches. Continue on sand and gravel, about 2 feet wide. As you emerge from the forest, the trail opens up to the sandy, gravelly area around the lake. There are a couple of little paths down to the lake between the trees. For the best view of the waterfall, continue straight across the broad sandy area and just before you get to the cliff side, there's another footpath on the right. It leads to the northwestern shore of the lake and gives you a direct view of the waterfall. There is a little shade along the cliff side, but otherwise not much shade around the lake. There are also few places to sit, so you may want to bring a chair if you can't sit on the ground. Several fire rings surround the lake, but please obey all fire restrictions and don't camp within 100 feet of the lakeshore.

MILES AND DIRECTIONS

0.0   Start at the trailhead at the parking area.

0.2   A short footpath on the left leads to the creek and a waterfall.

0.9   Begin a general incline to the lake.

1.4   Cross the bridge over the creek.

1.5   Reach June Lake and the end of the trail.

3.0   Arrive back at the trailhead.

SOUTHWEST WASHINGTON

Southwest Washington encompasses a large region south of Olympia to the Columbia River and west to the Pacific Ocean. It is characterized by extensive wetlands along the water in the south and west, and the Cascade foothills to the east, representing a broad diversity of ecosystems. It is also highly impacted by development, primarily along the I-5 corridor, and a history of logging, particularly along the coast.

Cowlitz and Chinook were the largest Tribes in the area. The Cowlitz never agreed to a treaty with the United States. This means that this is unceded territory and no agreement was made with the US government to allow for its use by Euro-American settlers. The Cowlitz Tribe received federal recognition in 2000 and currently operate a number of businesses. They continue to practice traditional lifeways and maintain their rights to the land.

The Chinook Indian Nation includes the five Chinookan-speaking Tribes along the Columbia River: the Willapa, Lower Chinook, Wahkiakum, Kathlamet, and Clatsop. They signed the Tansy Point Treaty, which promised that the Tribes could remain in their homeland and receive provisions and annuities. However, the treaty was not ratified and the Chinook Indian Nation continues to fight for federal recognition.

19 RIDGEFIELD WILDLIFE REFUGE AUTO TOUR

WHY GO?

Ridgefield Wildlife Refuge is an oasis tucked between the Columbia and Lake Rivers, not far from I-5. It contains wetlands, grasslands, forests and woodlands, riparian zones, and cropland, providing homes for hundreds of species of birds, mammals, and more. There are many ways to enjoy the refuge, but the auto tour is a personal favorite. Watch for wildlife in this incredibly peaceful spot without even leaving your car. Pamphlets and audio guides for the route are available on the refuge website.

THE RUNDOWN

Type: Scenic drive
Distance: 4 miles
Elevation: 10 feet
Typical width and surface: Single lane gravel road. Drivable in a standard passenger car.
Season/schedule: Open dawn to dusk
Amenities: Restrooms only. No picnic tables, water fountains, or trash cans.
Dog-friendly: No, must remain in the vehicle at all times
Cell phone reception: Excellent
Nearest town: Ridgefield

Land manager: Ridgefield National Wildlife Refuge Complex, (360) 887-4106
Pass/entry fee: Federal recreation pass or day-use fee
Land acknowledgment: The Chinookan People of the Lower Columbia have lived and cared for this land since time immemorial. The Chinookan village of Cathlapotle was located here, at the confluence of the Columbia River, Lake River, and Lewis River. A plankhouse in the refuge provides an important cultural link for the Chinook Indian Nation.

FINDING THE TRAILHEAD

Getting there: From I-5, take exit 14 towards Ridgefield. Turn onto Pioneer Street and continue for approximately 2.5 miles, continuing straight through two traffic circles. Turn left onto S. Hillhurst Road. In 0.6 mile, turn right at the dog park and continue through the gate. Address: 1071 S. Hillhurst Rd., Ridgefield. GPS: 45.807380, -122.733700
Start: At the information kiosk and pay station

THE HIKE

To reach the start of the auto tour route, travel 0.5 mile on a somewhat bumpy gravel road, then cross a bridge over the Lake River. The refuge stretches as far as you can see. Vault toilets, a pay station and information kiosk, and an occasionally staffed ranger booth are located at the entrance—start your odometer here. Drive to the right, following the two-lane gravel road past the auto tour route sign. A clock indicates closing time—be sure to exit the refuge before it closes, because the gates are on an automatic timer. The speed limit through the refuge is 15 mph, but it is unlikely that you will go that fast.

The auto tour road traveling through cottonwoods

View of the wetlands

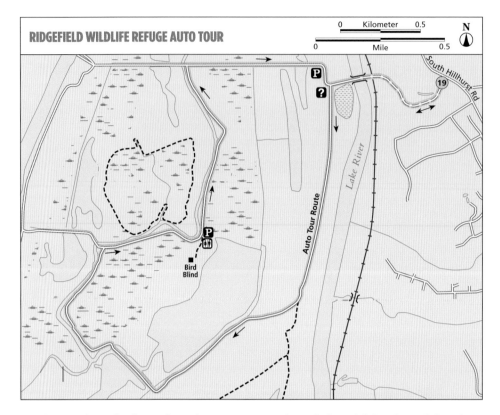

There are lots of pullouts along the way to stop and watch for wildlife. This is definitely a place to take your time, be patient, and enjoy the experience.

The road veers left and passes through the first part of the wetlands. At 0.5 mile the route veers left again and becomes a one-way loop. At 0.9 mile there's a large pullout on the right to watch for wildlife in the grasses. At 1.3 miles there is a parking area on the right with one accessible parking spot, an accessible vault toilet, and a short paved path that leads to a viewing blind. In another 0.1 mile around the loop, you arrive at a large gravel parking area and the trailhead for the Kiwa Trail. This wheelchair-accessible trail is generally open May 1 through September 30.

At 1.6 miles you leave the grassland and enter an area of cottonwoods along a stream. You're likely to see blue herons and other waterbirds here. The road can be narrow as you curve between trees. There are several pullouts where brush has been piled up to form a screen. At 2.1 miles the route curves left and starts traveling through open grassland again. At 3.2 miles you come to a large pullout on the left and expansive views all the way across the grassland. The loop ends back at the information station at mile 4.0.

Finally, a few notes on rules, regulations, and etiquette for the Auto Tour Route: Please use the pullouts to stop and observe wildlife so that other drivers may pass. It is a good idea to turn off your vehicle while stopped to reduce noise and pollution. You must stay in your vehicle between October 1 and April 30 to protect overwintering waterfowl, but from May through September you can get out to observe or even walk the entire route.

20 MOULTON FALLS REGIONAL PARK

WHY GO?

This area is home to four waterfalls and two parks along the East Fork Lewis River, connected by over 5 miles of trails and offering a variety of options. Picnic along the stunning Lewis River canyon, take a stroll or roll through lush forest, or hike from waterfall to waterfall—you might feel like you're in a choose-your-own-adventure book. This guide introduces you to Lucia Falls Park, takes you through the main section of Moulton Falls Regional Park on the East Fork Lewis River Trail, then the shortest route to Yacolt Creek Falls.

THE RUNDOWN

LUCIA FALLS

Spoon rating: 1 spoon. Partially wheelchair accessible.
Type: Loop
Distance: 1 mile
Elevation: 450 feet
Elevation gain: 20 feet
Max grade: 10%
Max cross-slope: 5%

Typical width: 3 feet
Typical surface: Pea gravel
Trail users: Hikers
Season/schedule: Open 7 a.m. to dusk year-round
Water availability: None
Special notes: Picnic area with viewpoint

MOULTON FALLS AND THE EAST FORK LEWIS RIVER TRAIL

Spoon rating: 2 spoons. Partially wheelchair accessible.
Type: Out-and-back
Distance: 2.4 miles
Elevation: 528 feet
Elevation gain: 60 feet
Max grade: 12%
Max cross-slope: 2%

Typical width: 8 feet
Typical surface: Compact gravel
Trail users: Hikers, horseback riders, mountain bikers
Season/schedule: Open 7 a.m. to dusk year-round
Water availability: None

YACOLT CREEK FALLS

Spoon rating: 2 spoons. A set of steep stairs and a grated bridge for the best view.
Type: Out-and-back
Distance: 0.3 mile
Elevation: 636 feet
Elevation gain: 20 feet
Max grade: 20%
Max cross-slope: 2%
Typical width: 5 feet
Typical surface: Gravel, rocks, stairs
Trail users: Hikers
Season/schedule: Open 7 a.m. to dusk year-round

Water availability: Water fountain
Special notes: 45 steps
Amenities: Flush toilets, benches, picnic tables, trash cans; park host at Moulton Falls Park
Dog-friendly: Yes, on leash
Cell phone reception: Spotty
Nearest town: Battle Ground
Land manager: Clark County Parks, (564) 397-2285
Pass/entry fee: None
Land acknowledgment: Cowlitz

FINDING THE TRAILHEAD

Getting there: From the town of Battle Ground, head north on WA 503N. In 5 miles, turn right onto NE Rock Creek Road. After 1.5 miles, the road veers left onto NE Lucia Falls Road. Continue 3.5 miles to Lucia Falls Park. Continue another 3 miles to Moulton Falls Regional Park. Yacolt Falls is another 0.3 mile. It is an easy drive on paved, two-lane roads.

Lucia Falls Park has a large paved parking area with two van-accessible parking spots. GPS: 45.84049, -122.4481

The Moulton Falls parking area is paved with fifteen parking spots and one van-accessible spot. It is a bit easy to miss—look for the paved entrance on the right just before a curve at 6.5 miles on Lucia Falls Road. GPS: 45.83178, -122.38883

The upper parking area for Yacolt Falls is a large paved loop with room for thirty cars and one van-accessible spot. It is located at a right turn just before NE Sunset Falls Road. GPS: 45.83324, -122.38425

Start: Lucia Falls: Trailhead at the east (left) side of the parking lot
Moulton Falls Regional Park: Trailhead at the corner of the parking area and NE Lucia Falls Rd.
Yacolt Falls: Trailhead in the upper parking area. Alternate: a gravel pullout just past the upper parking area on NE Lucia Falls Rd.

THE HIKE

LUCIA FALLS

Lucia Falls Park is a gorgeous park located on the north bank of the river. Steelhead leap Lucia Falls in spawning season. There is a picnic area, viewpoints, and a 1-mile loop trail along the river. A rose and rhododendron garden is located at the beginning of the park. It is wheelchair accessible, but there are some 10% grades in the picnic area to access the viewpoints. The loop trail is compact pea gravel and generally level with a couple of 2 to 5% grades, one 5 to 8% grade for 100 feet, and two 8 to 10% grades for 30 feet. There are a few low round wood barriers in the trail surface.

MOULTON FALLS AND EAST FORK LEWIS RIVER TRAIL

The best view of Moulton Falls is actually right at the parking area. Pass between two large boulders at the picnic area by the entrance, and the first overlook is on the left.

East Fork Lewis River

This overlook is wheelchair friendly if you take the short paved path that leads along the front of the parking area, but it gets a little narrow as you pass next to the trees. For closer viewpoints, continue to the right, stepping over some roots rising 3 to 4 inches above the surface, then take ten stone steps with a handrail on the left down to another view across huge rocks. Five more stone steps lead you down to the rocky river canyon, where you can walk out for a close-up view of the river.

To access the East Fork Lewis River Trail, go towards the parking area exit and turn right at the park map. Follow a gravel footpath along the road with a wooden fence on the left. A pedestrian crossing on the left takes you to the loop for Yacolt Creek Falls. Continue straight for Moulton Falls Park, then cross a boardwalk over a creek. There's a 1-inch rise onto the boardwalk, which immediately declines at 10% for 20 feet, with 1- to 2-inch-high wood strips across the surface for traction. The boardwalk then levels out for 30 feet, and inclines again the same way. Wheelchair users may have difficulty crossing the wooden strips, but it is worth it if you can—the trail ahead is level, firm, and very beautiful.

Continue on an 8-foot-wide compact gravel path and immediately come to two benches with plenty of room to maneuver a wheelchair and hang out for a while. In less than 0.1 mile, there is an overlook of the river on the right. It is a really sweet spot tucked underneath arching alders and western redcedars; however, it is surfaced with river rock, so it's pretty uneven and bumpy—some of the rocks rise a couple of inches. Another viewpoint waits just beyond this one on the right; it is easier to access, with a smooth gravel surface. Continuing straight on the trail, you pass over an area that is slightly washed out down the center, creating a couple of humps with a slight grade. You then come to an interpretive sign about Moulton Falls and the East Fork Lewis River watershed, with a map that pinpoints various waterfalls. The trail then forks to the right, leading to another rocky overlook with a view up to the bridge and down the river canyon—it is pretty slippery, though, and there are some very tall rocks to cross.

Continuing straight on the trail past the restrooms, take an 8 to 10% incline for approximately 100 feet. The trail is slightly washed out and rutted down the center. There is another fork at the top of the rise—the trail on the left is the other side of the loop for Yacolt Creek Falls. Go straight on the Lewis River Trail. The trail continues at 8 feet wide, with compact gravel and a firm natural surface. Curve slightly right on a 5 to 8% incline for 100 feet, increasing to 10% and crossing over a 1- to 3-inch round wood barrier in the trail. The trail then levels out as you approach the bridge.

At 0.4 mile you arrive at the bridge. There is an 8% incline for about 15 feet, then a 4-inch and 2-inch lip onto the bridge. The bridge is sturdy, with tightly placed horizontal boards and a level transfer back onto gravel on the other side. The East Fork Lewis River flows smoothly through the rocky, tree-lined canyon below you. The trail forks on the opposite side of the bridge—the right fork leads to a short loop through a picnic area. Continue straight on a 12% incline for 30 feet as the trail curves right then levels out on compact gravel. You are now traveling above the river through a beautiful, lush, green mature forest. There are filtered views of the river through the trees, but the sound of rushing water follows you the entire way. Unfortunately, so does noise from the main road. At 0.5 mile you get a glimpse of Moulton Falls from high above across the river. The trail continues generally level and firm.

At 0.9 mile you cross a culverted stream on a firm compact gravel bridge with metal rails on both sides. You then reach a trail board at the intersection with the Bells Mountain

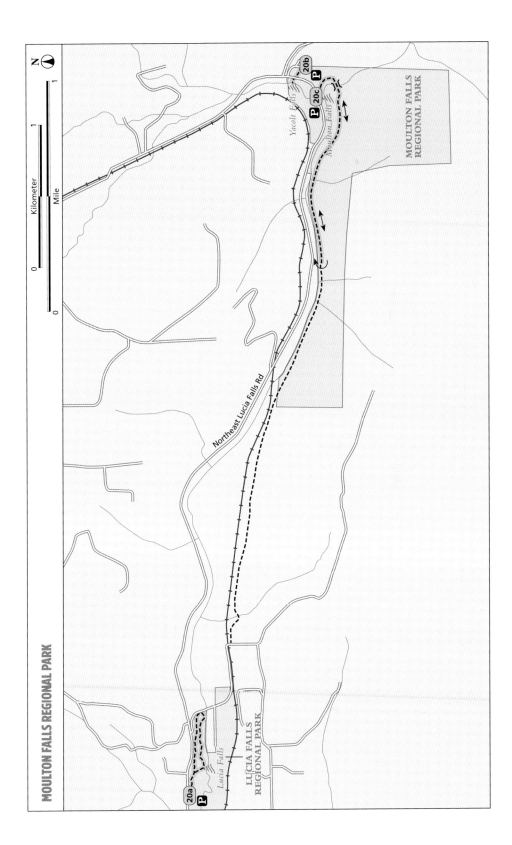

MOULTON FALLS REGIONAL PARK

Northeast Lucia Falls Rd

Lucia Falls

LUCIA FALLS
REGIONAL PARK

Yacolt Falls

Moulton Falls

MOULTON FALLS
REGIONAL PARK

20a

20b

20c

N

Kilometer

Mile

0 1

0 1

Trail. Continue straight ahead. At 1.2 miles there is a bench on the right overlooking an unnamed waterfall. This makes a nice place to rest and then turn around, or you could continue another 1.5 miles to Lucia Falls Park.

YACOLT FALLS

The shortest route to Yacolt Falls begins at the upper parking area. There is a large trail sign near the entrance to the parking lot—go straight past the sign on a compact gravel trail that is approximately 5 feet wide. Step over a round wood barrier and take a 10% decline for about 20 feet. Curve right, step over a couple more round wood barriers, and continue on a 2 to 5% decline. As you approach the road, the trail curves left and takes a 15 to 20% decline for 50 feet then curves right on a 12% decline for 30 feet. Be attentive for vehicles as you cross the road on a crosswalk. Note: You can avoid this section by parking in the gravel pullout on the left about 0.1 mile past the parking area and walking on the road to the picnic area.

Across the road is a picnic area with three picnic tables, a water fountain, and a partially obstructed view of the top of the falls. Take seven stone steps down to a large, level rock overlooking the falls. Take another seven stone steps and curve left, following the creek for about 100 feet, then arrive at a steep set of stairs. There are twenty-nine stone steps down with a wire barrier handrail on one side, then seven steps up to a metal grate bridge over the creek. There is a 10-inch step up onto the bridge. You have an up-close view of Yacolt Creek Falls as it cascades down the cliff and forms multiple small pools in the creek.

MILES AND DIRECTIONS

MOULTON FALLS AND EAST FORK LEWIS RIVER TRAIL

- 0.0 From the parking area, go right and travel along the road to enter the park.
- 0.2 Continue straight past the restrooms. There are a couple of river overlooks on the right.
- 0.3 The trail forks for the Yacolt Creek Falls trail. Continue straight.
- 0.4 Cross the bridge over the river, then continue straight at the fork.
- 0.9 The trail forks with the Bells Mountain Trail on the left. Continue straight.
- 1.2 Reach a bench overlooking a small waterfall. This is the recommended turnaround point.
- 2.4 Arrive back at the parking area.

YACOLT FALLS

- 0.0 Start at the trailhead in the upper parking lot.
- 0.1 Cross the road.
- 0.15 Arrive at the waterfall. Turn around here.
- 0.3 Arrive back at the parking lot.

21 **POOL OF THE WINDS**

WHY GO?

Pool of the Winds is one of three waterfalls along Hardy Creek. It drops down through a cavern into a pool, creating a constant spray of wind and water for which it is named. It is an incredible destination on its own, but the trail to get there brings you through iconic Columbia River Gorge views that includes two more waterfalls and a volcanic rock.

THE RUNDOWN

Spoon rating: 4 spoons. A generally gradual elevation gain with a few steep sections, rocks, and stairs. Few places to sit and no easy access to water.
Type: Out-and-back
Distance: 3 miles
Elevation: 587 feet
Elevation gain: 487 feet
Max grade: 25%
Max cross-slope: 8%
Typical width: 3 feet
Typical surface: Compact gravel, natural
Trail users: Hikers
Season/schedule: Year-round
Water availability: May be available in campground

Amenities: Flush toilets and picnic grounds at the Hamilton Mountain trailhead, a couple of benches
Dog-friendly: Yes, on leash
Cell phone reception: Yes, but spotty in areas
Nearest town: Washougal
Land manager: Washington State Parks, (509) 427-8265
Pass/entry fee: Washington Discover Pass
Land acknowledgment: Beacon Rock is known as Che-che-op-tin, or "navel of the world." The Watála, Upper Chinookan-speaking peoples, lived in a village here, where they fished the Wímał (Columbia River) and tended plants in the meadows.

FINDING THE TRAILHEAD

Getting there: From Vancouver, Washington, travel east on WA 14E for approximately 34 miles. Pass Beacon Rock Headquarters on the left, then veer left uphill at signs for Beacon Rock Campground, just before the large gravel parking area for Beacon Rock on the right. Continue all the way into the campground. There will be a gravel parking area on the right about a third of the way around the loop. The trailhead is located to your right, on the same side of the road—look for the Hadley Trail sign. GPS: 45.63519, -122.02219
Start: End of the loop in Beacon Rock Campground

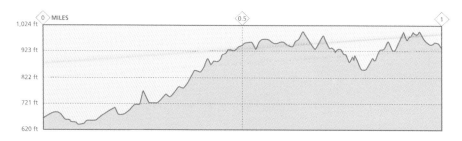

Viewpoint at Pool of the Winds

THE HIKE

The most common route to Pool of the Winds is the Hamilton Mountain Trail, but that trail gains over 450 feet in 0.7 mile at its start. The Hadley Trail is a little shorter and much easier, gaining less than 300 feet in 0.7 mile. It also offers a short side trip to Little Beacon Rock.

Start at the Hadley Trailhead, located at the end of the loop in the Beacon Rock State Park campground. There is a brown trail sign on the east side of the road. Take three steps down and then continue on the compact gravel path through a lush green understory. At 0.1 mile curve sharply right and continue on a generally 10% incline. A forest of tall Douglas firs rises ahead of you—look for a stump with a plaque for Hadley Grove just as you enter the trees.

At 0.2 mile, after gaining about 80 feet in elevation, you come to a fork. The right trail leads another 0.2 mile to Little Beacon Rock. This side trip is definitely worth it—it is generally level except for one switchback, and there is one scree-covered traverse with a sharp drop-off for about 100 feet. But there's an awesome talus field and expansive views of the Columbia River Gorge, including Big Beacon Rock, and Little Beacon rises above you. Note: Add 0.4 mile to the mileages given below if you take this side trip.

To continue to Pool of the Winds, take the left fork towards Hamilton Mountain on the Hadley Trail. The trail continues approximately 3 feet wide, natural surface and compact gravel, on a gentle 5% incline for a couple hundred feet. It then levels out and you step over a small log rising about a foot above the trail. Curve sharply right at 0.4 mile, then come to a 10 to 12% incline for about 30 feet and level out slightly. There's a slight hill on the left with a clearing for power lines, but you are traveling through a green forest of alder, surrounded by vanilla leaf, huckleberries, and vine maples. Come to another 10 to 15% incline as the trail curves slightly right again, decreasing to less than 8% as it curves slightly right and left again. Continue on a generally 8 to 10% incline. The trail levels out and narrows next to an old blowdown. Take another slight incline as the trail curves left.

At 0.6 mile the trail curves sharply left on a 12% incline and you exit the forest at the top of the hill, emerging to a power line clear-cut with incredible views of the gorge and Bonneville Dam. The trail levels out as it curves left and passes underneath the power lines. There is a picnic table surrounded by wildflowers; it's a great spot to rest or have lunch. The trail continues level on pea gravel.

At 0.8 mile come to the junction with the Hamilton Mountain Trail. There is another bench here. Take a short, steep decline, then continue straight on Hamilton Mountain. The trail begins level, traveling back into the forest, then you step over a log barrier and it starts to incline, gaining 200 feet in the next 0.25 mile. It is a firm but uneven gravel surface with roots and rocks in the trail, starting on a 10 to 15% incline. Curve left on a 20% incline, then continue on a general incline of 10 to 15%. At 0.7 mile the trail narrows and gets much rockier, some rocks rising 3 to 4 inches above the surface, continuing on a general incline.

At 1.0 mile the trail starts to level out but continues to be rocky and narrow. At 1.1 miles it levels out, widens to 4 feet, and the surface becomes more even. You may notice the sound of running water. The trail curves sharply left next to a tree and gets a little rockier and slippery on a 10 to 12% decline. Continue on a 10% decline as the trail curves left and right. The trail then levels out and you cross a boardwalk and then a footbridge with two 3-inch steps. On the other side, the trail curves right then bypasses next to some large roots. The trail continues generally level and uneven, but not rocky. There's a nice view as Hardy Creek funnels down the mountain.

At 1.3 miles pass to the left of a large Douglas fir and then take a rocky 12% incline as the trail curves right, followed by a 15% decline, stepping down and around a couple of roots. Pay attention to the feel of the air—you may start to feel it changing as you approach the waterfalls. The trail continues generally level but uneven, with some areas of steep cross-slope. At 1.4 miles you come to a signed fork in the trail. The Hardy Falls viewpoint is straight ahead, but you may want to skip it, especially if you have knee or balance problems—a very steep and eroded trail with tall steps leads down to a wooden deck overlooking the waterfall. It is beautiful, though—you're tucked back into a fold of the mountain, surrounded by green plants and giant fir trees—but I have to emphasize that the trail is pretty sketchy.

To continue to Rodney Falls and Pool of the Winds, go left at the signed intersection. Cross the footbridge—mind the 4-inch gap between the end of the bridge and the trail. Pass over a nice little stream, then step down onto some rocks, cross a wet area, and pass next to a snag on the right. Take a 15 to 20% incline on a rocky trail, increasing to 25% for a few feet, and then level out with a wood barrier on the right. You are traveling above Hardy Falls. Take a 15 to 20% incline on the other side of the barrier for about 100 feet, then level out briefly before it declines at 10 to 15%.

At 1.5 miles you arrive at a signed fork in the trail—the spur to Pool of the Winds is straight ahead. This is truly a magical spot—you are surrounded by ferns and mossy rocks with waterfalls above, across, and below you. Continuing to Pool of the Winds, the trail starts on a slight rocky incline. Pass narrowly to the left of a boulder and then come to

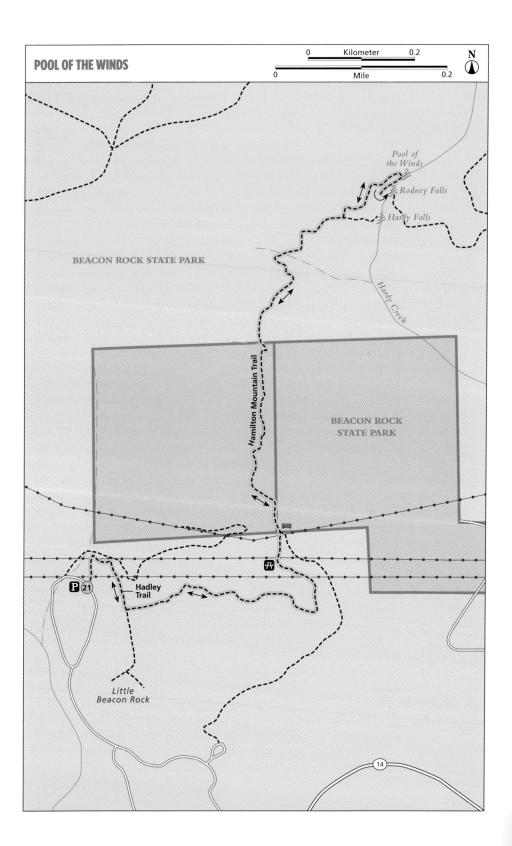

a set of stairs—the first step up is pretty eroded and almost 2 feet tall, but the next thirteen steps are shallow and only a couple of inches. You then decline at 10% with a sharp drop-off on the right, ducking very narrowly and closely to the cliff side on the left. You then arrive at the viewpoint for Pool of the Winds. It is very rocky and, depending on the water level, there may be pools of standing water. It takes you right out over Rodney Falls and under Pool of the Winds. If you are feeling pretty surefooted, you can go all the way out to the edge of the rocks—a metal barrier protects the edge—and get an up-close experience of the waterfall as it plunges down into a cave-like enclosure. I felt incredibly rejuvenated and refreshed by it.

Take all the time you want to here, and then I recommend a short detour to Rodney Falls and another view of Pool of the Winds. Head back on the spur to the main trail, go left, and take six steps down with a 4- to 6-inch rise. Take a 10% decline before it levels out and then switchbacks to the left. Take another set of twelve stairs with a 4- to 6-inch rise. The trail then generally levels out as it approaches a bridge over the creek. It is a 2-foot-wide wooden footbridge with rails on both sides, so you may have to wait for others to cross, but it brings you directly below the falls. Rodney Falls cascades down mossy rocks in front of you, with Pool of the Winds high above.

The trail continues across the footbridge to climb Hamilton Mountain, so head back the way you came to return to the trailhead.

MILES AND DIRECTIONS

0.0 Start at the Hadley Trailhead in the campground.

0.2 The trail forks. Go left to continue to Pool of the Winds. Right takes you to Little Beacon Rock.

0.6 Emerge to a power line clear-cut.

0.8 Junction with the Hamilton Mountain Trail. Continue straight.

1.4 The trail forks. The Hardy Falls viewpoint is straight ahead, but I recommend skipping it and continuing left.

1.5 The trail forks. The spur trail to Pool of the Winds is straight ahead. The bridge over the creek with a view of Rodney Falls is to the right. Visit both, then return the way you came.

3.0 Arrive back at the trailhead.

22 COASTAL FOREST TRAIL

WHY GO?

The Coastal Forest Trail in Cape Disappointment State Park is home to rare old-growth forest at the mouth of the Columbia River. You'll experience ancient trees and lots of birds, and have views of the Columbia River and the wetlands. It is relatively easy for a coastal old-growth trail, but there are some steep sections and slippery conditions. This trail is definitely worth the effort, and overall it felt more replenishing than taxing.

THE RUNDOWN

Spoon rating: 3 spoons. There are grades up to 25% for under 30 feet and rolling grades up to 20% for 0.1 mile, two sets of steep stairs, and some slippery areas. Benches are available.
Type: Loop
Distance: 1.6 miles
Elevation: 20 feet
Elevation gain: 266 feet
Max grade: 25%
Max cross-slope: 8%
Typical width: 2 feet
Typical surface: Natural
Trail users: Hikers
Season/schedule: Year-round

Water availability: Drink service at the camp store
Amenities: Benches, food and drink service at the camp store, a nearby boat launch for more river views
Dog-friendly: Yes, on leash
Cell phone reception: Yes
Nearest town: Ilwaco
Land manager: Washington State Parks, (360) 642-3078
Pass/entry fee: Washington Discover Pass
Land acknowledgment: Chinookan people know the mouth of the mighty Wímał (meaning big river) as Kah'eese.

FINDING THE TRAILHEAD

Getting there: From US 101 in Ilwaco, take WA 100, following signs for Cape Disappointment State Park. Drive all the way into the park, and turn left at the state park welcome sign before you enter the campground. The trailhead is located across the road from the camp store, at the far edge of the large gravel parking lot. GPS: 46.28419, -124.05447
Start: End of a large gravel parking lot

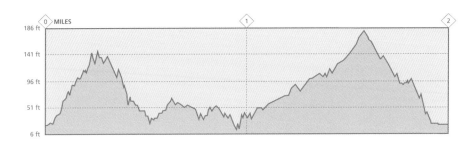

The Columbia River and wetlands

THE HIKE

The trailhead is hidden in the trees at the northern corner of the parking area, close to the road. Look for a metal post with a map and red caution sign. There is a bit of a steep incline on a grassy hill to reach the trailhead—it's approximately a 20% incline and 6 feet long—but you could walk on the road and access the trailhead more directly. You have two options for this trail: an easier 0.5-mile loop or a more difficult 1.5-mile loop. This guide is for the longer loop, but describes most of the shorter loop except for the section that cuts across the longer loop.

The trail begins on a narrow footpath heading uphill at a 10 to 15% incline then curves left and passes narrowly next to a large alder. Continue on a steady incline of 10 to 15%, passing under lots of red elderberry and stepping up over roots—a few rise about 4 inches above the surface. You'll still get peeks at the road below you on the left. Take five steps up narrowly between roots and then come to a set of steep stairs with a 12-inch rise. The trail then levels out slightly, continuing on a foot-wide path as you continue to climb away from the road. Pass over a small root mat rising up to 3 inches then curve left, stepping up on roots on a 20% incline. Pass underneath a very large red elderberry arching over the trail. Continue on a 10% incline.

At 0.1 mile you arrive at the start of the loop. A wooden sign gives the elevation at 93 feet and points to the right. The trail continues as a narrow, grassy footpath on a steady incline of 10 to 15% and a few sections with a 10% cross-slope. You'll start passing under a few large Sitka spruces as you continue rising through the forest. The surface is fairly uneven and rolling, continuing on a steady 5 to 10% incline. At 0.2 mile the trail starts to curve left with a view down to the water on the right, and you pass underneath four large Sitka spruces with a couple of small roots in the trail. Take a 10 to 15% incline; there is then a rustic bench on the left. Here is the signed intersection for the shorter loop; according to the map and what I saw, it appears to go uphill slightly then levels out for 0.1 mile, reconnecting with the longer loop at mile 1.2.

To continue on the longer loop, take a 20% decline for 50 feet and then rise at about 8%, passing underneath some large Sitka spruces and then declining again on a 15% grade. The trail widens to almost three feet, and there are nice views of the Columbia River to the right. A few roots run alongside and across the trail, so watch your step. The trail rolls a few times on 5 to 10% declines. Step across one root rising about 10 inches above the trail, then pass to the left of an old-growth Sitka spruce with large exposed roots. Take a 15% decline for approximately 50 feet. The trail continues to roll several times on a general decline with grades up to 25%, passing underneath many large Sitka spruces. Switchback to the right with more roots in the trail and continue on a general 10% decline. Continue through old-growth Sitka spruce and hemlock trees. Take a 20% decline as the trail curves right, stepping down on a couple of roots.

You're now at approximately 0.25 mile; the trail generally continues on a more level elevation along the ridge for the next 0.5 mile. The trail narrows to less than 2 feet wide as you travel between two hills and pass underneath an old fallen tree. Take six wooden steps down, watching out for the last one with a 1-foot rise. The trail then curves sharply to the left with peekaboo views of the river. Continue on an 8% decline for a couple hundred feet before the trail levels out slightly, then step over a couple of roots and continue on a general 5% decline. You'll pass between a cut-out blowdown and then cross two-by-fours that have been placed in the trail. You're surrounded by old-growth forest with lots of healthy understory plants including huckleberry, salmonberry, and thimbleberry. Berries bring birds, and you may hear the rising call of a Swainson's thrush or the chirping song of a Pacific wren.

Take an 8% decline as the trail curves left. You then arrive at a steep decline to a seasonal stream and incline on the other side with stairs. Take three steep steps down; the last step is about 18 inches and a bit unstable. Cross on a piece of wood placed in the trail over the mud, then take eight steep steps up. Continue on a 10% incline, passing to the left of old-growth Sitka spruce and hemlock trees; step down over roots rising about 8 inches. Continue on a 10% incline as the trail curves left and right a couple of times then levels out on a 2 to 5% incline. Step over a few more roots as you pass next to another spruce.

At 0.5 mile pass another large old-growth Sitka spruce. Cross over a root mat, taking a slight decline, and pass to the left of another large spruce and step down a couple of inches from its roots. You then enter a large area of old growth and come to a couple of steep hills. Take four steep steps down over roots, and then take a 20% decline for about 15 feet. Curve slightly right then come to a very old, amazing Sitka spruce. It's covered in ferns and other epiphytes, shelf mushrooms, and dripping sap. A stream runs through here during wet months. The trail levels out briefly then curves left and climbs a steep 25% incline for about 50 feet. You can step up on roots and log rounds that have been placed in the trail. Continue on a general 5% incline.

At 0.7 mile there is a rustic bench to rest on and enjoy the forest. A spur leads off to the right for about 0.1 mile that provides an overlook of the wetlands and the Columbia River. It is worth the side trip, but the path is narrow and slippery with some steep

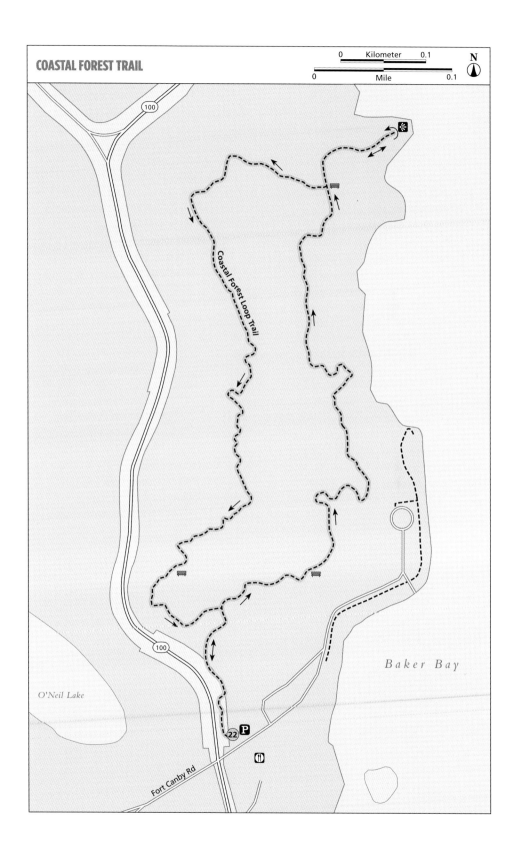

COASTAL FOREST TRAIL

0   Kilometer   0.1

0   Mile   0.1

N

100

Coastal Forest Loop Trail

100

22

P

O'Neil Lake

Baker Bay

Fort Canby Rd

drop-offs and lots of roots. But it leads out to a point with a really awesome view across the mouth of the Columbia and the surrounding wetlands.

If you take the spur trail, go right back on the main trail. Take a slight incline as it curves left and right through more old-growth forest. Step over a couple of 6-inch roots and then come to a 30-foot-long boardwalk made of two two-by-four boards. You then step over a large blowdown that has been cut out with a 1-foot step on either side. The trail continues generally level with up to 8% inclines. The canopy eventually opens up and you get a nice view across the forest to some of the tall old growth as the trail curves left and then starts to descend slightly, passing lots of thimbleberry, salal, and red elderberry. Continue on a slight descent and pass a very large old Sitka spruce on the right. The trail inclines slightly and you step 6 inches over and across a root. Come to an old-growth hemlock with a big open area under its roots.

At 1.0 mile take a slight incline stepping on roots, and pass between a fallen Sitka spruce. The trail continues generally level, curving right and left through thick understory. At 1.1 miles the trail rolls down, across, and then up an area that is muddy in the winter. Cross between an old mossy log and take a 20% incline, stepping up on an old semi-rotten log round in the trail. Continue on an 8% incline for a couple hundred feet, then curve right on a 10% incline, stepping over a couple of roots next to a Sitka spruce and a hemlock. Curve left on a 20% incline for 10 feet, then right on a 15% incline for 10 feet, then right on a 20% decline for about 8 feet. The trail then inclines at 10% for about 50 feet and continues on a general incline up to 5%. Over the 100 feet, curve left and right, then take a 15% incline before leveling out slightly and then inclining at 15%.

At 1.2 miles come to the intersection with the short loop—continue to the right, stepping over a couple of roots on a narrow trail through ferns and thimbleberries. You then pass between a really old nurse log that's covered in plant life. The trail descends slightly, curves left, and continues passing through younger forest. Step down over an 8-inch-tall root, then curve left and right, continuing on a gradual descent with a couple of 8 to 10% sections. Pass next to a large Sitka spruce, and continue on a level to slightly rolling trail. Step over a root and then the trail becomes a footpath through grass and brush. It gets a little more uneven and has some steep cross-slopes. At 1.4 miles you reach the end of the loop; go right to return to the parking area.

MILES AND DIRECTIONS

0.0   Start at trailhead at the corner of the gravel parking area.

0.1   Go right at the start of the loop.

0.2   Reach the junction for the short loop. Continue straight.

0.7   The spur trail on the right leads to an overlook of the wetlands and Columbia River.

0.9   Go right on the loop trail from the spur trail.

1.3   Reach the junction at the end of the short loop. Continue to the right.

1.5   Come to the end of the loop. Go right to return to the parking area.

1.6   Arrive back at the parking area.

23 MARINE PARK

WHY GO?

The Columbia River Renaissance Trail is an accessible, 5-mile paved path that begins at the downtown Vancouver Waterfront Park and ends at Wintler Park. It is a wonderful urban stroll or roll along the banks of the mighty Columbia River. This section, from Marine Park to Wintler Park, is typically much less busy and passes through wetlands, cottonwood forest, and sandy beaches.

THE RUNDOWN

Spoon rating: 1 spoon. Wheelchair accessible, with one 5% grade for over 40 feet towards the end of the trail.
Type: Out-and-back
Distance: 3 miles
Elevation: 30 feet
Elevation gain: 40 feet
Max grade: 5%
Max cross-slope: 2%
Typical width: 8 feet
Typical surface: Paved
Trail users: Walkers, runners, baby strollers
Season/schedule: Year-round
Water availability: Water fountains

Amenities: Flush toilets, benches, picnic tables
Dog-friendly: Yes, on leash
Cell phone reception: Excellent
Nearest town: Vancouver
Land manager: City of Vancouver, (360) 487-8311
Pass/entry fee: No parking fee at Marine Park; there is a fee to park at the boat launch. A fee is charged to park at Wintler Park from Memorial Day to Labor Day.
Land acknowledgment: Chinook and Cowlitz

FINDING THE TRAILHEAD

Getting there: Take I-5 to WA 14E, and take exit 1. Turn left onto SE Columbia Way. In 1.2 miles, turn right onto SE Marine Park Way. There is a large paved parking area with two van-accessible parking spots. GPS: 45.61464, -122.62726
Start: Paved path beginning at the parking lot

THE HIKE

From the parking area, head towards the restrooms on the right—the restrooms are closed long term due to budget cuts, but an interpretive sign just behind the building provides information about the area. The paved path leads through the grassy park with several wheelchair-accessible picnic tables. Pass a large group picnic site and a playground on the left—the restrooms here are generally open, but you have to access them over a brick paved

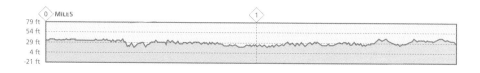

Start of the trail in Marine Park

path. The river is on your right just beyond some trees; you're actually traveling through wetlands, which will become more obvious soon. Pass over a couple of ¼-inch cracks in the pavement as you leave the park. The trail curves left and right then parallels the road as you approach the Water Research Education Center with wetland on the right.

At 0.3 mile you reach the Water Resource Education Center on the left, which is typically open to visitors. There are a couple of parallel parking spots next to the trail and a nice sitting area with benches, plants, and a peace pole. An interpretive viewpoint on the right overlooks the wetland and the river. This section is paved in wide, smooth brick and is pretty even. The paved path continues generally level and 8 feet wide, traveling through a wetland underneath cottonwood trees. Take a short, 5% decline and incline, cross over a 20-foot-long brick section, then the trail curves away from the road again.

At 0.5 mile you come to a little bridge with a wide shoulder overlooking a stream and a small green gully. At 0.6 mile you come to the first bench since you left the park. The trail then curves slightly to the right and passes a nice wetland area, then curves sharply left and opens up to views of the river. You are now leaving the forest and traveling along the banks of the river, with several condo buildings on the left. A sandy path on the right leads down to a little beach. The path is lined with benches here, and it is a great place to watch for wildlife or people boating in the river.

At 0.9 mile there is a little overlook at a marina with several benches. Continue along the river with views of wetlands on the right and lots of condos on the left. You then start on a slight 2% incline. At 1.2 miles the path reenters a wooded area with a wetland on the right. Pass some fencing, and then the trail curves sharply left on a 5% incline and transfers from pavement to concrete with a slight rise. Continue on a 5% incline for

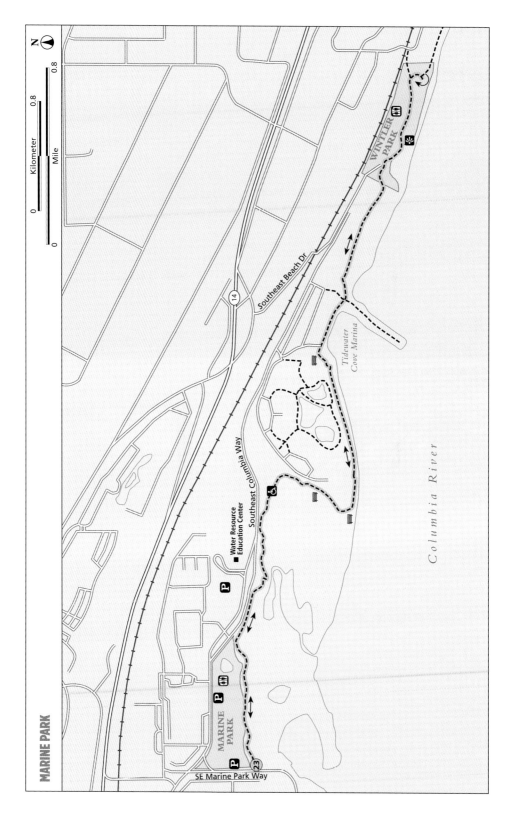

MARINE PARK

MARINE PARK

Water Resource
Education Center

Southeast Columbia Way

SE Marine Park Way

23

Southeast Beach Dr

14

Tidewater
Cove Marina

WINTLER
PARK

Columbia River

N

Kilometer   0.8
Mile   0.8
0

24 BRISTLECONE PINE TRAIL

WHY GO?

Hoyt Arboretum, located in Washington Park just two miles from downtown Portland, is an oasis in the city. This accessible trail passes trees from Chile and South America, Korea, China, Japan, the Pacific Northwest, and Europe. It ends at an accessible picnic area tucked back into a group of gingko trees, which blaze golden yellow in the fall. This quieter area of the arboretum is a perfect place for a mindful visit.

THE RUNDOWN

Spoon rating: 1 spoon. Wheelchair accessible, with one area of cracked pavement that may require navigating.
Type: Out-and-back
Distance: 0.8 mile
Elevation: 720 feet
Elevation gain: 25 feet
Max grade: 5%
Max cross-slope: 5%
Typical width: 4 feet
Typical surface: Paved
Trail users: Hikers
Season/schedule: Year-round, 5 a.m. to 10 p.m.

Water availability: Water fountains at visitor center
Amenities: Flush toilets and water fountains at visitor center, benches, picnic tables
Dog-friendly: Yes, on leash
Cell phone reception: Yes
Nearest town: Portland
Land manager: Hoyt Arboretum, City of Portland, (503) 865-8733
Pass/entry fee: No entry fee, but paid hourly parking is required at the two main lots.
Land acknowledgment: Multnomah and Atfalati (Tualatin Kalapuya)

FINDING THE TRAILHEAD

Getting there: From Portland, take US 26W to exit 72 and follow signs for Hoyt Arboretum. In approximately 1 mile, turn right onto SW Fairview Boulevard. In 0.2 mile, turn left onto SW Fischer Lane. The small parking lot is on the left, about 0.25 mile before the visitor center main parking area. It is a free lot with only five parking spaces, so it can fill up quickly. Two spots are designated accessible parking, but the access aisle is too narrow for a van. Address: 148 SW Fischer Ln., Portland. GPS: 45.51629, -122.71921

Public transit: The MAX light rail Blue and Red lines stop at Washington Park. An elevator takes you to the surface near the Vietnam Memorial at the south end of the park; the Overlook Trail is an accessible, but slightly steep, route up to the visitor center. Bus 63 from downtown stops at the visitor center.

Start: A small paved lot on SW Fischer Lane in Hoyt Arboretum

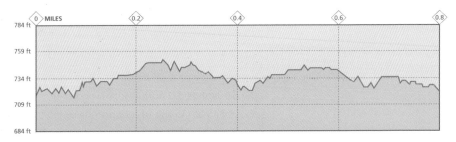

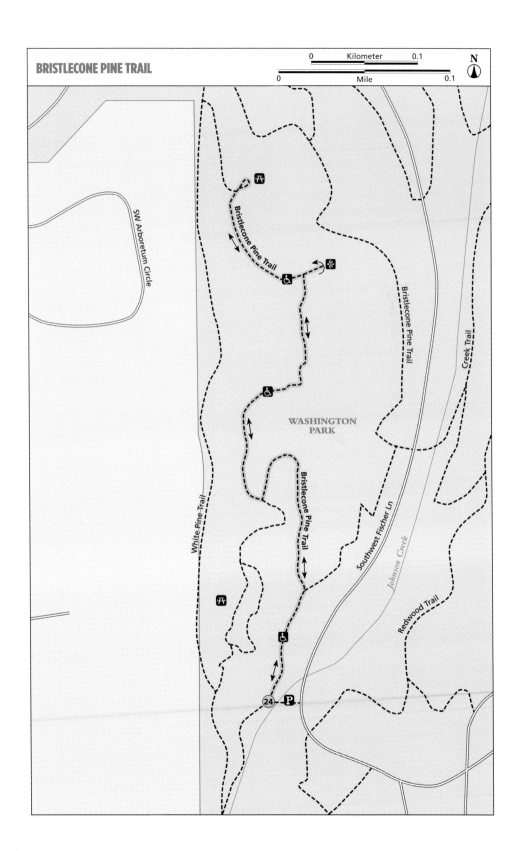

BRISTLECONE PINE TRAIL

N

0   Kilometer   0.1
0   Mile   0.1

SW Arboretum Circle

Bristlecone Pine Trail

Bristlecone Pine Trail

WASHINGTON
PARK

White Pine Trail

Bristlecone Pine Trail

Southwest Fischer Ln

Johnson Creek

Creek Trail

Redwood Trail

24 P

The start of the trail

THE HIKE

The trailhead is on the right (northwest) side of the parking area. The trail begins on a paved, 6-foot-wide path with maximum 5% grades for up to 20 feet. In about 250 feet the trail forks—continue straight on the paved section. A few roots have lifted the trail surface approximately 2 inches down the center of the trail for about 10 feet, but it can be navigated with at least 2 feet of clearance on either side. The trail surface is slightly uneven, with minimal cross-slope. There is a bench on the left facing a collection of native Douglas firs. The trail continues level, with a couple of small cracks in the surface.

At 0.1 mile arrive at a signed fork. To the left is a small, inaccessible picnic area in a quiet spot tucked into native forest. The pavement is pretty rough, with lots of cracks, holes, and raised sections. There are two 8 to 10% grades. The benches and picnic tables are not wheelchair accessible.

To continue to the accessible picnic area, go right at the fork. The path curves right then passes next to a large Douglas fir. The trail surface is cracked and raised up to 2 inches with a 5% cross-slope for 5 feet—sloping towards the inside of the trail. The trail continues smoothly and you come to a bench next to a stream. Shortly after that, there is a section of trail raised by a root. It is 3 inches high and 10 inches long, on a slight slope. The crack is about 7 inches wide and 1 inch deep. It is passable, but some wheelchair users may need assistance. The trail then continues on maximum 5% grades, with a few small cracks and uneven sections. A bench on the left overlooks a meadow, then there are a few more cracks rising 3 to 4 inches on a manageable slope.

At 0.4 mile you arrive at the Korean collection. An accessible viewpoint on the right overlooks a pine and Douglas fir forest, the tops of the redwoods towering above them all. The trail continues left, circling a meadow with gingko trees in the center. Pass a Chinese forest on the left, then arrive at the picnic area. You are tucked back against a hill, overlooking the gingkos and Chinese forest. Return to your car the way you came.

MILES AND DIRECTIONS

0.0   Start at the trailhead on the northwest side of the parking area.

0.1   Continue right at the signed fork.

0.4   Reach an overlook, then continue straight to the picnic area.

0.8   Arrive back at the trailhead.

25 **REDWOOD LOOP**

WHY GO?

This is my favorite trail at Hoyt Arboretum, and perhaps in all of Portland. It packs a lot into a mile, but the redwood grove is the crowning
jewel. This is the only redwood grove outside of northern California
and southwestern Oregon; they are cultivated, of course, but their
towering magnificence is not diminished. A redwood deck allows you
to sit in the canopy, surrounded by trees. You may forget that you are
just a couple of miles from downtown in Washington Park.

THE RUNDOWN

Spoon rating: 2 spoons. General 5%
grade, maximum 12% for up to 150
feet. Typically level and even with no
obstacles. Several forks in the trail,
but they are well signed.
Type: Loop
Distance: 1 mile
Elevation: 800 feet
Elevation gain: 120 feet
Max grade: 12%
Max cross-slope: 5%
Typical width: 2 feet
Typical surface: Natural, pea gravel
Trail users: Hikers
Season/schedule: Year-round, dawn
to dusk

Water availability: Water fountains
at visitor center
Amenities: Flush toilets and water
fountains at visitor center, benches,
picnic tables
Dog-friendly: Yes, on leash
Cell phone reception: Yes
Nearest town: Portland
Land manager: Hoyt Arboretum,
City of Portland, (503) 865-8733
Pass/entry fee: No entry fee, but
paid hourly parking is required at the
two main lots.
Land acknowledgment: Multnomah
and Atfalati (Tualatin Kalapuya)

FINDING THE TRAILHEAD

Getting there: From Portland, take US 26W to exit 72 and follow signs for
Hoyt Arboretum. In approximately 1 mile, turn right onto SW Fairview Boulevard. The parking area will be on your right. There are two van-accessible
parking spots. Be aware: This is a paid parking lot. Address: 4000 SW Fairview Blvd.,
Portland. GPS: 45.5156, -122.71649
Public transit: The MAX light rail Blue and Red lines stop at Washington Park. An
elevator takes you to the surface near the Vietnam Memorial at the south end of the
park; the Overlook Trail is an accessible, but slightly steep, route up to the visitor center. Bus 63 from downtown stops at the visitor center.
Start: At Stevens Pavilion near the visitor center

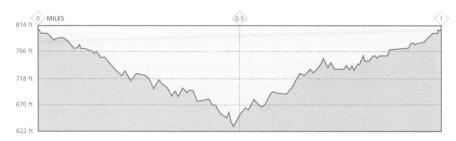

The redwood deck

THE HIKE

This loop is well marked—just follow the square symbols on the map and signposts for the 1-hour loop. From the visitor center, cross the street towards Stevens Pavilion. Facing the pavilion, head left on the Fir Trail. It starts on a firm natural surface, 3 feet wide and level. Take a 10% decline for 100 feet, then the trail levels out and passes under the sweeping branches of a spruce tree. At 0.1 mile the trail forks—follow the Redwood Trail to the right. Continue on compact pea gravel through a nice, open meadow. Descend at approximately 10% for 50 feet, then incline at 5% for 100 feet. Pass beneath sweeping fir branches, then come to a bench on the right. Take a 20% grade with a 5% cross-slope for 50 feet as you approach another intersection.

At 0.2 mile the trail intersects the Fir Trail. Continue straight on the Redwood Trail. Take a 10 to 15% decline for 100 feet, curve sharply right around a boulder, then take a 15% decline. Cross Fischer Lane and pick up the Redwood Trail on the other side. (Note: The SW Fischer Lane parking area is on the left.) Take a 5% decline from the road and continue on compact pea gravel. The trail curves right and passes a Deodar cedar from the Himalayas. It then curves left over a small culverted stream with an 8% cross-slope then inclines at 10% for 10 feet. The trail then levels out and becomes a semi-firm natural surface.

At 0.3 mile pass a connector trail on the right. The trail becomes a firm, packed gravel surface and continues level, then returns to natural surface with several roots rising 3 inches. The trail rolls a few times, traveling through lush forest with large western redcedars on both sides. Continue descending on grades up to 10%, and curve left across a small culverted stream. There is a sharp drop-off on the left as you travel above Johnson

Trail through the western redcedar forest

Creek. At approximately 0.35 mile curve slightly right around a hillside, passing beneath large western redcedars, with their branches sweeping over the trail—this is one of my favorite spots to take a break and appreciate the trees. Continue descending on grades up to 10%. The trail curves left and levels out, passing a variety of cedars from around the world (western redcedars are not true cedars).

At 0.4 mile another connector trail goes sharply downhill to the left—continue straight. The trail is generally level compact gravel, then comes to a 10% incline for 100 feet, levels out again, and descends on a slightly uneven 10% grade before coming to a bench on the right. Continue on a slightly rolling, uneven trail that is 2 feet wide. Continue straight past another connector trail, descending at less than 10% grades.

At 0.5 mile you enter the redwood grove. The trail curves left and levels out, traveling beneath towering coast redwoods, giant sequoias, and dawn redwoods. Stay to the right at the fork for the Wildwood Trail, continuing towards the redwood deck. Take a slight 5% incline, switchback right with another bench on the left, and take a 20% incline for 100 feet. Come to another 20% incline for 20 feet as you approach the deck. The redwood deck sits in the tree canopy; there are three wooden benches, and a sequoia tree protrudes through the center. Continuing past the deck, the trail switchbacks left on a 10 to 15% incline for a couple hundred feet as it leaves the redwood grove and heads higher up the hill, increasing to a 20% grade for a few feet at the top.

At 0.6 mile the trail levels out past an informational sign about the redwoods, takes a 5 to 10% incline, curves right, and comes to a fork with three trails at an informational sign and a trash can. Continue on the Spruce Trail in the center, following the 1-hour loop.

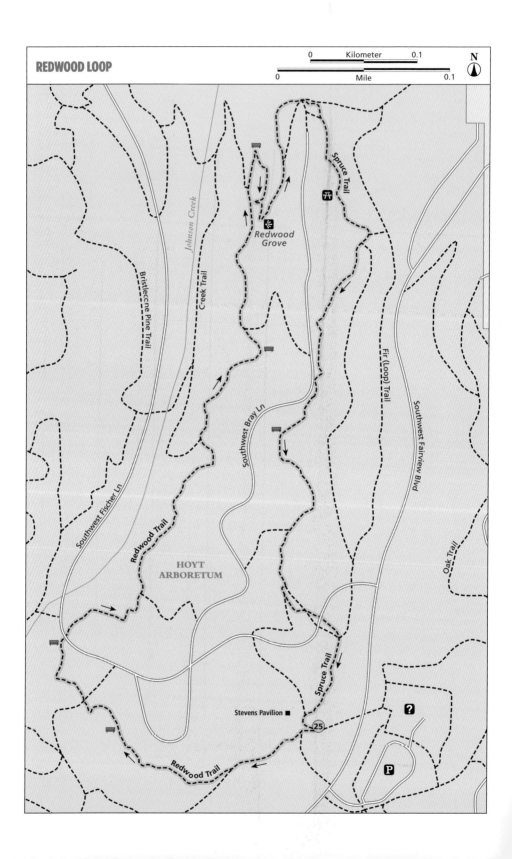

REDWOOD LOOP

Kilometer
0   0.1

Mile
0   0.1

N

Johnson Creek

Spruce Trail

Redwood Grove

Bristlecne Pine Trail

Creek Trail

Fir (Loop) Trail

Southwest Bray Ln

Southwest Fairview Blvd

Southwest Fischer Ln

Redwood Trail

Oak Trail

HOYT ARBORETUM

Spruce Trail

Stevens Pavilion ■

25

P

?

Redwood Trail

Begin on a 15 to 20% incline, curve right, and continue on a 10 to 15% incline. The trail surface is natural and semi-loose pea gravel.

At 0.7 mile pass the wedding meadow with picnic tables on the right. You then come to another trail intersection. (Note: The Fir Trail goes to the left for an additional 30-minute loop; you can take this as a side trip if you like. It loops 0.3 mile through a collection of firs from around the world and returns to this intersection.) Continue right on the Spruce Trail, following signs for the 1-hour loop. Continue on a 2-foot-wide compact pea gravel trail, passing the meadow. The trail curves slightly left, comes to a 10 to 15% incline for 100 feet, then levels out along the hillside—pitch pines grow along the trail here, and they smell wonderful in the summer sun. Take another 15 to 20% incline for 150 feet.

At 0.8 mile come to another intersection with a connector trail leading down steeply to the right. Continue straight and take a slight incline, with a bench on the left. The trail curves left, continuing on semi-loose pea gravel, and inclines at 10 to 15% up another slight hill. You then enter the spruce collection. The trail levels out, passing underneath Norway spruce, then curves right on a 10% incline. A bench is on the right at another connector trail—continue to the left. Take a slight incline and then enter a grove of oriental spruce.

At 0.9 mile stay to the left at another connector trail and continue on a 15% incline for approximately 150 feet. Cross the road and continue on the Spruce Trail. The pavilion will be in front of you; stay to the right at the next intersection, then take a 15% incline for about 75 feet to return to the pavilion. The visitor center is on your left across the road.

MILES AND DIRECTIONS

0.0 Start at the Stevens Pavilion across the street from the visitor center.

0.1 The trail forks. Go right on the Redwood Trail.

0.2 Cross Fischer Lane.

0.5 Enter the redwood grove.

0.6 Arrive at a three-way intersection. Continue on the Spruce Trail in the center.

0.7 Junction with the Fir Trail on the left. Continue right on the Spruce Trail.

0.9 Cross Fischer Lane. Continue to the pavilion in front of you.

1.0 Arrive back at the pavilion.

OREGON COAST

The 363 miles of the Oregon Coast is publicly owned; all of the beaches, extending from the lapping waves to the vegetation line, are protected for public access under the Beach Bill, earning it the moniker of "The People's Coast." It comprises three regions: the North Coast, from Astoria to Lincoln City; the Central Coast, from Lincoln City to Florence; and the South Coast, from Florence to Brookings. Each is ecologically and geographically unique. The North Coast is most notable as the place where the Columbia River meets the ocean, with sandy beaches and estuaries. The Central Coast includes numerous capes and rocky shorelines. The South Coast is the location of the renowned Oregon sand dunes and striking sea stacks.

This has come at the cost of the Indigenous peoples, however. Starting in the north, the Clatsop, Nehalem, Tillamook, Nestucca, Siletz, Yaquina, Alsea, Siuslaw, Kalawatset, and Hanis people all occupied territories along the coast and the mountains and valleys to the east. However, as Tribes were forced from their lands, 100 miles of the coast was set up as a reservation and many Indigenous peoples were marched to the coast. Even that reservation was gradually reduced, and now only 5 square miles of land is owned by the Confederated Tribes of the Siletz. The North Coast territories of the Tillamook were never ceded.

26 OLD GROWTH CEDAR PRESERVE

WHY GO?

Travel a well-constructed and -maintained accessible boardwalk to a 500- to 900-year-old western redcedar, the largest in Oregon. The tree rises over 150 feet above the forest, spreading into a magnificent candelabra crown. You'll pass over a wetland and through an old-growth forest on your way, with several more ancient trees. An optional footpath takes you into the forest.

THE RUNDOWN

Spoon rating: 1 spoon—wheelchair-accessible boardwalk for 1.4 miles out and back. 2 spoons—optional footpath for 1.2-mile lollipop loop with narrow, brushy corridor, several roots and blowdowns, and potentially confusing path.
Type: Out-and-back or lollipop loop
Distance: 1.4 miles out and back or 1.2-mile lollipop loop
Elevation: 16 feet
Elevation gain: 30 feet
Max grade: 5%
Max cross-slope: 2%
Typical width: 4 feet

Typical surface: Boardwalk, natural
Trail users: Hikers
Season/schedule: Year-round
Water availability: None
Amenities: Portable toilet at parking area, benches and picnic tables, several pullouts and viewing decks
Dog-friendly: Yes, on leash
Cell phone reception: Yes
Nearest town: Rockaway Beach
Land manager: City of Rockaway Beach, Rockaway Beach Nature Conservancy, (503) 355-8108
Pass/entry fee: None

FINDING THE TRAILHEAD

Getting there: The parking area is located north of Washington Street on the east side of US 101, just south of town. From the main beach access parking lot in central Rockaway Beach, head south 0.2 mile. The parking area will be on the left, just past the Rockaway Beach sign. It is not well marked and may be easier to see if you're heading north; if you get to Washington Street you just passed it. The paved parking area has ten parking spaces, including two van-accessible spots. GPS: 45.60112, -123.94554
Start: Paved parking area on US 101

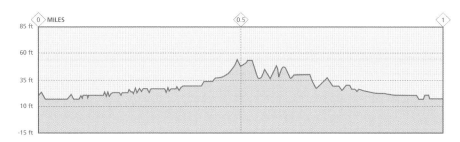

The old-growth western redcedar

THE HIKE

The boardwalk begins at the north side of the parking lot, next to a large interpretive sign and map. It is a level transition from the pavement to the boardwalk, which has edge barriers or railings along the entire length and pullouts approximately every 200 feet. The surface is tightly placed horizontal boards, very level with no rise above ¼ inch. The boardwalk continues for 0.3 mile over a lush wetland, surrounded by tall Sitka spruces and western redcedars, with vine maples and red alders arching over the trail. The skunk cabbage is some of the largest I've seen, growing taller than the boardwalk. It seems like you are entering an ancient secret garden, with plenty to feel, see, hear, and touch.

At 0.3 mile the boardwalk forks. Go to the left for 0.1 mile, passing the footpath on the left, to reach a wetland viewing deck. There are four benches and a picnic table here. The deck is tucked back and surrounded by trees and wetland plants. It is a great place for birding or just taking in your surroundings for a while. Turn around and head back to the main boardwalk, turning left at the fork. Continue through the wetland for about 0.1 mile, then the boardwalk curves left and enters a mature second-growth forest. There are tall western hemlocks, Douglas firs, and Sitka spruces. Large trees grow out of old stumps and fallen logs. Pass over a creek, then take a couple of 5% grades for less than 30 feet with level areas in between. Big Sitka spruces surround the boardwalk as you move further into old-growth forest.

Suddenly, the trail curves and a giant cedar comes into view. You reach the observation deck at 0.7 mile, which encircles the ancient tree. Take your time moving around this 154-foot-tall, 50-foot-circumference tree—there is a lot to notice here. One non-accessible picnic table and two benches provide a place to rest and enjoy this place. But your trip isn't done yet! Continue past the big cedar, heading left on the boardwalk. A couple more old-growth cedars wait at another viewing deck with a bench just a few feet away. From here, you can turn around and head back on the boardwalk, or travel through the forest on a footpath for 0.2 mile. This section is not wheelchair hikeable, and there are some tall roots and blowdowns to navigate, but it is a neat trip past more old growth.

Continuing on the footpath, take ten steps down to a natural surface trail. Continue level as the trail curves left and right a few times, with a few small roots and brush encroaching on the path. You then come to another old-growth cedar. Continue straight and pass between a Douglas fir and a large cedar. Step over a 6-inch-tall root then across two old logs with steps cut into them; the last one is a steep 12-inch step down. Continue curving left on the narrow footpath, step up on some more small roots, then pass a really old blowdown that is turning into a nurse log—ferns, huckleberries, and other plants growing from its decaying wood.

The footpath then gets very narrow and brushy. The route may be a little confusing to follow here as you cross some old fallen trees—just stay on the most worn path. Curve to the left and pass an old blowdown root ball; keep to the left and follow the faint path as it crosses narrowly between two alders, then step up on a large root and come to a massive old fallen tree. Go right around the tree, step up on roots, and then step down about 12 inches. You then come to an area that is muddy in the winter, but logs are placed in the trail to bypass it. Continue on the narrow footpath, ducking underneath some low-growing brush and blown-down trees. Curve left, pushing through an area of brushy salal, then step up on a couple of tall roots and pass an old blowdown root ball on the left. Cross over another potentially muddy area with some logs in the trail. Step up over a root

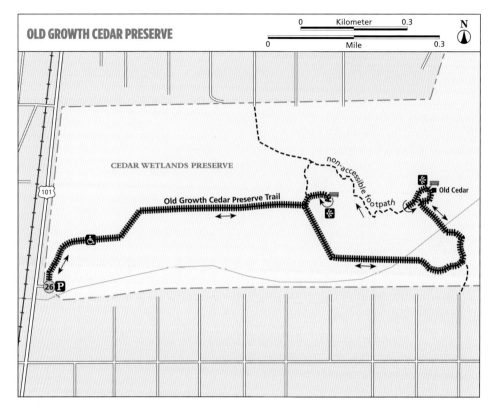

CEDAR WETLANDS PRESERVE

Old Growth Cedar Preserve Trail

non-accessible footpath

Old Cedar

mat and then reconnect with the boardwalk. Head right and then right again, staying on the boardwalk to return to the parking area.

MILES AND DIRECTIONS

0.0 Start on the boardwalk at the north side of the parking lot.

0.3 The boardwalk forks. Go left for 0.1 mile to a viewing deck.

0.5 Return to the main boardwalk and go left.

0.7 Reach the deck around the ancient cedar. Go left, then the boardwalk ends. Return the way you came, or take the footpath through the forest for the 1.2-mile lollipop loop option.

1.4 Arrive back at the parking lot.

27 KILCHIS POINT RESERVE

WHY GO?

Take a very level and partially wheelchair-accessible trail through a native garden and young coastal forest to a bird-watching shelter along Tillamook Bay. This little-known spot is well cared for and popular with disabled residents. You can even reserve a golf cart to travel to the birding shelter by calling the Pioneer Museum. Interpretive signs and well-marked maps guide your way.

THE RUNDOWN

Spoon rating: 1 spoon. Wheelchair accessible with caution for the first 0.5 mile; the remainder is wheelchair hikeable on level but potentially muddy terrain that may require all-terrain tires. Two boardwalks have a rise exceeding 1½ inches. No designated ADA parking.
Type: Out-and-back with two loops
Distance: 2.3 miles
Elevation: 20 feet
Elevation gain: 25 feet
Max grade: 8%
Max cross-slope: 5%
Typical width: 4 feet
Typical surface: Brick, gravel, boardwalk
Trail users: Hikers, birders

Season/schedule: Year-round
Water availability: Water fountains
Amenities: Benches placed at regular intervals, two all-gender accessible flush toilets, picnic tables, trash cans, dog cleanup bags, water fountains
Dog-friendly: Yes, on leash
Cell phone reception: Yes
Nearest town: Bay City
Land manager: Tillamook County Pioneer Museum, (503) 842-4553
Pass/entry fee: None
Land acknowledgment: Kilchis Point held one of the largest known Tillamook villages.

FINDING THE TRAILHEAD

Getting there: From Tillamook, head north on US 101 for approximately 5 miles to Bay City. Just as you enter the city limits, turn left on Warren Street, then left onto Spruce Street. The reserve is located at the end of a residential neighborhood. There is a small paved parking area with room for five cars and two overflow spots at the corner of Spruce and Warren, or a larger circular gravel parking area with about twenty parking spots and room for buses just past the trailhead. There are no designated accessible parking spots at either lot. GPS: 45.51248, -123.88156
Start: Small paved parking area

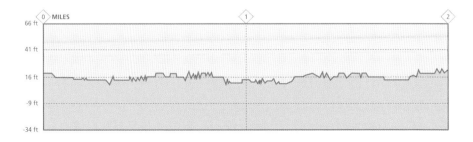

The birding shelter at Tillamook Bay

THE HIKE

The trail begins at the parking area on a brick path through a native garden with several picnic tables. There are interpretive signs about the Tillamook people, pioneer settlement, and the flora and fauna of the area. A short boardwalk lies a couple hundred feet down the path. Unfortunately, the brick has settled on both sides, resulting in a ½- to 1½-inch rise on the approaching side and a 2- to 3-inch fall on the other. The trail then comes to a round intersection with a circle made of brick and two benches on the perimeter.

The most accessible portion continues straight ahead on the brick path for about 0.1 mile, passing some interpretive signs about a lumber company and a couple of benches, and continues through the native garden, with brushy grass and blackberries, before ending at the gravel parking area. Go right to continue on the main trail, which continues on brick for a couple hundred feet. Several more benches are placed along the path. Travel through young, mossy forest onto a boardwalk; it is level onto the boardwalk, with a few slightly uneven and unsteady boards. The boardwalk encircles a tree, then ends onto compact gravel and natural surface for the remainder of the trail system. During the wet months, the trail may be too soft to travel on without all-terrain tires.

At 0.3 mile come to an intersection at a brick paved circle with a trash can and two benches. The trails are well signed and ultimately form a loop, reconnecting to continue towards Tillamook Bay. The Flora and Fauna Trail is on the right, Native American Way on the left. This route goes right on the Flora and Fauna Trail, but it may be very muddy and has a couple of steep cross-slopes.

Continuing on the Flora and Fauna Trail, at 0.4 mile come to another boardwalk with an 8% incline approaching the boardwalk, a ½-inch rise on the approach, a 2-inch

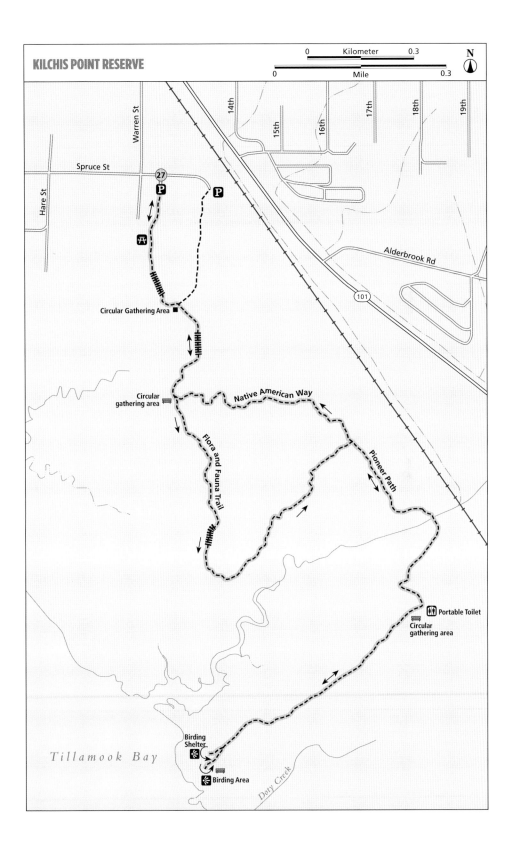

KILCHIS POINT RESERVE

Kilometer
0   0.3

Mile
0   0.3

N

Warren St

14th

15th

16th

17th

18th

19th

Spruce St

27

P

P

Hare St

Alderbrook Rd

101

Circular Gathering Area

Circular gathering area

Native American Way

Flora and Fauna Trail

Pioneer Path

Portable Toilet

Circular gathering area

Birding Shelter

Tillamook Bay

Birding Area

Doty Creek

fall on the other side, and an 8% decline to a very soft surface. The trail then travels on a turnpike with a natural surface and a couple inches of mud, and curves left and right between some firs. At 0.5 mile the trail becomes uneven with some cross-slopes up to 5%. It generally continues with a slightly rolling and uneven trail surface with some steep cross-slopes, soft surface, and potentially some mud for 0.2 mile.

At 0.7 mile you reach the intersection that forms a loop with Native American Way. Go right onto the Pioneer Path. Continue on a natural and compact gravel surface, then cross a short boardwalk with a 1-inch rise on either side. The trail curves through the forest, occasionally rolling on 5% grades. Cross another short boardwalk over a stream, then come to an 8% incline for 20 feet, level out, then take another 8% incline for a few feet. The trail reaches an intersection with what seems like an old road going to the left; there is a portable toilet and trash cans here. Continue towards the right, passing through a large convening circle with several benches arranged around the perimeter.

At 1.1 miles you reach the birding platform and shelter overlooking Tillamook Bay. The ramp may be slick—one set of skid-resistant shingles is on the right side and a handrail is on the left. There are benches and several signs with bird-watching tips at the shelter. A level gravel path leads left around the shelter to benches screened by foliage. There are gorgeous views of Tillamook Bay and the estuary near the mouth of the Kilchis River. When you are done here, return the way you came. Go left at the big convening circle.

At 1.7 miles arrive back at the intersection with Native American Way. Continue straight on Native American Way to finish the loop. The trail continues on soft compacted gravel. Come to an 8-foot-long boardwalk with no rise onto it and a 1.5-inch rise on the other side. At 1.8 miles, just past the boardwalk, there is a short natural surface path to a picnic table in the trees on the right. The trail rolls on 5% grades, then continues level on soft surface with some areas of 2-inch mud, passing old stumps and many interpretive signs about Tillamook Tribe culture and lifeways. The trail curves left and right a couple of times, then at 2.0 miles arrives back at the small convening circle—go right to return to the trail you came in on.

MILES AND DIRECTIONS

0.0 Start at the paved parking area.

0.2 Reach a trail intersection. Go straight for the most accessible portion, right to continue on the trail.

0.3 Reach the intersection of the Flora and Fauna Trail and Native American Way. Go right.

0.7 Reach the intersection of Native American Way and the Pioneer Path. Go right.

0.9 Pass an old road on the left. Go right, through a convening circle with benches.

1.1 Arrive at the birding platform and shelter. Return the way you came in.

1.7 Reach the intersection of Native American Way and the Flora and Fauna Trail. Continue straight.

2.0 Reach a trail intersection. Go right to return to the parking area.

2.3 Arrive back at the parking area.

28 DRIFT CREEK FALLS

WHY GO?

This iconic trail winds along forested coastal hills above a gully, then crosses a suspension bridge spanning 100 feet above Drift Creek. The waterfall plunges 75 feet down basalt cliffs in a lush green canyon. It is a very popular hike, and one or more roads to it are frequently washed out, but the trail is well maintained and the elevation gain is fairly gradual.

THE RUNDOWN

Spoon rating: 4 spoons. Prolonged grades of 5 to 10%, max 15 to 20%. Very muddy in winter. Suspension bridge may cause dizziness. A few benches are available.
Type: Out-and-back
Distance: 3.5 miles
Elevation: 970 feet
Elevation gain: 560 feet
Max grade: 20%
Max cross-slope: 5%
Typical width: 2 feet
Typical surface: Natural, muddy
Trail users: Hikers
Season/schedule: Year-round
Water availability: Creek

Special notes: Steady incline on the way back
Amenities: Vault toilet at trailhead
Dog-friendly: Yes, on leash
Cell phone reception: None
Nearest town: Lincoln City
Land manager: Siuslaw National Forest, Hebo Ranger District, (503) 392-5100
Pass/entry fee: Federal recreation pass
Land acknowledgment: Alsea Tribe hunted and gathered berries in the area of Drift Creek.

FINDING THE TRAILHEAD

Getting there: There are two routes to access the trailhead, from the north on OR 18 or the south from Drift Creek Road. As of this writing, the south route is blocked by a landslide on FR 17. Directions from the north: From US 101 and OR 18 north of Lincoln City, travel east 4.5 miles on OR 18. Turn right (south) on Bear Creek County Road for 3.5 miles. Continue 7 miles on FR 17 to the parking area on the left. FR 17 is a wide one-lane paved road with several hidden curves; there is enough room to pass cars with caution. The trailhead has two van-accessible parking spots with spaces for thirty cars, toilets, and trash cans. GPS: 44.9361268, -123.8546705
Start: Next to a trailhead sign and toilets at the edge of the parking area

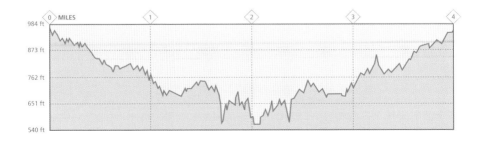

Typical trail

THE HIKE

The trail begins on compact pea gravel then turns to a semi-firm and slightly muddy natural surface. Take a 10 to 12% decline for a few feet before leveling out, and step over a couple of roots and a slightly muddy area. The trail switchbacks left on a 10% grade then narrows to 2 feet wide. Continue on a general rolling decline up to 10% as the trail curves along the hillside, passing (sometimes narrowly) between small Douglas firs and western hemlocks. Swordferns and salal blanket the hill above you and a narrow, wet gully is below you.

At 0.3 mile pass a numbered sign—these signs mark locations on an interpretive map that is available on the Siuslaw National Forest website. Step over a few roots rising up to 3 inches above the surface. The trail widens to 4 to 5 feet and continues on a semi-firm natural surface with a gradual decline up to 10%. Step over and around more roots rising 3 to 6 inches above the surface in several spots. The trail curves left between Douglas firs, and you may notice the sound of rushing water down below—you are actually high above Drift Creek Falls on the opposite hill. The trail narrows briefly as it traverses the hillside with a sharp drop-off on the right.

At 0.5 mile curve left and right, then the trail becomes much more rocky. There are trees in the middle of the trail to pass around; it's wide enough for one person passing on either side. A bench provides a nice place to take in the lovely mossy trees and ferns surrounding you. The trail then levels out slightly before coming to a short 10% incline, then levels out again. It curves gently to the west around a ridge, then enters a narrow canyon. The trail continues directly opposite from you, across a creek. Approach a small bridge on a 15% incline for approximately 200 feet with one level section halfway. The bridge is sturdy with a rail on the right, and is partially covered in chicken wire for traction. On the other side, the trail continues on natural surface with some rocks and roots. Take a short 15% incline then decline and curve right over a culverted stream.

At 0.8 mile the trail forks. To the left is the North Loop, which travels uphill, adding 0.5 mile with 100-plus feet of elevation gain, and provides access to stands of old-growth forest before reconnecting with the main trail. Go right to stay on the main trail, continuing on a 4-foot-wide natural and slightly muddy surface. Several roots rise 6 inches above the surface; one requires stepping over and down. Pass to the left of a bigleaf maple

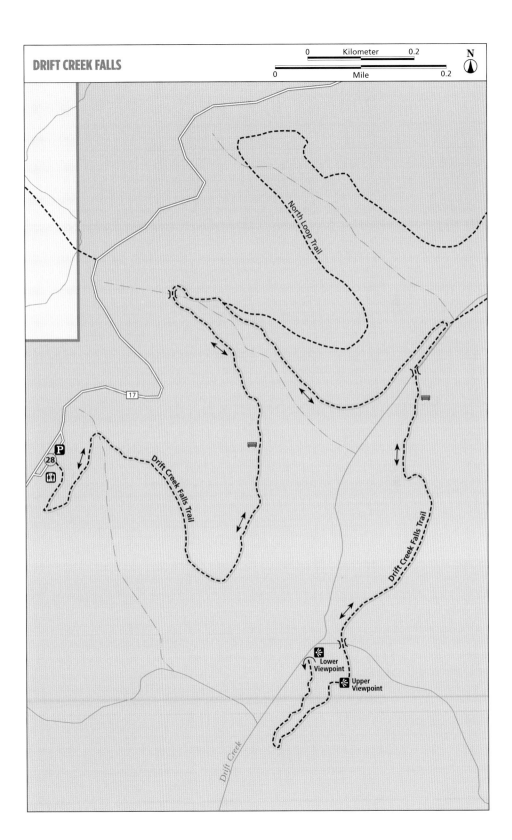

DRIFT CREEK FALLS

0   Kilometer   0.2

0   Mile   0.2

N

North Loop Trail

17

P

28

Drift Creek Falls Trail

Drift Creek Falls Trail

Lower
Viewpoint

Upper
Viewpoint

Drift Creek

with exposed roots, then continue on a 10 to 15% decline passing between Douglas firs. Continue on a general decline, stepping down over some roots.

At 0.9 mile you get the first views of Horner Creek and a long bridge down below. You then cross a sturdy footbridge covered in wire with a railing on the right. The surface becomes firmer and rockier as you approach the canyon floor, continuing on a general 10 to 15% decline.

At 1.1 miles the North Loop reconnects with the main trail on the left. Continue right towards the long bridge. Pass between large bigleaf maples, then there is creek access on the left—this is an easy spot for water if you need it. As you approach the bridge there may be a very large muddy area with standing water; it can be passed by maneuvering around trees and branches on the outer edge, but it may be just as easy to walk through with good boots, which is also better for the trail. The bridge is sturdy and spans about 100 feet across Horner Creek, with a railing on the right. A bench awaits on the other side. You then climb up a very steep, muddy bank between large Douglas firs, using their roots as some steps. Continue on a 10% incline for a couple hundred feet; there is a stump to sit on at the top of the hill.

The creek is below you again and you are traveling through a mature second-growth forest, with several large trees. Continue on a general 10% incline on a 3- to 4-foot-wide trail. Curve left on a 15 to 20% incline then right over a culverted stream. Take a steep, muddy 20% decline for 100 feet, then come to a gravel turnpike section with a steep drop-off on the right. The trail levels out slightly, with a few roots rising over 6 inches above the surface. Western redcedars, hemlocks, firs, and a few Sitka spruces surround you as you continue on a gradual decline, the creek rushing down below you on the right.

At 1.5 miles you start to approach the suspension bridge and the falls. There is a chain-link fence on the left, protecting the edge of the cliff, and the trail curves right and left around firs. A steep decline leads to the bridge, with several large rocks to step down onto. The bridge is pretty sturdy and can hold over 165,000 pounds, but it is narrow and sways slightly at 100 feet above the canyon, so it may be dizzying. The experience is incredible if you can stop on it, with the waterfall rushing below you, but if not, there are equally impressive views on the other side. Take two tall steps down from the bridge to another viewing area across from the falls.

For another vantage point at creek level at the base of the falls, continue on the trail to the left. The trail continues on up to a 20% decline, switchbacks right, then comes to a fallen log followed by rough steps. It continues on a steep, rocky descent as you approach Drift Creek below the falls. There are a couple of benches and several large boulders along the bank of the creek. You have a long, gradual incline ahead of you; take some time to appreciate the roaring waterfall in front of you and Drift Creek rushing downstream to eventually meet the mouth of the Siletz River.

MILES AND DIRECTIONS

0.0   Start at the trailhead at the edge of the parking area.

0.8   Junction with the start of the North Loop Trail. Go right.

1.1   Junction with the end of the North Loop Trail. Go right and cross the bridge.

1.5   Cross the suspension bridge to a viewpoint of the waterfall.

1.7   Reach the creek-side viewpoint of the waterfall. Return the way you came.

3.5   Arrive back at the trailhead.

29 YAQUINA HEAD OUTSTANDING NATURAL AREA

WHY GO?

Yaquina Head extends 1 mile into the Pacific Ocean. It is a wonderful place for tide pooling, whale watching, and birding, and the interpretive center is very educational. The historic lighthouse is the tallest in Oregon, and sits picturesquely at the tip of Yaquina Head. The Lighthouse Trail provides a walking route from the main parking area to the lighthouse, or you can park in the upper lot. Several other trails take you through the grassy headlands.

THE RUNDOWN

Spoon rating: 1 spoon. Wheelchair accessible to overlooks at the interpretive center and the lower overlook at Yaquina Head. Wheelchair hikeable along the Lighthouse Trail.
Type: Scenic viewpoint, out-and-back
Distance: 0.6 mile
Elevation: 135 feet
Elevation gain: 50 feet
Max grade: 8%
Max cross-slope: 8%
Typical width: 4 feet
Typical surface: Paved
Trail users: Hikers
Season/schedule: Trails open 8 a.m. to sunset year-round
Water availability: Water fountains
Special notes: Prolonged grades up to 8% on the Lighthouse Trail. Restroom doors may be difficult for wheelchair users to open.

Amenities: Accessible single-stall gendered restrooms with flush toilets, water fountains, benches, picnic tables, staffed visitor center
Dog-friendly: Yes, on leash
Cell phone reception: Yes
Nearest town: Newport
Land manager: Bureau of Land Management, (541) 574-3100
Pass/entry fee: Federal recreation pass, Oregon Pacific Coast Passport, or day-use fee
Land acknowledgment: The Yaquina once had dozens of villages along the shores of the Yaquina River. Yaquina Head was home to one village, whose inhabitants fished the waters and hunted elk and deer on the grassy headlands. They spoke a unique language, Yaquina, a Yakonan dialect. Descendants of the Yaquina Tribe are members of the Confederated Tribes of Siletz Indians.

FINDING THE TRAILHEAD

Getting there: From Newport, travel 4.5 miles north on US 101. Turn left onto Lighthouse Drive to enter Yaquina Head. There are eight van-accessible parking spots at the interpretive center. There is one accessible parking spot in the upper lot, but the curb cut may be difficult to access. GPS: 44.67486, -124.07418
Start: Next to the interpretive center

THE HIKE

A paved area with picnic tables and interpretive signs is behind the Yaquina Head Interpretive Center. A 0.3-mile paved trail to the lighthouse begins to the left of the interpretive center. The trail is wheelchair accessible through a tunnel to an ocean overlook, with

Yaquina Head and lighthouse from the Lighthouse Trail

views down to Quarry Cove. The tunnel is less than 50 feet long, paved and barrier free; the lights inside the tunnel weren't working when I was there, so it may be a bit dim.

Continuing right from the overlook, the trail turns into a sidewalk on a 2 to 5% incline for a few feet, then turns to pavement. It continues parallel along the road and the cliff with barriers on both sides on a steady 5 to 8% decline for 0.2 mile with areas of 5 to 8% cross-slope, sloping towards the road. There are interpretive signs and views from the cliff along the way. Take a 5% decline for the last few hundred feet as you approach the upper parking area.

You can also park in the upper lot for a scenic view. From the parking lot, there is a ramp down to a wooden overlook of the cliffs, beach, and lighthouse. Only the first level is wheelchair accessible, with two benches, then a few stairs down to the next level. There are over 160 stairs to access the beach.

The interpretive center is ADA accessible, and wheelchairs are available for rent. Exhibits include a captioned video and tactile elements. Access to Quarry Cove is available by vehicle—request a gate opener at the entrance station or interpretive center.

YAQUINA HEAD OUTSTANDING NATURAL AREA

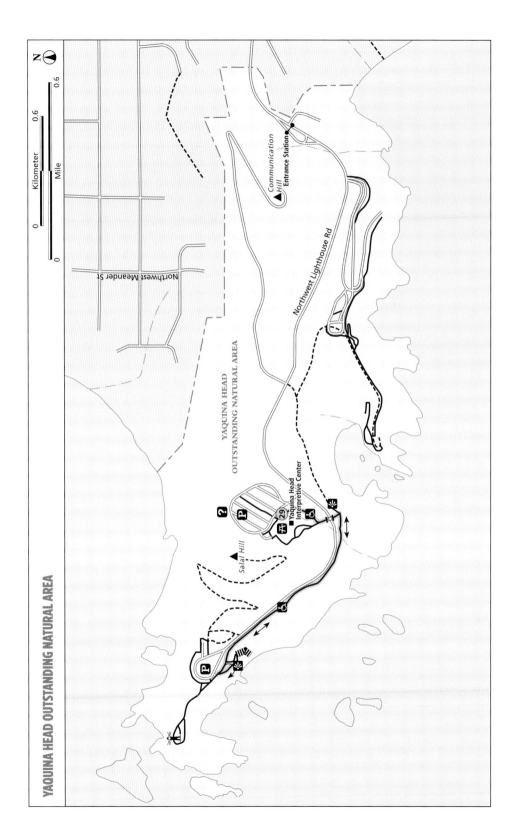

Northwest Meander St

YAQUINA HEAD
OUTSTANDING NATURAL AREA

Salal Hill

Yaquina Head
Interpretive Center

29

Northwest Lighthouse Rd

Communication
Hill

Entrance Station

Kilometer

Mile

N

Lighthouse Trail along the road

MILES AND DIRECTIONS

0.0 Start at the trailhead at the interpretive center.

0.05 Pass through a tunnel, then arrive at an ocean overlook. Go right to continue on the trail.

0.3 Reach the upper parking area and lighthouse.

0.6 Arrive back at the interpretive center.

30 THOR'S WELL AND SPOUTING HORN

WHY GO?

Cape Perpetua Scenic Area on the central Oregon Coast is a wonder of coastal experiences, including one of the largest spruce trees in Oregon, historic rock shelters, and ocean geysers. It is developed for tourism and can be very busy, but there are still areas of quiet nature to be found. This loop takes you through coastal rain forest and grassy headlands, with several ocean viewpoints along the way, before reaching a magnificent display of the ocean's power.

THE RUNDOWN

Spoon rating: 1 spoon. Paved trail, partially wheelchair hikeable with caution on prolonged grades of 5 to 10%.
Type: Lollipop loop
Distance: 1 mile
Elevation: 156 feet
Elevation gain: 135 feet
Max grade: 15%
Max cross-slope: 5%
Typical width: 4 feet
Typical surface: Paved
Trail users: Hikers, wildlife-watchers
Season/schedule: Year-round
Water availability: Fountains at visitor center

Amenities: Flush toilets, water, benches, picnic tables, public Wi-Fi
Dog-friendly: Yes, on leash
Cell phone reception: Yes
Nearest town: Yachats
Land manager: Siuslaw National Forest, (541) 547-3289
Pass/entry fee: Federal recreation pass
Land acknowledgment: The cape was known as Halaqaik to the Alsea, for the vast coastal prairies that were maintained by the people. A village occupied the base of the cape, and the area remains crucial to Indigenous lifeways.

FINDING THE TRAILHEAD

Getting there: From Yachats, head south on US 101 for approximately 3 miles. Turn left into the Cape Perpetua Visitor Center. There are two accessible parking spots at the lower parking area, with a long level path to the center across the main driveway. GPS: 44.28091, -124.10843
Start: At the trailhead in front of the visitor center

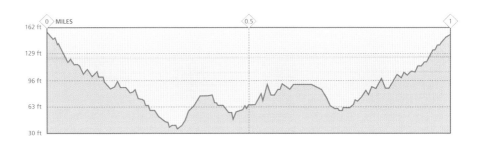

Spouting Horn on the left and Thor's Well to the right

THE HIKE

The Captain Cook Trail begins in front of the visitor center, at a basic map that lists the trails in the area. Take the paved path to the right of the sign, continuing on a 10% decline for 0.1 mile with a level pullout every 250 feet and one sharp curve at a 5% cross-slope. Reach a bench at 0.1 mile. The trail continues on a 5 to 8% decline for another 500 feet, with two more level pullouts, passing a sign at the remains of a Civilian Conservation Corps building and then crossing a creek. Pass the Oregon Coast Trail on the left and continue on the paved Captain Cook Trail. It continues generally level with a couple of roots raising the surface about 6 inches, and up to a 5% cross-slope as you approach US 101.

At 0.2 mile pass through a tunnel under the highway—it is about 50 feet long with a slight decline and moderately low light; be careful of the dip and grate directly in front of the tunnel exit. Straight ahead is an overlook of Good Fortune Cove; it has a fence and the view is blocked at sitting height by shrubs. At low tide you can see tide pools and at high tide the water rushes into the narrow cove, pounding dramatically at the hillside. Go left to continue to Spouting Horn. The trail continues generally level along the coastal headland.

In less than 0.1 mile reach a signed fork at the beginning of the loop. Continue straight towards the tide pools. The trail is paved on a 2 to 5% decline. Curve right, approaching views of the coastline, and take a 12% decline for approximately 75 feet. Just before a footbridge over a creek, there is a short, steep, and uneven path that leads down to the rocky coastline and tide pools. Shell mounds, known as middens, in this area date back thousands of years. Though considered to be refuse piles, they hold cultural significance for the Alsea and Yachats people.

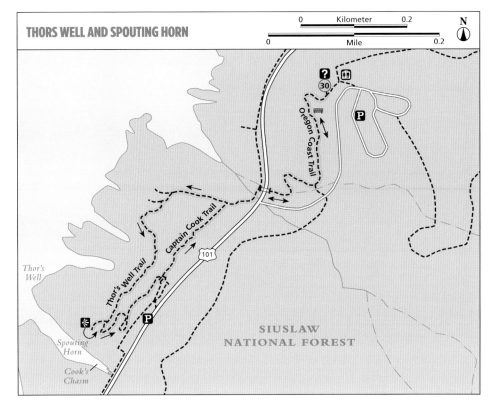

Continue across the footbridge, then take a 10% incline for 20 feet, level out, and curve left on a 10% incline as you follow the edge of the cliff with a fence on the right. This is a great place to stop and watch for whales, birds, and other wildlife, but the trail is under 4 feet wide, so it can be difficult to pass people. The trail then inclines more steeply at 15% for a couple hundred feet, curves right, and levels out. It then declines at 12% for 30 feet, then generally levels out and approaches the overlook of Spouting Horn and Thor's Well.

Reach the overlook at 0.5 mile. A path down to the right has a bench overlooking the coast. A steep set of eight stairs leads to another bench and overlooks Cook's Chasm. A very steep set of stairs leads down to the tide pools at low tide. The trail continues on a slight incline to another overlook above Cook's Chasm—this is the best view of Spouting Horn and Thor's Well. These geologic features are most active at high tide. Thor's Well is directly in front of you—look for a large well-like hole in the rock, where water rises from underneath. Spouting Horn is on the left, in the deep narrow cove called Cook's Chasm. Water spurts out of a narrow hole in the rock—you may notice a sound similar to a whale expelling water through its blowhole. The well, horn, and chasm combine to create an incredibly dramatic experience.

To finish the loop, continue on the paved trail as it curves sharply left up a slight grade then switchbacks right and left continuing on generally 5% grades for approximately 300 feet. Enter an area of Sitka spruce as you approach the highway, then come to a fork. The right fork leads to the day-use parking area and an accessible overlook of the chasm, horn, and well. This is a great place to stop on the highway, but it can be very busy. The trail from the parking area is wheelchair accessible though steep on 5% grades to the overlook.

The footbridge and view overlooking the tide pools

Take the fork to the left to continue back on the loop. It continues on a 10% decline for approximately 100 feet before leveling out and then taking a 5% incline to reconnect with the Captain Cook Trail. Continue right to return to the visitor center.

For some additional options in the area, you may want to check out the Whispering Spruce Trail (1 spoon), which travels on a well-maintained surface with maximum 10% grades through a Sitka spruce forest high up on the headland to a historic rock shelter along the cliff. It has astounding views all along the coastline. The Giant Spruce Trail (2 spoons) is a little rougher, traveling along a hillside and a creek with short 20% grades to one of the largest spruce trees in Oregon.

MILES AND DIRECTIONS

0.0   Start at the trailhead in front of the visitor center.

0.2   Pass through a tunnel under the highway. Go left at the overlook.

0.28 Reach the beginning of the loop. Continue straight.

0.3   A short footpath on the right, just past a footbridge, leads to the tide pools.

0.5   Reach an overlook of Cook's Chasm, Thor's Well, and Spouting Horn.

0.6   Continue on the switchback uphill. At the fork, go left.

0.8   Reach the end of the loop. Go right to return to the visitor center.

1.0   Arrive back at the visitor center.

31 **SUTTON CREEK LOOP**

WHY GO?

This narrow trail follows winding Sutton Creek through old forested dunes. The thick understory and contorted trees make it feel like a forest out of a fairy tale. The first half of the loop offers views of the sand dunes and ocean, and the second half moves deeper into a mature coastal forest of spruce and pine. Spur trails provide access to the dunes.

THE RUNDOWN

Spoon rating: 2 spoons. Generally level and firm surface with a few short grades and roots. Benches along the way.
Type: Loop
Distance: 1.5 miles
Elevation: 25 feet
Elevation gain: 65 feet
Max grade: 15%
Max cross-slope: 5%
Typical width: 3 feet
Typical surface: Natural
Trail users: Hikers
Season/schedule: Year-round
Water availability: None
Special notes: Beach access closed March 15 to September 15 for snowy plover nesting season

Amenities: Flush toilets, picnic tables, benches
Dog-friendly: Yes, on leash
Cell phone reception: Spotty
Nearest town: Florence
Land manager: Siuslaw National Forest, (541) 563-8400
Pass/entry fee: Federal recreation pass
Land acknowledgment: Siuslaw people lived around the estuaries of the Siuslaw river, and regularly traveled inland as far as the Willamette Valley.

FINDING THE TRAILHEAD

Getting there: From Florence, head north on US 101 for 4.5 miles. Turn left onto Vist Road and continue until the end. There is a large paved parking lot with no designated accessible spots. GPS 44.06817, -124.12296
Start: At the restrooms by the parking area

THE HIKE

Start by taking a short detour to the Holman Vista point, to the left of the trail sign by the restrooms. This wheelchair-accessible path starts paved and then leads to a boardwalk overlooking the creek and sand dunes, with views out to Sea Lion Point and the coastline.

The Sutton Creek Loop begins to the right of the trail sign. The paved path immediately comes to a fork. The left trail is an optional side trip—it leads 0.1 mile through tall salal to a sandy beach along the creek. There is a bench on the left. It is a nice place to hang out on the sand, with a gorgeous view of the creek and the dunes.

Go right at the fork to begin the Sutton Creek Loop Trail. The trail enters an old forested dune and starts on a 1½-foot-wide dirt surface with some rocks. Take a 10% incline for about 50 feet, then level out with views of the dunes to the left. You may hear or see

Sutton Creek, the sand dunes, and coastline

bald eagles, which nest in the tall trees. Curve right on a 5% decline, passing underneath Sitka spruce, then roll up and down a slight hill. The trail then levels out before taking a short 10% incline around a tree, then another short 10% incline. It continues to roll slightly on 5% grades. The ocean waves roar in the distance, and birdsong fills the forest. Come to a dense grove of trees, and the trail inclines at 10% for about 30 feet.

At 0.2 mile you reach a bench with a view through the forest of the dunes and the creek. Continue through a dense forest of spruce and pine, with berries, salal, and coast silk tassel. The trail continues generally level, with a few gentle rolling grades. You are moving gradually farther inland, following the curve of the creek, and the trees get taller and larger. Come to a 5% incline for about 70 feet, then step around a large root rising about 10 inches above the surface. You then come to a large spruce tree with a branch that has grown to curve over the trail and then into the ground. It is a very cool spot that gives even more enchanted hobbit forest vibes. The trail then curves right and left a few times on 10% inclines, with several roots crossing the trail.

At 0.4 mile a very short footpath on the left leads to a bench overlooking Sutton Creek. The trail then curves right and starts heading generally south, following the bend in the creek. Continue on a narrow, natural surface with a few small roots in the trail. Take a slight decline then a 15% incline for 15 feet. Step over several large roots. You're now further into the forest and away from the coastline, so the trees are much taller. Pass between two large Sitka spruces. On the left is another viewpoint of the creek, with a large spruce and maple arching over the water. Continue straight ahead on a slight incline

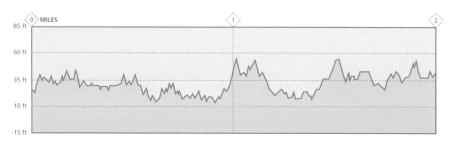

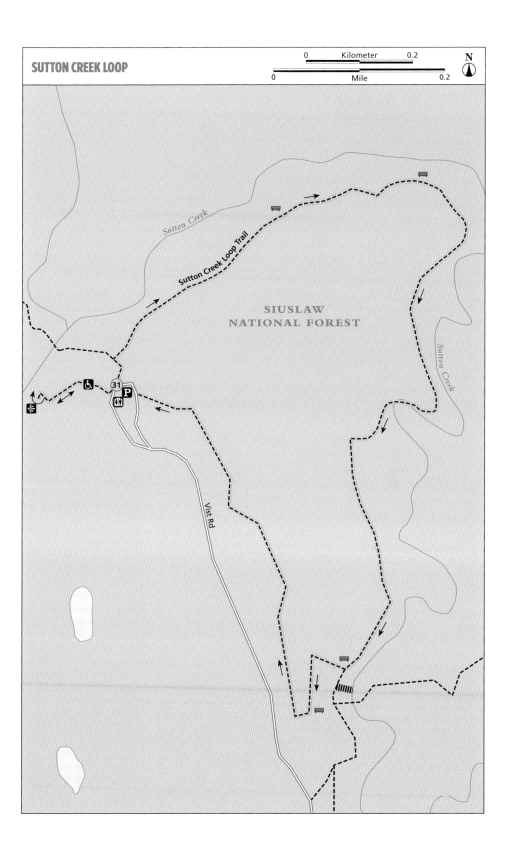

SIUSLAW
NATIONAL FOREST

Sutton Creek

Sutton Creek Loop Trail

Sutton Creek

Vist Rd

31

P

as you approach two more large spruces and a section of roots rising 6 to 12 inches above the surface. They are generally easy to walk around, but you do have to step down about 10 inches from the last one. Take another 10% incline for 100 feet, then be attentive for a few more roots in the trail as you pass under vine maples and huckleberries. The trail then levels and widens out to 4 feet, with many places to step off the trail if you need to. The forest cover opens up slightly, with views of the creek on the left. The trail continues generally level, with occasional roots rising up to 6 inches.

At 0.7 mile come to a sharp bend in the creek, traveling narrowly along its bank with a few eroded sections. It is a beautiful view of the creek-side habitat. Continue on the level trail as it curves right and left and starts to move away from the creek, traveling underneath large spruce and fir trees. Come to a very large spruce, stepping 6 to 8 inches down on three roots. Take a 10% incline for 40 feet then level out. You're now traveling through a thick rhododendron forest, which blooms in late spring. Switchback left on a 15% incline, then continue on a slight incline for a couple hundred feet, stepping over several roots in the trail.

At 0.8 mile you reach one of the highest points on the trail, with a view across the creek to the forest on the opposite hill. Continue generally level, traveling through spruce, rhododendron, and berries. Take a short 5% incline as the trail curves left and right and then starts declining at 10%, passing very narrowly between three trees. It then levels out as you approach a boardwalk at 0.9 mile. The boardwalk is about 8 feet long with 4-inch steps on either side. The trail levels out on the other side of the boardwalk and continues through a forest of salal and spruce.

At 1.0 mile come to an intersection with a bench. The trail to the left crosses a board-walk and connects with another loop that leads over the dunes to the campground. Go right to continue on this loop. The trail reenters a dense forest with lots of mossy trees and tall Sitka spruces. Pass next to a large spruce, stepping easily over some of its roots. The trail curves right on a 10% incline for 100 feet, then curves left at the top of the hill and levels out. Continue through a thick rhododendron forest.

At 1.1 miles come to another bench on the left. Take a 10% decline for approximately 50 feet. The trail narrows to 2 feet as it curves along the hillside through lots of berries and rhododendron. Pass a large Sitka spruce on the left and take two short declines. You then pass a few madrones. The trail then rolls and curves a few times and a few roots cross the trail up to 4 inches tall. Take a 10% incline as the trail curves right and left for 100 feet. Continue to roll slightly as you pass through a thick forest of tall rhododendrons.

At 1.4 miles come to a 20% decline, stepping down over some roots for about 50 feet. The surface gets a little muddier. Continue to two 10% inclines for approximately 50 feet each. Begin a gradual decline with a few rolling inclines up to 10%, stepping over and around occasional roots. At 1.5 miles you approach the parking area. Take a 15% decline for 75 feet and then arrive back at the parking lot.

MILES AND DIRECTIONS

0.0 Start at the trailhead sign near the restrooms. Go left to Holman Vista, then return to the trailhead and turn left to continue on the loop trail. The trail immediately forks. Go right to continue on the loop trail.

0.4 A footpath on the left leads to a bench overlooking Sutton Creek.

1.0 Junction with the Sutton Dunes Trail. Go right.

1.5 Arrive at the opposite side of the parking area.

32 DARLINGTONIA STATE NATURAL SITE

WHY GO?

This short boardwalk leads over a fen filled with the carnivorous Darlingtonia californica plant. Also called the cobra lily, this plant is very rare and grows only in serpentine soil and bogs. The flowers bloom in spring, but the plant is striking all year, with yellow-green hoods and mottled purple-red leaves. A small picnic area surrounded by a forest of spruce, cedar, pine, and rhododendron provides a nice lunch spot.

THE RUNDOWN

Spoon rating: 1 spoon. Wheelchair-accessible boardwalk.
Type: Lollipop loop
Distance: 0.14 mile
Elevation: 60 feet
Elevation gain: None
Max grade: 3%
Max cross-slope: 0%
Typical width: 4 feet
Typical surface: Paved, boardwalk
Trail users: Hikers, nature viewers

Season/schedule: Year-round
Water availability: None
Amenities: Toilet, picnic tables
Dog-friendly: Yes, on leash
Cell phone reception: Yes
Nearest town: Florence
Land manager: Oregon State Parks, (541) 997-3851
Pass/entry fee: None
Land acknowledgment: Siuslaw

FINDING THE TRAILHEAD

Getting there: From Florence, head north on US 101 for 4.5 miles and turn right onto Mercer Lake Road. The parking area is immediately on the right. It is a large paved parking area with no designated accessible spots. A curb cut leads to the trail. Several picnic tables are accessible from the parking area. GPS: 44.04744, -124.09745
Start: Trail next to picnic area

THE HIKE

The trail starts roughly paved. There is a level transfer onto a short bridge, and then the trail becomes compact gravel. Another picnic table sits under large cedars and firs on the left. The trail then becomes roughly paved again, traveling through a lush forest with large skunk cabbage and salal.

After about 100 feet the trail forks for the loop—continue to the right. There are a couple of gently raised sections but no cracks. The boardwalk has a 1-inch rise and then continues level and even. You are surrounded by Darlingtonia. Interpretive signs explain the ecology of the area and the uniqueness of this rare plant.

A large viewing area is halfway around the boardwalk, with a pullout at both the beginning and the end. The boardwalk curves left and then right. If you are using a wheelchair, I recommend turning around at the end of the boardwalk.

Start of the boardwalk

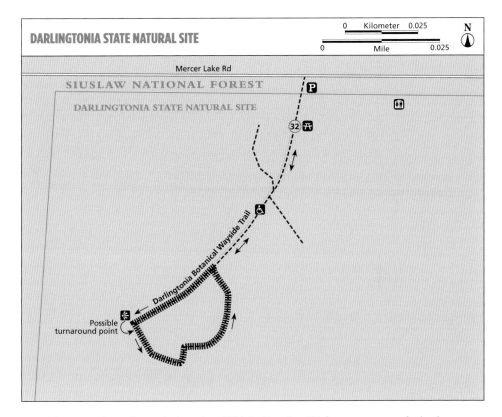

Mercer Lake Rd

SIUSLAW NATIONAL FOREST

DARLINGTONIA STATE NATURAL SITE

Darlingtonia Botanical Wayside Trail

Possible
turnaround point

If you continue forward, there is a 15% decline for 1½ feet as you transfer back onto the pavement. The trail then passes narrowly between trees and rolls a few times on 5% grades, and then the pavement gets very rough and uneven with some cracking. One set of cracks has a 1½-foot-wide gap and a 2-inch rise. It then reconnects with the trail—go right to return to the parking area.

MILES AND DIRECTIONS

0.0   Start at the trailhead at the parking area. Go right to the boardwalk.

0.05 Reach the boardwalk and viewing area. Wheelchair users may want to turn around here.

0.1   Arrive at the end of the loop. Go right to the parking area.

0.14 Arrive back at the parking area.

33 COQUILLE RIVER SCENIC DRIVE

WHY GO?

The drive along OR 42, also known as the Coos Bay–Roseburg Highway, is often overlooked as a scenic drive. It is not as striking as the scenic byways, but it is an easy drive through pastoral farmland and mountains with some unique stops along the way. You'll follow the Middle Fork of the Coquille River, which serves as the dividing line between the Coast Range and the Klamath Mountains, making it a unique area. The highway provides easy access to Bandon and all of its wonderful beaches and marshes.

THE RUNDOWN

Type: Scenic drive
Distance: 180 miles round-trip
Typical width and surface: Two-lane paved highway and county roads
Season/schedule: Road and all sites open year-round
Dog-friendly: Yes, on leash
Cell phone reception: Yes
Nearest town: Services available in Winston, Camas Valley, Myrtle Point, Coquille, and Bandon

Pass/entry fee: No passes required at viewpoints
Land acknowledgment: Nah-so-mah (Coquille) people lived in the Coquille River watershed, stewarding over one million acres of forests, meadow, prairie, and beaches. The Coquille Indian Tribe has regained 10,000 acres of their ancestral lands.

FINDING THE TRAILHEAD

Getting there: From Roseburg, head south on OR 99 for 5 miles to the town of Winston, famous for the Wildlife Safari. Turn right onto OR 42 west, and begin the 72-mile trip to the coast.
Start: OR-99 in Roseburg

THE HIKE

After the city of Winston, you'll pass through several small towns before meeting up with the Middle Fork of the Coquille River just past Camas Valley. At mile 36, stop at the Sandy Creek Covered Bridge Wayside on the right, just past the exit for the town of Remote. The bridge was constructed in 1921 and functioned until 1949. It is now the site of a small park along the Middle Fork. There are picnic tables and accessible restrooms, a footbridge, and an information booth.

Continue on OR 42, leaving the open farmland and entering the Coast Range. I highly recommend taking a short detour onto OR 542/Powers Road at mile 50. Drive 10 winding miles through some beautiful rural countryside to the Coquille Myrtle Grove State Natural Site. This small picnic area is tucked into an old myrtlewood grove, one of very few left in the state. The trees are massive and stately, and if you've never smelled fresh myrtle leaves, you are in for a treat. The picnic area is not ADA accessible, but there

Viewpoint at Face Rock

are tables close to the gravel parking lot. You can also enjoy the trees from your car. A short but steep and deeply rutted gravel boat ramp leads down to a sandy beach along the Coquille River. It's a perfect spot to enjoy the sun or sit in the shade along the cool water.

Alternatively, you can stop at the Hoffman Memorial State Wayside, just past the exit for Powers Road. However, it is a left turn across the busy highway heading west, and the parking area is a gravel pullout along the road. The path down into the myrtlewood grove is at a 20% grade and very uneven. You can also hear highway noise the entire time. But it doesn't require a detour, and the trees are just as wonderful.

Continue another 12 miles on OR 42 to the city of Coquille. You can turn left onto OR 42S/Coquille-Bandon Highway to go directly to the city of Bandon, traveling through the pretty Coquille River valley, but I recommend continuing on OR 42 for 5 miles and turning left onto North Bank Lane at the Coquille Valley Wildlife Area. There is a parking area here to observe possible wildlife. Continue 2.5 miles on this paved two-lane road to East Beaver Hill Road. Turn right and continue for 2 miles, curving gently through coastal foothills, to US 101. Turn left onto the Oregon Coast Highway/US 101.

Your next stop is Bullards Beach State Park. The park is located at the mouth of the Coquille River. The marshes offer excellent wildlife viewing, and Bullards Beach is a long stretch of sandy coastline. Continue 6.5 miles on US 101 and turn right on Bullards Beach Road. Continue past the campground, and the parking area for Bullards Beach is straight ahead. However, the easiest access is from the Coquille Lighthouse—continue until the road ends and park in the paved lot. Take the paved path for less than 100 feet to the historic lighthouse, which no longer guides mariners but still has a solar-powered light, then continue past the jetty to one of the level, sandy access points to the beach.

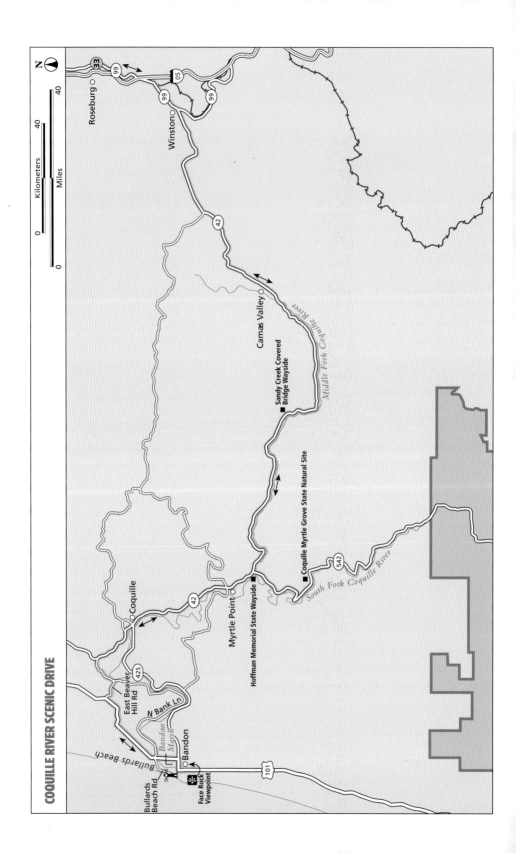

COQUILLE RIVER SCENIC DRIVE

Coquille Lighthouse

Next I recommend a stop at an accessible site at Bandon Marsh. Continue south on US 101 from Bullards Beach Road, and turn west onto Riverside Drive just north of Bandon. A small paved parking lot with accessible parking leads directly to an accessible overlook of the marsh.

Your final stop is Face Rock Scenic Viewpoint. Continue on US 101 through Bandon. Turn right onto 11th Street SW, continue through a park on a roundabout, then turn left onto Beach Loop Road. Continue 0.6 mile to the viewpoint on the right. There is no accessible parking here, but there is a curb cut near the restrooms. The path around the viewpoint is only about 50 feet long and paved, but there is often a large section of sand at the far end, so you may need to go out and back on both sides. Face Rock has important cultural significance to the Nah-so-mah (Coquille) people, as the location of a legend about the daughter of Chief Siskiyou and the spirit of the ocean, Seatka. The legend is told on a sign overlooking the rock. There are views of the surrounding caves and sea stacks, which are incredibly striking. A set of stairs leads down to the beach.

WILLAMETTE VALLEY

The Willamette Valley surrounds the Willamette River, extending from Portland and the Columbia River in the north to Eugene in the south. It is bordered by the Coast Range to the west, the Cascade Range to the east, and the Calapooya Mountains to the south. I-5 runs the length of the valley, and the entire region is home to 70% of Oregon's population. Originally home to vast oak savannas and wetlands, the region is now renowned for its wine production.

The Willamette Valley is the traditional territory of the Kalapuya people, who lived in several related groups who spoke three dialects: Northern Kalapuyan, Central Kalapuyan, and Yoncalla. Each group occupied traditional areas along the Willamette, Umpqua, and McKenzie Rivers. Several treaty-making cycles were made with the people of the Willamette Valley. The last treaty was the Kalapuya Treaty in 1855, made with several remaining bands of the Kalapuya, Molalla, Clackamas, and other Tribes of the Willamette Valley. The Tribes ceded the entirety of the valley. They were promised reservations and other long-term support. However, the people were forcibly marched to the Grand Ronde Reservation. The federal government ceased recognition of the Grand Ronde Reservation in 1954. The Confederated Tribes of Grand Ronde fought for re-recognition based upon the Kalapuya Treaty, and regained it in 1983.

34 CALLOWAY CREEK LOOP

WHY GO?

The McDonald and Dunn Research Forests offers a network of over 26 miles of trails and 100 miles of forest roads. This loop travels through a variety of forest, from plantation to natural mixed forest, crosses a lovely creek, then ascends briefly to a lake for a perfect birding and picnicking spot.

THE RUNDOWN

Spoon rating: 3 spoons. Gentle grades except for a 10 to 20% incline for 0.2 mile and an 8 to 10% decline for 0.7 mile. Few obstacles. Two benches and a picnic table along the route.
Type: Loop
Distance: 2.6 miles
Elevation: 367 feet
Elevation gain: 279 feet
Max grade: 20%
Max cross-slope: 5%
Typical width: 3 feet
Typical surface: Dirt, compact gravel
Trail users: Hikers, seasonal bikers on Calloway Creek, bikers and horseback riders on Road 500
Season/schedule: Year-round, 5 a.m. to 9 p.m.
Water availability: None
Special notes: Trail use not allowed when there is significant standing water or mud

Amenities: Restrooms typically available at the arboretum
Dog-friendly: Yes, on leash or under voice or other command
Cell phone reception: Spotty
Nearest town: Corvallis
Land manager: Oregon State University, College of Forestry, (541) 737-2004
Pass/entry fee: None
Land acknowledgment: Corvallis sits in the traditional homelands of the Mary's River or Ampinefu Band of Kalapuya. Kalapuyans consisted of more than a dozen groups with an estimated population of 15,000 people. Their descendants are now part of the Confederated Tribes of Grand Ronde and Confederated Tribes of the Siletz Indians.

FINDING THE TRAILHEAD

Getting there: From Corvallis, head north on OR 99W past Lewisburg. In approximately 6 miles, just past milepost 78, turn left onto NW Arboretum Road. Turn left into Peavy Arboretum. Stay to the left, following signs for parking. Go past the business office and park in a large gravel lot. GPS: 44.65684, -123.2323
Start: Next to trail sign at end of gravel lot

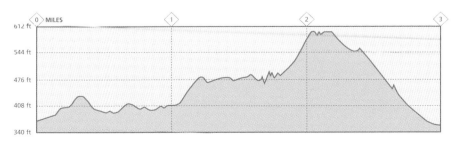

Pretty Calloway Creek

THE HIKE

Begin your hike on the Intensive Management Trail at the northern end of the parking lot, next to an information sign about the forest. The trail begins on a natural surface and compact gravel bordered by low rocks on a 2 to 5% incline as it curves left, passing under Douglas fir and madrone. The trail curves right and comes to a sign about the Intensive Management Trail and forest practices developed by the OSU Forest Managers. Cross a muddy area as the trail comes to an 8 to 10% incline for about 75 feet. You're traveling through plantation forests with houses beyond the tree line on the right, surrounded by Douglas fir, ivy, blackberries, and some ferns and holly. Take a 10% incline for 100 feet.

At 0.3 mile the trail widens to 4 feet and descends at 10 to 15% on a rocky surface for a couple hundred feet as you enter a more mature forest with yew and Douglas fir. Take a sharp right at an arrow, then level out on compact gravel. The trail then starts to rise on a 5% incline, passing through a Douglas fir plantation. At 0.5 mile you come to a T-intersection with a carved wood map. Go right to the Calloway Creek Trail. The trail continues through mossy forest on a gradual 5 to 8% incline—houses are visible on the right.

At 0.6 mile come to a fork—go right on the Calloway Creek Trail. The trail continues as a wide dirt track and generally level. It curves left and right a couple of times on a compact gravel turnpike, takes a 10% incline for 50 feet, then continues on a turnpike. The trail takes some gentle rolling grades of 5 to 8%. The forest here feels more natural, with big Douglas firs and mossy maples.

At 0.8 mile cross a culverted creek. There is a 15-foot-long concrete path over the culvert that has collapsed, so there's an 8% grade going down and a 10% grade going up with a slight cross-slope. Take a 10% incline for about 10 feet on the other side, then the trail levels out again and returns to natural surface and compact gravel, continuing through a nice forest. Step over a 4-inch root in the trail then come to a 5 to 10% incline for a couple hundred feet. Cross over a small culverted stream, then curve left and continue on a 10 to 15% incline for approximately 200 feet.

At 1.0 mile the Calloway Creek Trail forks—go left to continue on the main loop (the right fork forms a connector loop that returns 0.1 mile up the trail). Continue on a 10% incline, with some sections reaching 15%, for another 250 feet. The trail finally levels out, with several rocks and roots rising up to 4 inches above the surface. At 1.1 miles come to a T-intersection—go left to continue the loop. Pass next to large Douglas firs on the right and bigleaf maples on the left. Several roots cross the combination gravel and natural surface trail. Descend slightly to a turnpike area over a stream, then pass a large, branching, old bigleaf maple on the right covered in moss and ferns. Cross another turnpike section over a small stream, stepping across a couple of roots and dips in the trail.

At 1.2 miles there is a bench in an oak grove—the giant tree is named the Honeybee Oak. The trail continues gently rolling on maximum 8% grades, with slightly muddy sections, through a lovely mixed forest of oak, fir, and maple. At 1.4 miles cross a sturdy, level footbridge over Calloway Creek. The creek ribbons through mossy forest, with a few short paths down to the water. The trail curves left on compact gravel and rocks with a slight drop-off on the left, then curves right on a 10% incline for 50 feet. Continue generally level underneath big Douglas firs.

At 1.5 miles you arrive at an intersection with the Cronemiller Lake Trail. This route leads to Cronemiller Lake, gaining 100 feet in 0.2 mile, then connects with a gravel logging road and descends 220 feet in 0.7 mile. It is worth the trip, but you can go left at the

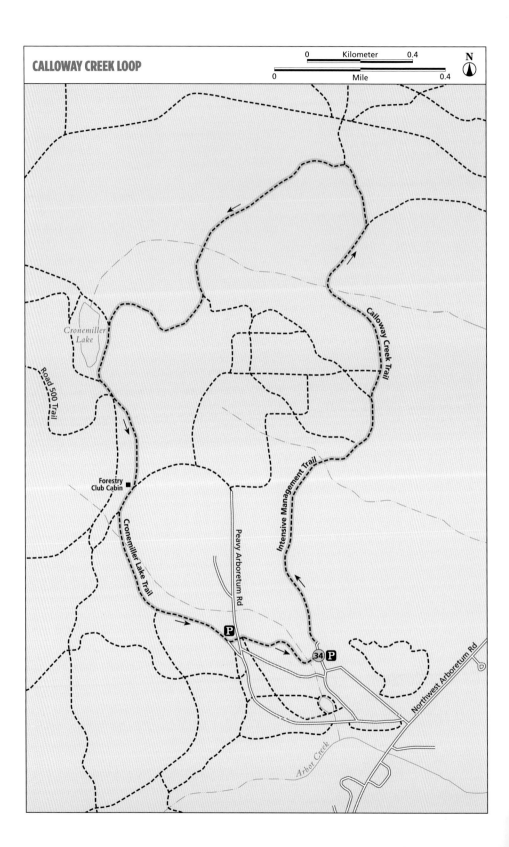

0   Kilometer   0.4

0   Mile   0.4

N

Cronemiller
Lake

Road 500 Trail

Calloway Creek Trail

Intensive Management Trail

Forestry
Club Cabin

Cronemiller Lake Trail

Peavy Arboretum Rd

34

Northwest Arboretum Rd

Arbor Creek

intersection instead and follow the Intensive Management Trail back to the beginning of the loop for a shorter and more level route. Continuing towards the right, the trail is compact gravel with some rocks and dirt. Come to a 10% incline for a couple hundred feet. The trail curves right, passing narrowly between two Douglas firs, and continues on a generally 10% incline. Switchback to the right and step over a few roots rising 6 inches. The trail continues on a generally 5 to 10% incline, with several low roots. A few fallen trees provide a place to sit, but there are no benches.

At approximately 1.6 miles the grade increases to 15% and passes between a blow-down. The incline increases to 15 to 20% for 100 feet, then continues at 10 to 15% as you curve narrowly between Douglas firs. Level out slightly, then come to a 20% incline for 50 feet, curving left and then continuing on a generally 10% incline as you approach the lake. At 1.7 miles you arrive at Cronemiller Lake and a picnic area. Continue towards the left, following the shore of the lake. There are filtered views across the valley. Several signed trails branch off at the end of the lake—continue to the left and take Road 500 back to the arboretum. The wide gravel road continues on a 5% decline then comes to a fork with a sign for Road 520 on the left—continue straight on Road 500.

At 2.1 miles you pass the Forestry Club Cabin on the right and a large set of wheels used for logging with an interpretive sign. Continue on a generally 8% decline, continuing straight on the gravel road past several other trails. It is a nice walk beneath large bigleaf maples and Douglas firs with the sound of flowing water in the distance. At 2.3 miles pass an intersection with Road 510 going off to the right—continue straight on Road 500. Pass around an orange gate and go through a parking area with a portable toilet (this parking lot is the most direct access to the lake—there is an information sign and picnic table here). Continue straight through a small redwood grove, following the Firefighter Memorial Trail as it crosses a creek and goes past a memorial shelter. You then arrive back at the gravel parking area.

MILES AND DIRECTIONS

0.0 Start at the trailhead at the northern end of the parking area.

0.5 Reach a T-intersection. Go right to the Calloway Creek Trail.

0.6 Reach a trail junction. Go right on the Calloway Creek Trail.

1.0 The trail forks. Go left to continue on the main loop.

1.1 Reach a T-intersection. Go left on the Calloway Creek Trail.

1.5 Reach the intersection with the Cronemiller Lake Trail. Go right.

1.7 Arrive at Cronemiller Lake. Follow the shore of the lake to the left, then continue on the wide gravel road.

2.1 Pass the Forestry Club Cabin.

2.3 Continue straight on Road 500.

2.4 Pass the parking area and cross the road. Continue straight through the small redwood grove on the Firefighter Memorial Trail.

2.6 Arrive back at the parking area.

35 JACKSON-FRAZIER WETLAND

WHY GO?

Tucked back on the edge of a suburban Corvallis neighborhood, you might be tempted to skip this 4-acre park. But it is worth the trip. A wheelchair-accessible boardwalk takes you on an intimate journey through a thriving wetland with complex biodiversity, amidst a much larger conserved area. Plant and bird lists are available, and interpretive signs are scattered throughout.

THE RUNDOWN

Spoon rating: 1 spoon. Wheelchair-accessible boardwalk. Manual wheelchair users may have difficulty with the vertical boards, and there are a couple of damaged areas with a steep cross-slope.
Type: Lollipop loop
Distance: 0.9 mile
Elevation: 220 feet
Elevation gain: None
Max grade: 5%
Max cross-slope: 8%
Typical width: 3 feet
Typical surface: Boardwalk
Trail users: Hikers, birders

Season/schedule: Year-round
Water availability: None
Special notes: Boards run lengthwise and are slightly rough and uneven; small wheels may stick in the grooves.
Amenities: Benches
Dog-friendly: Yes, on leash
Cell phone reception: Yes
Nearest town: Corvallis
Land manager: Benton County Parks, (541) 766-6521
Pass/entry fee: None
Land acknowledgment: Mary's River or Ampinefu Band of Kalapuya

FINDING THE TRAILHEAD

Getting there: From Corvallis, head north on OR 99W/Pacific Highway W. In approximately 3 miles, turn right onto NE Conifer Boulevard. Turn left onto NE Lancaster Street in 0.5 mile and continue until the end. There are two signed accessible parallel parking spots along the sidewalk near a curb cut, four pull-in non-accessible spots, and plenty of street parking. Address: 3600 NE Lancaster St., Corvallis. GPS: 44.60409, -123.23993
Start: End of a suburban cul-de-sac

THE HIKE

The trail begins at the end of a cul-de-sac. Follow the sidewalk along the wooden fence; there's a slight break between one of the sections, with a sloped 2-inch rise that is passable with most wheelchairs. There is a 2% cross-slope as the trail curves right, then a 5% incline for about 10 feet as you approach a short boardwalk. There is a 1-inch rise on either side of the boardwalk, which transfers back to a sidewalk. Continue towards the left and you'll arrive at the trail information board and a map. The sign gives a little history of the area and a description of the environment.

The boardwalk continues behind the sign. A reflector turns blue if there has been frost or freezing to warn of slippery conditions, so take note if you're there in the winter.

Typical boardwalk

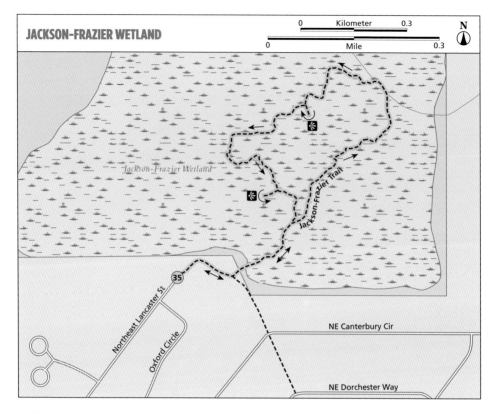

There is a 1-inch rise onto the boardwalk, with a little bit of grass growing between the sidewalk and boardwalk. The boardwalk is only 4 feet wide, but there are several pullouts and overlooks along the way with beautiful views of the surrounding hills.

At 0.2 mile the boardwalk forks for the loop. Go right on a 2 to 4% incline. At 0.3 mile there are two sections of boardwalk that are slightly collapsed with an 8% cross-slope, but there are guards along the outer edge. At 0.4 mile cross Frazier Creek and come to another bench. There may be standing water on the boardwalk. At 0.5 mile a boardwalk on the left leads out into the wetland for another viewpoint.

At 0.6 mile come to two overlooks with benches overlooking the wetland. There are a few holes in between the boards, so watch your wheels. There is another section ahead where the boardwalk has collapsed slightly on the left side, with an 8% cross-slope. You then come immediately to another viewpoint at a deck with trees covered in moss; this is a really cool forested spot. Continue a few more feet to close the loop and go right to return to your car.

MILES AND DIRECTIONS

0.0 Start at the trailhead at the end of the cul-de-sac.

0.2 Reach the start of the loop. Go right.

0.5 A viewing platform leads out to the wetland on the left.

0.6 End the loop. Go right to return to the trailhead.

0.9 Arrive back at the trailhead.

36 **MARY'S PEAK**

WHY GO?

Mary's Peak is the highest point of Oregon's Coast Range. At 4,097 feet elevation, there are incredible views of the Pacific Ocean and the Cascades. The meadows burst into color in the spring and summer, and a rare noble fir forest thrives on the mountain. You can enjoy this unique area from a picnic area at the parking lot, or take a steep hike to the top of the peak.

THE RUNDOWN

Spoon rating: 4 spoons for the hike to the peak. Over 500-foot elevation gain in 0.7 mile, exposed trail with no water or benches. Trail is loose gravel or narrow, uneven footpath.
Type: Scenic viewpoint, lollipop loop
Distance: 1.5 miles
Elevation: 3,760 feet
Elevation gain: 537 feet
Max grade: 20%
Max cross-slope: 10%
Typical width: 4 feet
Typical surface: Dirt, gravel
Trail users: Hikers
Season/schedule: Spring through fall
Water availability: None
Special notes: Exposed trail, no water

Amenities: Accessible vault toilet and picnic tables
Dog-friendly: Yes, on leash
Cell phone reception: None
Nearest town: Philomath
Land manager: Siuslaw National Forest, Central Coast Ranger District, (541) 563-8400
Pass/entry fee: Federal recreation pass or day-use fee
Land acknowledgment: Kalapuyans know the peak as *tcha Timanwi* meaning "place of spiritual power." It is a sacred place to Indigenous peoples, and features strongly in ancestral stories.

FINDING THE TRAILHEAD

Getting there: From Corvallis, head south on OR 99W/Pacific Highway W and take the exit for US 20W. In 6 miles, turn left onto OR 34W/Alsea Highway. Continue 9 miles and turn right onto Mary's Peak Road. Drive 9 miles to the peak. The way is all two-lane highway and paved forest road. GPS 44.5102, -123.55076
Start: At a large paved parking area

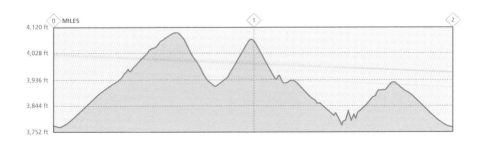

Overlooking the meadows on Mary's Peak

THE HIKE

This drive is really all about the destination; it's not particularly interesting until you reach Mary's Peak. From the turn onto Mary's Peak Road, continue on a paved two-lane, very curvy road with several pullouts. You'll travel through typical US Forest Service land, with patchwork forests in various stages of growth. Wildflowers line the road.

At 2.5 miles pull off at the Mary's Peak Road Layby on the left, with views across the Coast Range through the trees. The first glimpse of the peak is just past a clear-cut hill. At 3.6 miles there's a large parking area on the left for the East Ridge Trail. At 5.3 miles pass a sign with a forest road going off to the left—continue straight ahead to the view-point. The road is gated at approximately 6 miles; it is typically open year-round but may be closed for snow. Pass a small waterfall on the left at 6.7 miles. Another pullout at 8.3 miles offers a teaser of what's ahead, with incredible views across the Coast Range. Pass a nice campground at 8.7 miles, and then you reach the parking area at the peak.

It is a very large paved parking area with three van-accessible spots. Several picnic tables provide vantage points to take in the experience. You are surrounded by expansive meadows that give way to an old noble fir forest. You may notice many birds and other wildlife in the grass. The wind makes its own unique sounds as it travels through the peaks and valleys below you and up the mountain. On a clear day, the Pacific Ocean glistens in the west and Cascade peaks rise in the distance to the east.

Experienced wheelchair hikers with an all-terrain chair may be able to travel a short distance on the dirt and gravel road that leads to the top of the peak and travels through rolling meadows. The gravel is pretty loose, and the road eventually erodes into some large rocks.

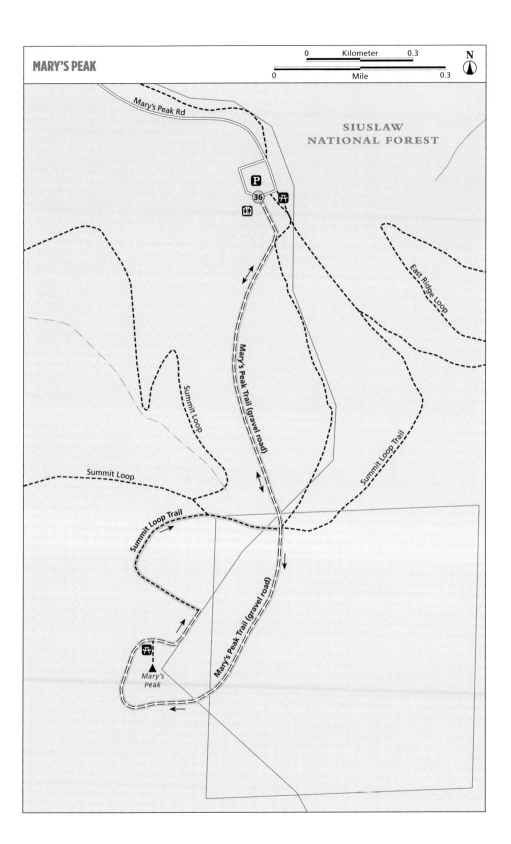

MARY'S PEAK

SIUSLAW
NATIONAL FOREST

Mary's Peak Rd

East Ridge Loop

Summit Loop

Summit Loop

Summit Loop Trail

Summit Loop Trail

Mary's Peak Trail (gravel road)

Mary's Peak Trail (gravel road)

Mary's
Peak

0   Kilometer   0.3

0   Mile   0.3

N

There are several trails in the area, but the most direct route to the peak is the gravel road. Pass the gate and begin on loose gravel at an 8% incline, then continue on a steady 10 to 12% incline. At 0.3 mile it levels out on a 5 to 8% grade with a couple of shady spots then comes to a fork—continue straight on the gravel road. Continue on a 10% incline, increasing to 15% for a hundred feet. The road gets rocky and eroded at 0.5 mile, with several ruts and rocks rising up to 6 inches. Continue on a steady 10% incline as the trail rounds the ridge and rises to the top of the peak.

You reach the summit at 0.7 mile. It may feel a bit anticlimactic at first—there is a large fenced mechanical station blocking part of the view and a single picnic table, and it feels a little boxed in. I recommend continuing downhill and into the meadow, where it feels much more natural and there are better views. Look for a footpath on the left with a sign numbered 1325 for the Summit Loop. Start traveling on a narrow, rocky footpath through the meadow; depending on the season, there may be lots of lupine, tiger lily, yarrow, and other wildflowers. Continue on an 8% decline, then come to an unsigned intersection. Go left, continuing through the meadow (the trail straight ahead is decommissioned and in bad shape).

This portion of the Summit Loop Trail continues through the meadow on a narrow, uneven footpath with 10 to 15% declines. It is pretty unstable footing with lots of holes, rolls, and uneven patches of grass. The trail has been widened in some spots due to overuse. If you take this route, please stay on the established path as much as possible to protect the meadow. In approximately 0.2 mile you enter a noble fir forest. Continue towards the right and reconnect with the gravel road in another 0.1 mile.

If you want to enjoy the meadows a bit more, you can cross the gravel road and continue for a short distance on the Summit Loop Trail along the eastern slopes of the mountain. This trail is also a narrow footpath through the meadow, but takes a more gentle 8% decline. It is a little more shaded, but you may need to turn around when you enter the tree line—massive blowdowns block the trail back to the parking area.

Whether you decide to continue through the meadows or not, make your way back to the gravel road to return to the parking area.

MILES AND DIRECTIONS

0.0   Start at the trailhead at the parking area.

0.4   Reach a trail intersection. Continue straight on the gravel road.

0.7   Arrive at the summit of Mary's Peak. To return through the meadow, take the footpath on the left with a sign numbered 1325.

1.0   Reach an intersection with the gravel road. Go left to return to the parking area. To continue a little further through the meadow, go straight then turn around when you enter the forest.

1.5   Arrive back at the trailhead.

37 ALTON BAKER PARK

WHY GO?

Alton Baker Park, sitting on the north bank of the Willamette River, is the largest developed park in Eugene at over 400 acres. There are a variety of things to enjoy here, including trails and river access, public art, native gardens, and the Kalapuya Talking Stones with words from the Kalapuyan language. The trail system offers options from short loops to over 5 miles of paved trails that connect with a larger urban system.

THE RUNDOWN

Spoon rating: 1 spoon. Wheelchair accessible, with some caution to Hays Tree Garden due to possible loose gravel and one large rut.

Type: Lollipop loop or out-and-back

Distance: 1-mile lollipop loop or up to 10 miles out and back

Elevation: 410 feet

Elevation gain: 30 feet

Max grade: 5%

Max cross-slope: 5%

Typical width: 6 feet

Typical surface: Paved

Trail users: Hikers at Hays Tree Garden, multiuse on North Bank Trail

Season/schedule: Year-round

Water availability: Water fountains

Amenities: Flush toilets, water fountains, picnic shelters, benches

Dog-friendly: Yes, on leash

Cell phone reception: Yes

Nearest town: Eugene

Land manager: City of Eugene Parks, (541) 682-4906

Pass/entry fee: None

Land acknowledgment: The area now known as Eugene and Springfield is the traditional lands of Kalapuya peoples, Cha Tumenma (Land of the Ancestors). Whilamut Natural Area, in the east part of the park, was renamed in 2002 to honor the Kalapuya who have been in relationship with that land for thousands of years.

FINDING THE TRAILHEAD

Getting there: From downtown Eugene, head north on Coburg Road for 0.5 mile. Take the exit for Martin Luther King Jr. Boulevard on the right, then make a right onto Club Road. Turn left into the park and park in the first lot on the right. It is a large paved lot with at least eight accessible parking spots. Address: 200 Day Island Rd., Eugene. GPS: 44.05629, -123.08107

For alternative access to Hays Tree Garden, continue straight on Martin Luther King Jr. Boulevard past Club Road. Turn right onto Leo Harris Parkway, then make an immediate right into the parking area. Cross the bridge over the canal and go left.

Start: Next to the restrooms at a large paved parking area

THE HIKE

Head towards the entrance to the parking lot and then cross the road (there are curb cuts on the sidewalk) and continue straight on a wide, level pea gravel path. Pass a duck pond on the left with many benches for watching the ducks, then a public art statue. The trail then splits and runs parallel to each other—both are compact pea gravel, but the section

Hays Tree Garden

closer to the river may have some muddy spots and curves on a steep cross-slope to reconnect with the main path, so you may want to continue on the path on the right.

At 0.2 mile there's another bench with views to the river. You then come to a fork at a big metal art installation—continue to the right. Continue on the dirt and pea gravel trail as it follows the Canoe Canal (a vendor rents kayaks here during the summer). There is a deep, rutted spot about 2 feet wide in the center of the trail as it curves right past the canoe launch—it is possible to bypass along the outer edge, but there may be clumps of grass and loose sand. The trail then curves right and returns to a paved path that loops through the tree garden. The 2-acre garden features trees from around the world and is particularly resplendent in spring and fall, when the blooms and foliage burst into color. It is a welcoming oasis in the city, and there are plenty of benches and tables to enjoy it.

Head back on the trail that you came in on. When you return to the duck pond at 0.9 mile, you can continue to the left or stay to the right and take the boardwalk to a little island. There are a couple of loose boards and gaps up to 1 inch wide. It transfers level onto a compact pea gravel path on an island with a little native garden in the center. Circle the island then take another short bridge and return to the gravel path—continue left around the pond to reconnect with the main trail. Cross the road again to return to the parking area.

To extend your hike, you can continue on the North Bank Trail. This paved path travels generally level along the north bank of the Willamette River, passing a scale model of the solar system and other art installations, picnic areas, river access, and more. It is a popular multiuse trail, so you'll have to share the 8-foot-wide path with runners, skaters, bikers, and strollers, but there are lots of benches and places to step off if you need to.

ALTON BAKER PARK

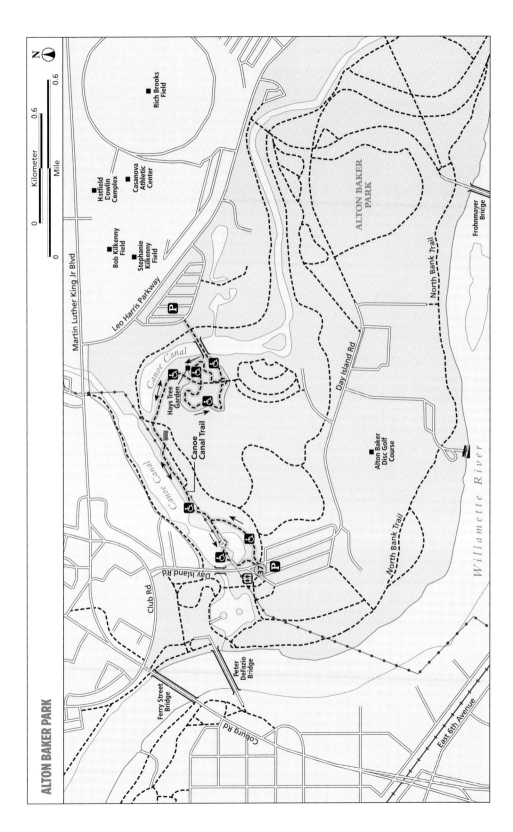

Duck Island

Follow the paved trail past the restrooms and Duck Island. The trail then forks left to travel through the picnic area—continue right, towards the river. You'll pass a 1:1 billion scale model of the solar system and a playground, then curve left and continue along the Willamette River. The North Bank Trail continues for up to 5 miles, and is generally level with maximum 8% grades. At approximately 1.0 mile you reach the Frohnmayer Bridge, formerly known as the Autzen Footbridge, over the Willamette. The trail continues for another 0.5 mile through the city park, then enters the Whilamut Natural Area. Several trails here can create a loop, but this is the only paved path, so you may want to return the way you came.

MILES AND DIRECTIONS

0.0   Start at the entrance to the parking lot. Cross the road and pass the duck pond.

0.3   Go right at the trail intersection.

0.4   Reach the Hays Tree Garden. Travel the loop and return the way you came. Or, take the paved trail along the river for up to 5 miles.

1.0   Arrive back at the parking area.

OREGON CENTRAL CASCADES

The western slopes of the Central Cascades are made up of a series of foothills generally defined by rivers. They include the Santiam Foothills along the North and South Santiam Rivers; the Willamette Foothills along the eastern portion of the McKenzie River and the Middle Fork Willamette River; and the McKenzie Foothills along the western portion of the McKenzie River. The foothills rise to the picturesque peaks of Mount Jefferson, Mount Washington, and the Three Sisters. This area has seen a large increase in recreation, and a Central Cascades Wilderness Permit system has been implemented by the US Forest Service. The hikes in this book are not currently impacted, but you should verify requirements if you plan to visit any of the wilderness areas.

Like other places in Oregon, the settlement of this area resulted in the forced removal of the Indigenous peoples. The hikes represented in this book are in the traditional territory of the Santiam Kalapuya, Santiam Molalla, and Calapooia Band of Kalapuya, who signed the 1855 Treaty with the Confederated Tribes of Willamette Valley. Many of their descendants are members of the Confederated Tribes of Grand Ronde, discussed in the previous section.

38 MCDOWELL CREEK FALLS

WHY GO?

McDowell Creek Falls County Park is home to three very impressive waterfalls—Royal Terrace drops 119 feet over two tiers, Majestic Falls cascades 39 feet down a basalt cliff, and Lower McDowell Falls cascades gently down the creek. Three miles of trails and four access points provide a variety of options.

THE RUNDOWN

Spoon rating: 5 spoons. Two long sets of steep stairs and one steep grade for over 0.2 mile. Few benches. Options for easier routes.
Type: Lollipop loop
Distance: 2 miles
Elevation: 817 feet
Elevation gain: 300 feet
Max grade: 25%
Max cross-slope: 10%
Typical width: 3 feet
Typical surface: Natural
Trail users: Hikers
Season/schedule: Year-round
Water availability: Creek
Special notes: Total of 250 stairs, including one series of 100 steps

Amenities: Vault toilets, picnic tables
Dog-friendly: Yes, on leash
Cell phone reception: Spotty
Nearest town: Lebanon
Land manager: Linn County Parks, (541) 967-3917
Pass/entry fee: None
Land acknowledgment: Santiam Kalapuya have lived in this area for thousands of years. The forks of the Santiam River, particularly where the North and South Santiam River converge, are important traditional lands that supported dozens of villages.

FINDING THE TRAILHEAD

Getting there: From I-5, take exit 228 for Lebanon/Corvallis towards OR 34. Turn east onto OR 34. Continue to the town of Lebanon, and turn right on US 20E. Continue approximately 9 miles, turn left onto Old Santiam Highway then immediately right on Fairview Road, then turn right on McDowell Creek Road. Continue 8 miles to McDowell Creek County Park. Address: 43170 McDowell Creek Dr., Lebanon. GPS: 44.4692, -122.68239

The lower parking lot is on the right just below the road. It is a large lot with one van-accessible parking spot and picnic tables right along the creek. The upper parking lot has spaces for ten cars plus parallel parking (no accessible spots) and picnic tables overlooking the creek.

Start: At the footbridge in the lower parking lot

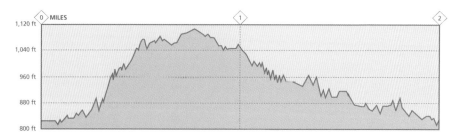

Stairs at Majestic Falls

THE HIKE

This route starts from the lower parking area and completes the entire loop through the park. You can do a series of shorter hikes to each of the falls if you prefer, or begin the loop from another parking area if the lower one is full. If you do this loop in reverse, the steep wooden stairs will be on the way up to Majestic Falls, the long incline will be a decline, then the stone stairs will be on the way down—it just depends on what is most comfortable for you. A basic map of the trail system and parking areas is available at the trailhead.

The trail begins at the edge of the parking lot across a bridge over McDowell Creek; there is a 2-inch rise onto the bridge, which curves on a slight grade over the creek. There is a view of the top of Lower McDowell Falls from the bridge. Continue on a generally level trail with a natural surface, following the creek for the first 0.2 mile. The trail then begins a gentle 5 to 8% incline, starting to rise up the side of the hill. Take a 50-foot-long uneven 10% decline over rocks and then incline for 50 feet with many rocks and roots in the trail. Pass next to a large Douglas fir on the right, then take a slight decline as the trail curves right. A footpath on the left leads to a small waterfall. Continue straight ahead, following the rushing creek down below, with glimpses of a waterfall up ahead. Take a 15 to 20% incline, stepping over rocks and roots for approximately 100 feet.

At 0.3 mile you approach a set of stairs leading to Majestic Falls straight ahead and a bridge on the left to Royal Terrace Falls. This is the shortest and easiest route to Royal Terrace Falls, but if you're doing the loop, I recommend saving it for the return—it's a nice reward at the end of your hike, and there is another view up ahead. Continuing to the stairs, the first step is eroded at the bottom, so it is 1½ feet tall. Take a hundred very steep, uneven stone stairs, some with an 8- to 12-inch rise. There are no handrails on this section. The trail levels out on natural surface briefly and then comes to another set of steep stairs, these with a handrail. The first step is also eroded with a 2-foot rise. Take another thirty-seven very steep stairs. The trail then levels out briefly and comes to an old stump in the middle of the trail; the trail is very eroded here and can be muddy. It is very narrow stepping around the stump on the outer edge with a steep drop-off, or you can step over it very carefully.

At 0.4 mile the trail descends on a short 20% grade then comes to a deck over Royal Terrace Falls. The trail continues with soft natural surface on a 5 to 10% incline then crosses Fall Creek on a footbridge with a 4-inch rise on either side. You then begin a long incline through the forest, on a generally rocky surface. Begin on a 15 to 20% incline for a couple hundred feet, with a few rough steps cut into the natural surface. The trail then levels out briefly and there is a fallen tree here that you can sit on if you need to. The trail continues on a 15 to 20% incline for a couple hundred feet, increasing to 20 to 25% as you follow the ridgeline. It narrows to 2 feet and continues muddy, with some views to the opposite ridgeline. Take a 15% muddy decline for 15 feet, very narrow and slick with a sharp drop-off on the left. The trail then levels out and curves right.

At 0.6 mile cross a short footbridge over a stream, then come to a fork in the trail. Go right to follow the loop. The trail inclines at 10% for about 100 feet as it approaches the road. Cross McDowell Creek Drive and continue through a small gravel parking area. The trail continues on compact gravel and is generally level with maximum 8% grades for the next quarter mile. Cross over a small culverted stream with a steep cross-slope.

At 0.8 mile there is a nice place to sit by two old bigleaf maples with exposed roots. You then descend on an 8 to 10% grade for about 20 feet before leveling out and passing through a boggy area with lots of skunk cabbage. Curve sharply left on a 10% incline, and then you may notice the main road on the left. Come to a 20% decline for 50 feet, with a few rough steps cut in, passing another small stream. Continue to follow the hillside with the main road to the left. The trail curves right, moves away from the main road, and starts to run parallel to the road for the upper parking lot.

At 1.0 mile you reach the upper parking lot. Take a 25% decline for 30 feet as you approach the road. Cross the road, then follow the compact gravel trail down to the right, taking a 20% decline for 10 feet. Come to two sets of six stone steps leading down, then a gradual set of stairs with thirteen uneven stone steps. You're now at McDowell Creek next to the rapids as water rushes towards Majestic Falls. Continue along the creek on a natural surface trail; you'll pass a section of chain-link fence that has partially fallen down and cross a wet and muddy area. Pass beneath some very large western redcedars and a Pacific yew, stepping over their roots. At 1.1 miles you reach the viewing deck for Majestic Falls. It is a large wooden deck with two benches overlooking the top of the falls. Beyond this point is a long series of steep stairs leading to a view at the bottom of the falls, so you may want to take some time here to rest.

Continue past the viewing deck. A short set of stairs leads up to the parking area on the left. To continue on the loop, go straight and immediately come to a long series of stairs. Take sixty steep, slippery wooden stairs to a platform directly in front of the falls (I do mean steep—I had to butt-scoot down them). Take another fifteen steps, cross a long footbridge over the creek, then take fifteen more steep steps, another footbridge, and then another fifteen steep steps. You're now traveling southwest on the opposite side of the creek.

The trail continues on a narrow, muddy natural surface with lots of rocks (some rising 4 to 6 inches). Cross over four exposed metal culverts, and take an 8% decline followed by an 8% incline. The trail curves along the hillside, following the creek down below. At 1.4 miles you can see a small waterfall down below with a barricade on the left and a very steep path down to the creek—this is Crystal Falls. The trail then switchbacks steeply down left and right, with another view of the falls at the lower switchback. Decline at 15% for 50 feet and cross another exposed culvert. Continue descending on generally 10% grades. The trail rolls a few times on loose gravel then levels out and crosses a culverted stream.

At 1.5 miles cross the road very carefully—there's a tall hill to the left and a hidden curve to the right, and people tend to drive too fast down. The trail returns to natural surface and declines at 8 to 10%. Step down over some roots, continuing on a 10% decline with the creek on the left. Rise and fall on 8% grades, then pass a large broken Douglas fir on the left. Reach a junction and continue towards the left, following the creek. Step over or around a 2-foot-tall log, then take two steps up and continue on an 8% incline. The trail rolls a couple of times and passes between a blowdown that's been cut out.

Continue to the left at the next junction, towards a footbridge. Step down on a 15% decline over roots and rocks, curve sharply left, and continue on a 15% decline as you approach the footbridge over McDowell Creek. The footbridge is sturdy but a little uneven. The trail then inclines at 5 to 10%, stepping up over roots, then curves left and arrives at Royal Terrace Falls. There's a bench set off to the left. Take a very steep, slippery decline, then cross the footbridge with a direct view of this magnificent two-tiered waterfall. Go right on the other side of the bridge to return to the parking area.

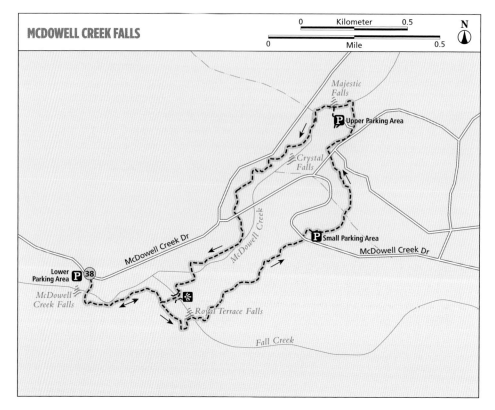

MILES AND DIRECTIONS

0.0 Start at the trailhead at the lower parking area.

0.3 Take two sets of steep stone stairs with no handrail.

0.4 Cross a footbridge over Fall Creek.

0.6 Cross a short footbridge, then go right at the fork.

0.7 Cross McDowell Creek Drive and continue straight.

1.0 Cross the road and continue into the upper parking lot, heading towards the creek.

1.1 Reach the viewing deck for Majestic Falls. Continue to the left, taking several sets of steep wooden stairs and crossing a bridge over McDowell Creek below the waterfall.

1.4 A steep footpath leads down to Crystal Falls.

1.5 Cross McDowell Creek Drive very carefully and continue straight.

1.6 Stay to the left at the next two forks in the trail. The paths on the right are old trails.

1.7 Cross a footbridge over McDowell Creek.

1.8 Cross a bridge at Royal Terrace Falls. Go right to return to the parking area.

2.0 Arrive back at the parking area.

39 DECEPTION CREEK

WHY GO?

This trail is actually named the Deception Butte Trail, but it was destroyed in the 2014 Deception Butte Fire, making the climb to the butte impassable. It is now a creek-side trail, and the first 1.75 miles is well maintained. It travels over rocky hills in a lush forest before descending to a riparian area and ending at a footbridge over the creek with an incredible view and a nice place to sit by the water.

THE RUNDOWN

Spoon rating: 4 spoons. Consistent rolling grades of 10 to 15%, with a maximum 25%, interspersed with some level areas. Rocky and narrow surface with sharp drop-offs. No benches. Generally well shaded.
Type: Out-and-back
Distance: 3.4 miles
Elevation: 1,040 feet
Elevation gain: 525 feet
Max grade: 25%
Max cross-slope: 10%
Typical width: 1½ feet
Typical surface: Natural
Trail users: Hikers
Season/schedule: Year-round
Water availability: Creek

Amenities: None
Dog-friendly: Yes, on leash or under voice command
Cell phone reception: Yes
Nearest town: Oakridge
Land manager: Willamette National Forest, Middle Fork Ranger District, (541) 782-2283
Pass/entry fee: None
Land acknowledgment: Chakgeenkni-Tufti Molalla Band lived in present-day Oakridge and several Santiam Molalla groups lived in the valley and surrounding foothills. Their descendants are members of the Confederated Tribes of Warm Springs.

FINDING THE TRAILHEAD

Getting there: From Oakridge, head west on OR 58W for 4 miles. Just past the ranger station, turn left onto Deception Creek Road. The trailhead is on the right, opposite the maintenance lot. It is a small gravel pullout with room for up to eight cars. Alternatively, you could park at the ranger station and walk down the road. GPS: 43.76039, -122.5346
Start: A small gravel parking area on Deception Creek Road

THE HIKE

Pass behind the wooden barrier and start on the 3-foot-wide path as it leads into a young mixed forest. You immediately come to a fork on the right—this creates a nice little loop through large western redcedars and Douglas firs, reconnecting with the main trail in 0.2 mile. It would be a nice wheelchair-accessible trail with some gravel and grading, but currently there are roots and rocks pinching the trail. I recommend checking it out on the way back.

Continue straight ahead on the level natural surface trail. The trail continues on a level natural surface with lots of rocks in the surface. At 0.2 mile you reach the junction with the small loop—continue to the left. The trail narrows to about 1½ feet as you

The author's dog on the trail along Deception Creek

pass between large western redcedars and bigleaf maples, with lots of trillium and other wildflowers along the path. The trail rolls slightly a couple of times and then takes a 10% decline for about 8 feet. You're following closely along the highway, with some considerable road noise, but you're buffered by large, old western redcedars.

At 0.3 mile cross a boardwalk over a wet area, with a 4-inch step up and 1-inch step down, then take a 15% incline for about 10 feet. The trail continues generally rolling up the hillside, and there are lots of rocks in the surface. Take another 15% incline with some rocks in the surface that work as steps. Continue on general 10 to 15% inclines with some level areas for about 200 feet as you start to round the ridgeline. Decline slightly for about 50 feet, curve slightly left, and then take a slight incline next to a blown-down tree with a root ball on the right. The surface continues rocky and even, and the trail continues to roll on 5% grades.

At 0.4 mile pass between two cut-out blowdowns. Take a 10% incline for about 30 feet, then level out with a rocky cliff rising above you on the left. There's a 10 to 15% cross-slope for 30 feet as you skirt along the hillside above the highway. Come to a 20% incline for about 30 feet, a 10% incline for another 30 feet, and then level out. Continue on a 20% incline for a few feet and then decline at 10% before leveling with a sharp drop-off on the right.

At 0.5 mile the trail curves sharply left and rounds the ridge, now following the course of Deception Creek. Take a 25% incline for 100 feet, decline slightly, and then curve slightly left again and level out on a fairly even natural surface. Continue curving left and right a few times as you move deeper into the forest, passing old cedars and firs, snags and blowdowns. At 0.6 mile there is a rustic bench made with a slab of wood over an old tree. Continue on a generally level trail with a few slight rolling grades. You may start to notice the sound of the creek.

At 0.8 mile the trail starts to get a little more difficult, with steep narrow grades and uneven surface as you rise and fall along the hills above the creek. It inclines slightly at 8 to 10% for about 100 feet, levels out, and skirts closer to the hillside. Take a 10% incline then decline for about 30 feet. Continue on a 15 to 20% incline for 50 feet, passing next to a rock wall and then some large blown-down trees. Take a 10% decline then an incline on a maximum 25% grade for about 50 feet. It could be slightly muddy here if it's been raining. Pass a blowdown, then incline again at 25% for 50 feet. You can see the creek rushing down below on the right, with lots of little waterfalls. The trail generally levels out with a few short inclines under 10%, continuing to skirt narrowly along the hillside with a sharp-drop off on the right. You then come to a muddy section with some rough steps cut in on a 15% incline.

At 1.0 mile you come to a pretty challenging steep grade that has been cut narrowly into the hillside next to a blowdown and a boulder. It rises on a 15% incline, passes narrowly on slick rocks, and then declines at 15%; there is a steep drop-off on the right and a steep hillside on the left, so be careful and watch out for berry vines and possibly poison oak on the hillside. Continue on a 15% decline for 15 feet with a steep cross-slope towards the hillside. Curve left and right around an old stump then decline slightly, continuing narrowly along the hillside with the creek below. Take an 8 to 10% incline, then a slight decline, and pass around some roots that are narrowly pinching the trail. The trail then inclines at 20%; step up on a rock, then curve left on a 10% incline. Pass between large rocks and moss-covered downed trees. Continue on a slightly rocky decline, then the trail rolls on more gentle grades several times. Come to an 8% incline for 50 feet. Deception Creek is still rushing below you. The trail curves right and left on a 10 to 15% incline, then left on a 10% decline. You then level out briefly as you closely hug the hillside. Continue on a generally rolling 10% decline for 150 feet.

At 1.2 miles you finally reach creek level. Cross a small stream on some rocks. You're now in a more riparian habitat with lots of mossy maple and cottonwood. The trail continues generally level and 1½ feet wide. You then come to the first view of the creek from its southern bank. Pass a trail that leads uphill on the left. The trail curves right and left, moving slightly away from and then close to the creek again. Take a slight hill on 5 to 10% grades, then level out and you can start to see damage from the fire up on the hillside on the left. At 1.4 miles you come to another nice view of the creek. You then cross on a level and even rock surface, passing narrowly next to the hill and the creek. The trail then starts a gradual incline of 5 to 10%.

At 1.5 miles you come to a small stream crossing—it's only about 3 feet wide and there are rocks or logs to cross on. The trail continues generally level with some rocks in the surface, traveling under cottonwoods along the creek. At 1.6 miles come to a little

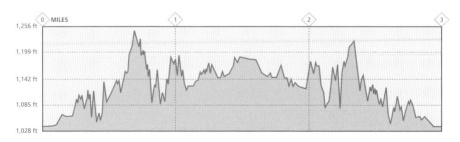

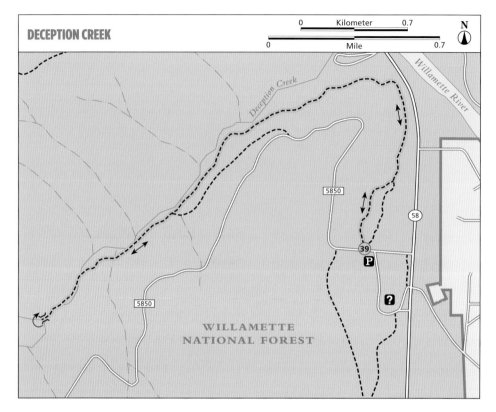

DECEPTION CREEK

0   Kilometer   0.7

0   Mile   0.7

N

Deception Creek

Willamette River

5850

58

39

P

?

WILLAMETTE
NATIONAL FOREST

5850

waterfall on the creek on the right. The trail then gets a little uneven and rocky but generally level with a few slight rolls.

At 1.7 miles you reach the footbridge over the creek. It is level onto the bridge, which has rails on both sides and two steps on the opposite side—the last one is about a foot high. There are beautiful views of the creek as it rushes over rocks. A short, steep footpath on the opposite side leads down to the creek, with some rocks to sit on. Once you've had enough time to enjoy this tranquil spot, turn around and return to the trailhead.

MILES AND DIRECTIONS

0.0   Start at the trailhead at the parking area.

0.05 Continue straight at the fork.

0.2   Go left at the fork.

0.3   Cross a short boardwalk.

0.5   The trail curves sharply left and rounds the ridge, following Deception Creek.

1.0   Traverse a short, steep, narrow grade with a sharp drop-off on the right.

1.2   Reach creek level. Cross a small stream on some rocks.

1.5   Cross a small stream on rocks or logs.

1.7   Reach the footbridge over Deception Creek. Turn around here and return the way you came.

3.4   Arrive back at the trailhead.

40 LARISON CREEK

WHY GO?

Travel along the rolling hills above Larison Cove on the Hills Creek Reservoir of the Willamette River, then follow Larison Creek. Experience dry rocky cliffs and lush old-growth forest. This trail is challenging, with consistent rolling grades, but you get to enjoy a waterfall and a deep pool in the creek at the end.

THE RUNDOWN

Spoon rating: 5 spoons. Consistent rolling grades with a few prolonged grades up to 20%. Narrow rocky trail with steep drop-offs and little shade on the cliffs above the cove, lots of roots and creek crossings in the forest.
Type: Out-and-back
Distance: 6.6 miles
Elevation: 1,550 feet
Elevation gain: 650 feet
Max grade: 20%
Max cross-slope: 10%
Typical width: 1½ feet
Typical surface: Natural
Trail users: Hikers, mountain bikers, horseback riders
Season/schedule: Summer and fall (high water crossing in winter and spring)

Water availability: Creek
Special notes: Poison oak along first half of trail
Amenities: None
Dog-friendly: Yes, recommend on leash
Cell phone reception: No
Nearest town: Oakridge
Land manager: Willamette National Forest, Middle Fork Ranger District, (541) 782-2283
Pass/entry fee: None
Land acknowledgment: Hills Creek Reservoir, which is an artificial lake behind Hills Creek Dam, did not exist prior to 1961. This area of the Middle Fork Willamette River is within ancestral Santiam Molalla territory.

FINDING THE TRAILHEAD

Getting there: From Oakridge, travel east on OR 58 for 2 miles to Kitson Springs County Road. Turn right and continue 0.5 mile to FR 21. Turn right and continue for 3 miles. Turn right into the trailhead at Larison Cove, and park in the lower trailhead parking area, which is a large gravel lot. GPS: 43.6877, -122.44109
Start: At a large gravel parking area

THE HIKE

The trailhead is at the edge of the parking area next to a large Douglas fir. The trail begins 3 feet wide on natural surface, traveling along the hillside above Larison Cove. Continue straight ahead, curve left, and incline at 10 to 15% for 20 feet, then decline on 10% for about 5 feet. The trail then levels out to rolling on slight grades. Pass another footpath on the left with an overlook of the cove. Take a 10% incline for 10 feet, level out, then take another 10 to 15% incline for about 100 feet. The trail then narrows to 2 feet, with some rocks and roots in the surface.

Curve left and cross a small stream; it is less than 2 feet wide and barely a trickle in the dry season, but in the rainy months it may be deeper. Take a very slight incline on the

The waterfall and pool on Larison Creek

other side, then level out with a few slight rolls. Pass a large blowdown on the right with a broken tree propping up another fallen tree—you then come to a washed-out section of trail where the outer edge has fallen away at a blowdown. The trail is about 16 inches wide with a steep drop-off on the left. Pass under some madrone, stepping over roots on a 5 to 8% incline for 150 feet. The trail then rolls slightly to another 10% incline, then step up on some roots and rocks. You then come to another place where the trail has fallen away on the outer edge with a large blowdown; the trail is about 1 foot wide with a 10% cross-slope.

The trail continues at 1½ to 2 feet wide with a slight drop-off on the left and a hill rising on the right. Step over or around some roots rising 4 to 8 inches above the surface of the trail next to a large Douglas fir on the left. The trail surface then becomes rather uneven with a 10 to 15% cross-slope and narrows to 1 foot with many rocks in the surface. Pass between a cut-out blowdown with some large boulders up above on the right. Incline at 5% as you approach another small stream crossing—this one is about 3 feet with some slick rocks to cross on. Incline at 10% for about 50 feet then level out, continuing on a rocky and uneven surface. The trail then declines at 10% for 15 feet, with a root pinching the trail to under 1 foot wide and a drop-off on the left. There is another creek crossing up ahead; this one is rockier and about 4 feet wide, with a sharp drop-off on the left over a gully as the water flows downhill.

At 0.5 mile there is a larger creek crossing at a deep curve in the hills. The creek is about 8 feet wide, but in the dry months the water is only a couple of inches deep. The trail then curves sharply left and starts to travel further uphill from the cove, on a generally steep incline for 0.1 mile. Take a 10% incline for a couple hundred feet as it rises up the hill, then curve right and continue on a slight incline. Several large roots cross the trail rising up to 4 inches. The trail widens to 2 to 3 feet with level shoulders on both sides, so there is finally some space to move off the trail if you need to. The trail then curves left and comes to a steep, muddy dip where a tree has fallen over; there is a short but steep incline on the other side. Continue on a 10% incline for 200 feet. You are still traveling through a forest of young fir, cedar, and swordferns.

At 0.7 mile cross a muddy section where the trail has eroded to about 1 foot wide; take another 10 to 15% incline as the trail curves right and then levels out at the top of the hill. You then start a general decline for the next 0.2 mile as you round the ridgeline and move back downhill. The trail continues at 1 foot wide, skirting along the hillside with no places to move off the trail. Take a 10% decline next to a large western redcedar with lots of roots crossing the trail, then take a 10 to 15% decline for about 20 feet. The trail continues slightly rocky and uneven on rolling 5 to 10% grades up to 20 feet long.

At 0.9 mile the trail curves right then opens up on a rocky and exposed ridgeline above the cove with a steep drop-off on the left. The view across the cove's aqua blue water is beautiful; depending on the water levels you may see layers of exposed stumps rising up the hill, evidence of the changes to the forest to create the reservoir. Continue on a rolling gradual decline with several sharp drop-offs and loose gravel. The trail curves around a rocky outcropping with the cliff rising above you on the right—there are some lovely stonecrops here.

At 1.0 mile the trail generally inclines at 5 to 10% for about 100 feet, continuing on a narrow, rocky, and exposed cliff side. Decline slightly at approximately 8%, then pass between some large Douglas firs for a little shade. You're a little closer to water level now. You then come to a long gradual incline for about 200 feet. Pass a large boulder with more stonecrops on the right, then the grade increases to 20% for a few feet and levels out. At 1.2 miles the trail reenters the forest. Take a couple of slight inclines, then level out and pass between a couple of blowdowns with an 8-inch-tall root in the trail. Continue on a 15% incline for a few feet, then the trail opens up again, following the exposed cliff side until 1.4 miles when it reenters the forest.

At 1.5 miles cross between two fallen trees. The surface is uneven and rocky, with some roots to step over across the trail. Take a generally 10% incline for about 150 feet, then fall and rise on 15% grades for about 50 feet. Continue on an eroded, rocky, and uneven trail with a few rolling grades for another 0.2 mile. At 1.7 miles the trail curves right and left and then crosses a large stream at the head over the cove. An old washed-out footbridge lies at an uneven angle across the water. Even in the dry season there is some water flowing here, and there are some nice spots to sit. The trail continues narrow but generally level to slightly rolling through the forest, with lots of places to step aside.

At 1.8 miles step over a large area of multiple root mats, then continue with several roots crossing the trail rising up to 2 inches. Take a 10 to 15% incline, stepping up on roots of Douglas fir and western redcedar, then down over an 8-inch root. Continue crossing over more roots and rocks as you pass between a large cut-out Douglas fir. Curve left and right a few times, then come to a very narrow section next to a tree with lots of large roots. Take an incline with up to 15% grades for a couple hundred feet. You're traveling through a lovely, mossy, mature forest. The trail then rolls on steep declines for 75 feet on a very eroded surface with lots of roots crossing and a maximum 25% grade for 10 feet. Pass through lots of blowdowns, stepping down and around roots rising up to 6 inches. Curve left next to an old western redcedar.

Rocky cliff above the cove

At 2.1 miles there's a nice overlook of Larison Creek on the left. The trail continues curving narrowly through old-growth forest along the creek with lots of roots, generally level with a few short rolling grades. At 2.2 miles take an incline for about 100 feet with a maximum 10% grade, weaving between large trees. Continue on a general incline for 0.1 mile, increasing to 18% for 50 feet at the end, with one large root to step up on. The trail rolls a few times and then descends slightly for a couple hundred feet, passing narrowly along the hillside with the creek down below and a sharp drop-off on the left. Pass next to a large Douglas fir, stepping over its roots, then take a 10% incline, curve left, and continue on a 20% incline for 10 feet. Pass next to another small fir, then continue on a steep 20% incline and then a 20% decline for about 50 feet. You then come to a 25% decline for 30 feet, stepping down over roots and rocks next to a large Douglas fir. Take a 15% decline for a few feet, then the trail rolls slightly on an uneven surface with lots of roots and rocks. Take a few more 20% declines.

At 2.5 miles the trail generally levels out but remains narrow and very rooted, continuing to pass through lovely forest and lots of large trees. The trail then rolls on 8 to 10% grades, with some level areas, as you continue through the forest for 0.2 mile. Pass several large blowdowns, then take two inclines with 20% grades for about 100 feet. Step up over a couple of roots and continue on a rolling incline with grades up to 15%. At 2.8 miles the trail rises on a 15 to 20% incline for about 100 feet then levels out again. Pass next to a Douglas fir, stepping over its root, then step over a couple more root mats on an uneven surface. The trail gets slightly brushy and continues generally 1 foot wide.

At 3.0 miles come to a rocky decline of 10 to 15% for about 50 feet. Continue level along the creek, stepping over several roots, then take a 10% incline for about 25 feet

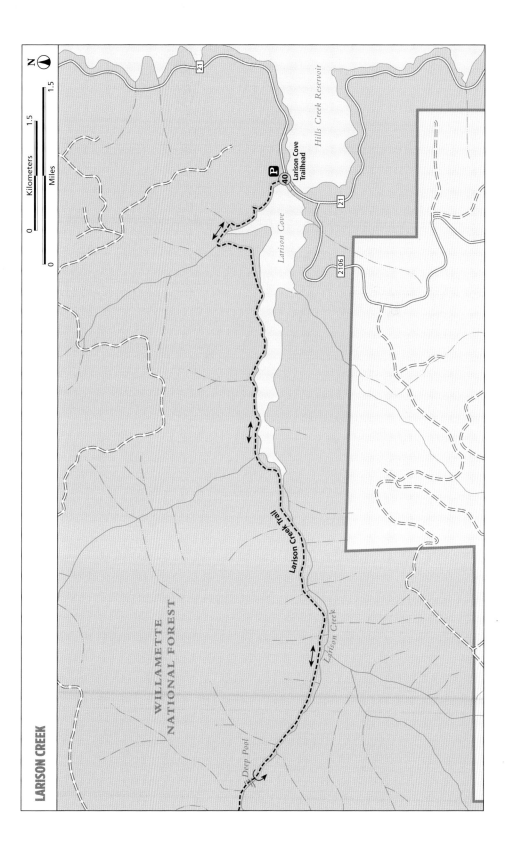

LARISON CREEK

WILLAMETTE
NATIONAL FOREST

Larison Creek Trail

Larison Creek

Deep Pool

Larison Cove

Larison Cove
Trailhead

Hills Creek Reservoir

N

0   Kilometers   1.5
0   Miles   1.5

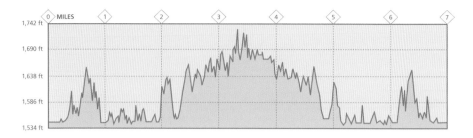

as you approach a large, old blowdown. Cross over some large rocks in the trail over a stream, then take a 25% incline on a very uneven surface with lots of roots and rocks for about 20 feet and then a 15% incline for about 100 feet. Level out again for a few hundred feet before rising on a 10 to 15% incline, then level out to slightly rolling grades and curve left around a blowdown. There are lots of loose rocks here. Take a 10% decline with a 10% cross-slope then level out. The trail gets more brushy, curves right and left a couple of times, then takes a 15% decline. The sound of rushing water gets very loud, then at 3.3 miles there is a footpath on the left. This leads steeply down to a small waterfall and deep pool in the creek. It is very brushy, with up to a 25% decline and several roots, but it's only a few feet long. The scramble is worth it—it is a very special spot, perfect for dipping into on a hot day.

The trail continues for another couple of miles along the creek before rising steeply up the hills, but this makes a good turnaround spot. Enjoy a different view of the creek and cove on the way back.

MILES AND DIRECTIONS

0.0   Start at the trailhead at the end of the parking area. There are two narrow stream crossings in the first 0.25 mile, each 3 to 4 feet wide with slippery rocks.

0.5   Cross the creek at a deep curve in the hill. It is 8 feet wide, but shallow in the summer.

0.9   The trail traverses a rocky and exposed ridge above the cove.

1.2   The trail reenters the forest.

1.7   Cross a wide stream at the head of the cove. The water flows a few inches deep, even in the summer.

2.1   Reach a nice overlook of Larison Creek. The trail continues to generally follow the creek.

3.3   The footpath on the left leads steeply down to the creek, with a small waterfall and deep pool. Turn around here and return the way you came.

6.6   Arrive back at the trailhead.

OREGON SOUTHERN CASCADES

Particularly famed for its waterfalls, the region along the North Umpqua and Little Rivers in the southern portion of the Cascades is full of surprises. The volcanic and seismic history of the mountain range is obvious in the many basalt rocks and folded cliffs. The lush forests and wild rivers have long been perfect habitat for steelhead, chinook, and coho, as well as lamprey and other species of fish. Over 230 bird species, including eagles, owls, ospreys, and peregrine falcons, are found here, as well as over 65 species of mammals and 27 reptiles and amphibians.

Unfortunately, large wildfires have had a growing impact on the region over the past decade. At the time this book was being written, several fires burned in the area, restricting access to many popular hikes for the foreseeable future.

The Umpqua people have resided in the main Umpqua Valley since time immemorial. The Upper Umpqua, who lived along the South Umpqua River, spoke a unique language (Etnemitane). Permanent winter villages stood along the lowland rivers. The Nezic Band had a village at Colliding Rivers, which was called kuri-khanumakwst tseqw. They signed the Treaty with the Umpqua and Kalapuya in 1854, and were forced to move to the Grand Ronde Reservation. Their descendants are members of the Confederated Tribes of Grand Ronde, Confederated Tribes of Siletz Indians, and Cow Creek Band of Umpqua Indians.

41 THE WATERFALL HIGHWAY SCENIC DRIVE

WHY GO?

The Rogue-Umpqua Scenic Byway is a 172-mile loop that follows the North Umpqua and Upper Rogue Wild and Scenic Rivers into the heart of the Southern Cascades. This area is rich in geological and ecological diversity, traveling from rolling oak hills to high mountain peaks, past cascading waterfalls and volcanic rocks. The section presented here makes an easy day trip from Roseburg, traveling along the North Umpqua River to the High Cascades. This area is known as the "waterfall highway" for the more than twenty-five waterfalls in the area. Here are five accessible sites for you to visit.

THE RUNDOWN

Type: Scenic drive
Distance: 140 miles round-trip
Typical width and surface: Two-lane paved highway
Season/schedule: The byway is open year-round, but many sites close in the winter and weather may make travel difficult.
Special notes: This area has seen a sharp increase in large wildfires in recent years, yielding regular road and site closures. Always confirm closures before heading out.
Dog-friendly: Yes, on leash

Cell phone reception: Spotty
Nearest town: Services are available in Roseburg, Glide, Idleyld Park, and Lemolo and Diamond Lakes. Most sites have restrooms.
Land manager: Roseburg Bureau of Land Management District, Umpqua National Forest, (541) 672-6601, TDD (541) 957-3459
Pass/entry fee: Federal recreation pass required at some sites
Land acknowledgment: North Umpqua

FINDING THE TRAILHEAD

Getting there: Starting from Roseburg, head east on OR 138.
Start: NE Diamond Lake Boulevard / OR 138 In Roseburg

THE HIKE

The first 40 miles of the scenic byway follows the North Umpqua Wild and Scenic River. Your first stop is Colliding Rivers Park in Glide. Sixteen miles from Roseburg, turn left onto Glide Loop Road at the ranger station. The park is immediately on your left. This unique geological spot is formed by the collision of the Umpqua and Little Rivers. The upper viewpoint is wheelchair accessible; ten steps lead down to a lower viewpoint. The visitor center has restrooms and is staffed during the summer. Interpretive signs offer a geologic and cultural history of the area.

Continue east on the byway, winding along the river and through some of the devastation of the Archie Creek Fire. At mile 32, turn right into the Susan Creek Day Use Site. This recreation site sits on a grassy area above the river, surrounded by tall cedars and firs. It has a wheelchair-accessible path to a picnic area and overlook of the North Umpqua

THE WATERFALL HIGHWAY SCENIC DRIVE

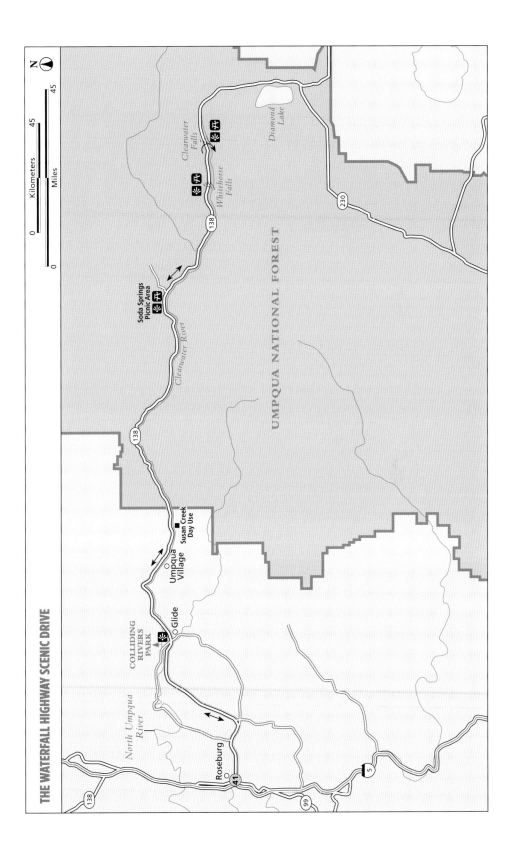

Whitehorse Falls

River. There are flush toilets. Unfortunately, Susan Creek Falls across the street was badly damaged in the fires and remains closed at this time.

The byway now starts winding through the Cascade foothills and into the High Cascades. The volcanic origins of this area become increasingly apparent, as you pass basalt columns, folded rock, and unique mountain peaks. At mile marker 60, turn left onto Medicine Creek Road/FR 4775 at Soda Springs. Take an immediate left onto a gravel road—FR 4775-011. Continue 1.5 miles to the Soda Springs Picnic Area and viewpoint. This road feels very private, traveling closely to the river then coming to the Soda Springs Dam—keep going to a large gravel parking area. There are a few picnic tables and interpretive signs, but the real draw is the incredible basalt column cliffs along the river. The colorful rock columns are part of a High Cascades lava flow that snaked its way down the deeply incised North Umpqua Canyon sometime between 25,000 and 125,000 years ago. A viewpoint above the dam is accessible from the gravel parking area.

Continue another 6 miles on the byway, then turn left into the Whitehorse Falls Campground. The day-use parking area is on the left, just before you enter the campground. You can see and hear the waterfall right from the picnic area, but for the best experience continue past the picnic tables and take the wheelchair-accessible boardwalk ramp on the right, which leads to a large platform at the waterfall. Whitehorse Falls drops 15 feet into a punchbowl surrounded by rocky cliffs on the Clearwater River. The power of the water on even this "small" waterfall is astounding. It is a very peaceful spot.

Another waterfall in a campground awaits 5 miles up the byway. Turn right at the sign for the Clearwater Falls Campground and follow the road into the day-use parking area. A compact pea gravel and firm natural surface trail starts at the restrooms and continues for a couple hundred feet to an overlook of Clearwater Falls. It is wheelchair accessible, but may be a bit rough in spots. This pretty waterfall cascades 30 feet over mossy rocks and logs. Interpretive signs describe the unique ecosystem here, including the variety of mosses.

The Rogue Umpqua Scenic Byway continues another 100 miles, curving south to Diamond Lake—a year-round recreation site—then continuing towards the north entrance of Crater Lake. OR 138 diverges east, and the byway continues on OR 230 and OR 62, winding along the Upper Rogue River to Gold Hill, just south of Grants Pass.

42 WOLF CREEK FALLS

WHY GO?
Cross over the Little River then hike through an old-growth forest along Wolf Creek to a magnificent two-tiered waterfall. Wolf Creek Falls drops 75 feet in the upper falls and 50 feet in the lower fall, tumbling into a pool below. The water flow varies from a powerful fan to a narrow spout, offering a different experience in every season.

THE RUNDOWN

Spoon rating: 3 spoons. The first half of the trail is generally level and even; the second half has short grades up to 20%. A few large roots and rocks, but otherwise few obstacles. No benches.
Type: Out-and-back
Distance: 2.8 miles
Elevation: 1,045 feet
Elevation gain: 272 feet
Max grade: 20%
Max cross-slope: 10%
Typical width: 3 feet
Typical surface: Natural, roots and rocks

Trail users: Hikers
Season/schedule: Year-round
Water availability: Creek
Amenities: Restroom, picnic table
Dog-friendly: Yes, on leash
Cell phone reception: None
Nearest town: Roseburg
Land manager: Bureau of Land Management, Roseburg District, (541) 440-4930
Pass/entry fee: None
Land acknowledgment: Upper Umpqua

FINDING THE TRAILHEAD
Getting there: From Roseburg, travel 16 miles on OR 138 to Little River Road. Turn right and continue 11 miles. There is a trailhead sign with a small paved parking area on the right and a large gravel parking area on the left. There is one accessible parking spot on the right. GPS: 43.23373, -122.95127
Start: At the bridge over the Little River

THE HIKE
Cross a footbridge that curves over the Little River on a 10 to 13% grade. The trail then becomes compact gravel and takes a 5% incline for 30 feet, passing next to a large Douglas fir on the right. It then levels out and transitions to a firm natural surface about 4 feet wide, with vanilla leaf and trillium lining the trail. Take a short decline, then cross

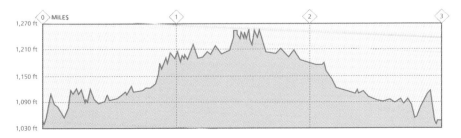

Wolf Creek Falls

a 5-foot-long bridge with no guards. Pass between an old cut-out log, being attentive for a couple of roots that rise 1½ inches above the surface. Continue underneath lots of vine maple, take a slight decline, and then come to a footbridge over Wolf Creek with a steep set of four stairs. The footbridge curves over the creek on a 10% grade, passing by dogwoods along the creek, to steep steps with up to a 1-foot rise leading down on the opposite side. The trail then continues on a natural surface with some rocks, with rolling 5 to 10% grades as it follows the edge of the hill. There are lots of wildflowers and typical Pacific Northwest trees, including Pacific dogwood and Douglas fir.

At 0.3 mile there is a small waterfall in the creek down below. The trails narrows slightly, with a 2-foot-wide level section and a steep cross-slope on the outer edge for a couple hundred feet. Take a 5 to 8% decline for about 20 feet, continuing on the slightly uneven trail with up to a 10% cross-slope. Pass a footpath on the left down to the creek at 0.4 mile. Take a short 10% decline, then you reach creek level. You're traveling on an exposed rock shelf, generally level but uneven. On the left is a large smooth rock on the creek that is perfect for sunbathing or dipping into the water. On the other side, the trail returns to natural surface with lots of roots and rocks. Pass between large western redcedars and Douglas firs, then cross a root mat with roots rising up to 4 inches. At 0.5 mile take four shallow wood steps in the trail. There's a small waterfall on the left as the creek flows through a narrow, mossy and rocky gorge. The trail continues generally level, 2 to 3 feet wide, with some small roots and rocks to step over.

At 0.6 mile there's another short footpath on the left to the creek. The trail widens out on an area that gets muddy in the rainy season. Take a 10 to 15% incline as the trail curves right for 15 feet, then continues on a very gentle incline, passing next to old-growth trees. Curve slightly left and right on a 15% incline. The trail narrows and then crosses over a fairly level rock that is about 10 feet long, with a 1-foot-wide natural

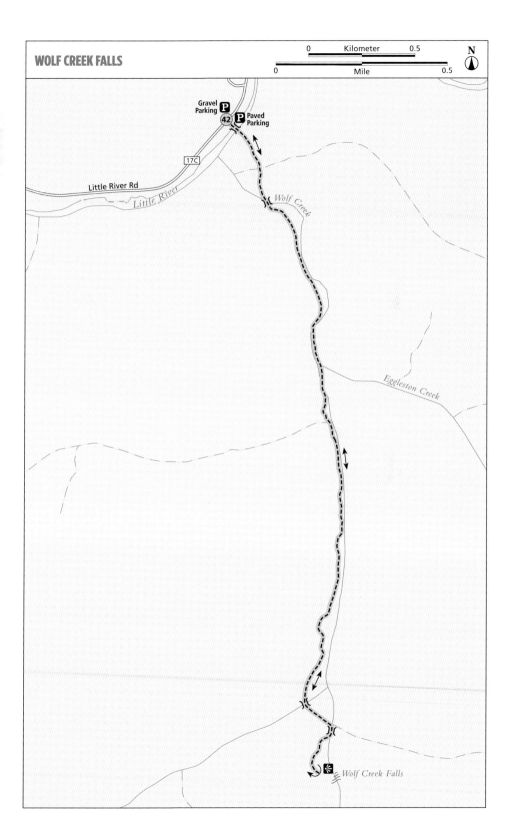

WOLF CREEK FALLS

Gravel
Parking

42

Paved
Parking

17C

Little River Rd

Little River

Wolf Creek

Eggleston Creek

Wolf Creek Falls

0   Kilometer   0.5

0   Mile   0.5

N

surface trail on the left. Cross a footbridge over the creek, then curve left and right on a 10% decline, passing through large western redcedars and Douglas firs. Step up about 6 inches onto a large root. You're surrounded by large boulders on both sides of the trail, with the creek on the left. The trail continues about 4 feet wide, uneven with lots of rocks, some steep cross-slopes, and narrow sections. Come to another section of trail that gets muddy in the winter—there are log rounds to step on or you can cross on the left if it's dry. Continue generally level through gorgeous old-growth mossy forest.

At 0.8 mile come to another small waterfall on the left. Step over one large root, then continue level with a few roots and rocks before crossing over a narrow stream across the trail. The trail then starts to get more difficult, traveling up the hill on occasionally steep grades. Take a 15 to 20% incline for 100 feet. The trail curves left over a culverted stream then continues on a 15% incline for another 100 feet, curving a couple of times. The grade increases to 20% and curves sharply right then continues for another 50 feet. It then decreases to a generally 10% incline, curving between large trees and passing over some roots and rocks.

At 0.9 mile you reach the top of the hill. The trail narrows to 2 feet and continues over lots of rocks and a large root, rolling on 5 to 10% grades. At 1.0 mile there's a board set on a decaying log on the left that you can sit on. The trail continues to travel through a really beautiful mossy, ferny forest. Take a 10 to 15% incline for about 15 feet, then level out to gently rolling trail. Cross an old, uneven footbridge. Take another 10 to 15% incline, then continue on an uneven, rocky natural surface with a sharp drop-off on the left. Come to a 20% decline on a narrow uneven surface, then cross a very wet and muddy section on a slight decline.

At 1.2 miles cross a level 8-foot-long footbridge over a stream. The trail levels out, with several large western redcedars lining the trail for a few hundred feet. You then come to a 15 to 20% incline, stepping up on several large roots for about 50 feet. The trail then curves right and left on a 10% incline, increasing to 15%, stepping up on a few rocky sections. You then get the first glimpse and sound of the waterfall on the left as you take another rocky 5% incline.

At 1.4 miles you reach the waterfall. Take two rocky 5 to 10% inclines as you approach the overlook. The viewpoint is generally level but a little rocky. There are steep stairs leading down to another viewpoint closer to the creek, but getting down to creek level is very rocky, slippery, and steep. The view of the falls from the overlook is definitely worth the hike.

MILES AND DIRECTIONS

0.0   Start at the trailhead at the bridge over the Little River.

0.2   Cross a footbridge over Wolf Creek with four steep stairs.

0.4   Reach creek level with a nice exposed rock shelf for sunbathing or dipping into the water.

0.8   The trail starts to incline.

1.0   Cross an old, uneven footbridge.

1.2   Cross a level 8-foot-long footbridge over a stream.

1.4   Reach the overlook of Wolf Creek Falls. Return the way you came.

2.8   Arrive back at the trailhead.

43 TOKETEE FALLS

WHY GO?

This is a very popular hike, for good reason. Travel through old-growth forests of Douglas fir, western redcedar, bigleaf maple, and Pacific yew to a viewing platform overlooking a tall two-tiered waterfall. The North Umpqua River cascades through a narrow rock gorge, and there are many boulders and interesting rock formations.

THE RUNDOWN

Spoon rating: 4 spoons. The trail is less than 1 mile round-trip, but there are several sets of stairs and narrow, rocky traverses. Barriers protect the steepest drop-offs, and there are two benches at necessary rest stops.
Type: Out-and-back
Distance: 1 mile
Elevation: 2,366 feet
Elevation gain: 105 feet
Max grade: 20%
Max cross-slope: 5%
Typical width: 2 feet
Typical surface: Natural, rocks, stairs
Trail users: Hikers
Season/schedule: Spring through fall
Water availability: None
Special notes: Total of 222 steps in several series of stone and wood stairs with landings and benches along the way
Amenities: Vault toilet, picnic table
Dog-friendly: Allowed on leash, but not recommended due to a narrow trail with steep drop offs
Cell phone reception: Yes
Nearest town: Glide
Land manager: Umpqua National Forest, North Umpqua District, (541) 496-3532
Pass/entry fee: None
Land acknowledgment: *Toketee* means "pretty" in Chinook Wawa, a trade language developed by Indigenous peoples of the Pacific Northwest.

FINDING THE TRAILHEAD

Getting there: Take OR 138 east from Roseburg. At mile 58.6, turn left onto FR 34/Toketee-Rigdon Road. Cross the bridge and immediately turn left. The paved parking area is on the left, with parking for only ten to fifteen cars. It can be very busy on weekends. A large metal pipe that is part of the North Umpqua Hydroelectric Project runs along the parking area—it frequently spouts leaks, so anticipate getting your car, and possibly yourself, wet. The trailhead is at the end of the parking area. GPS: 43.2639, -122.42709
Start: At the end of the parking area, next to a trail information sign

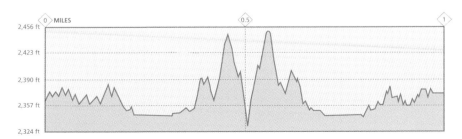

Partial stairs down to the overlook
of Toketee Falls

THE HIKE

The trail starts on level compact gravel and crosses a small footbridge over a stream. A large bigleaf maple shades the trail on the right. Curve left and right, crossing a large root mat with some roots rising 4 inches above the surface. You then cross a very wet and muddy area that has logs laid into it, then several more roots rising up to 6 inches. Cross between two blowdowns and then take a 15% decline for 20 feet. The trail levels out, passing between lots of large redcedars and Douglas firs. Pass next to a large boulder and an old cedar on the right, and notice the North Umpqua River rushing through a canyon on the left. Take a slight incline, stepping over lots of roots rising 3 inches above the surface, then step down on a rock, passing next to several very large boulders. Continue weaving narrowly in between trees and boulders, crossing over more roots and rocks.

At 0.2 mile come to a set of stone stairs. Take ten steps with a 6-inch rise and then reach a level area and another set of eleven steps with a 4-inch rise. The trail then levels out on a rocky and uneven section for about 100 feet. Come to another set of fifteen stone steps leading down, with a landing every five steps. Continue on another level but rocky section above the river, with a chain-link fence protecting the outer edge. Take another four steps down—the last one is about 1 foot tall. You then come to a viewpoint with a chain-link fence on the left overlooking a waterfall as the river tumbles down the gorge. The trail continues up to the right, passing next to lots of large boulders on the left. Step up on rocks on a 10% incline for about 50 feet.

At 0.3 mile the trail curves around a large Douglas fir, then there is a bench next to a large boulder. You then approach the first set of steep wood stairs leading up, with metal handrails on both sides. Take sets of eight, six, eleven, six, four, and four stairs with a landing in between each, then another four stairs and reach the top. There's a short level section and then the trail inclines steeply on a rocky 20% grade for about 75 feet. It then generally levels out for 100 feet and comes to another set of stairs. Take three stone steps, then ten wood steps with a landing, then three more wood steps with a landing to the end.

You're now at approximately 0.4 mile and there's a bench on the right, tucked into large boulders along the cliff. The trail continues level briefly, passing between boulders with several large rocks in the surface. You then come to a set of twelve stone steps leading down, with a rise between 3 and 6 inches. Level out then go up another set of twenty stone steps with a 3-inch rise. Cross another level but uneven and rocky section between large boulders. You then come to another very long set of stairs leading down with metal handrails on both sides. Take sets of four, five, four, five, and four stairs with a landing in between, then twelve stairs and you're at the bottom.

The trail is now about 2 feet wide, with a level and natural surface and a chain-link barrier on the left and boulders on the right. Curve sharply right around boulders, with a gorgeous view across the river canyon. Incline at about 15% for about 50 feet, then pause to take in another really incredible view. Take a few steps down on rocks and then decline at 8%, increasing to 10% and stepping over rocks. The trail narrows and then comes to a very shallow set of stone steps. The trail levels out and continues narrowly along boulders in the hillside then comes to another set of wood stairs leading down to the viewing platform. Take twelve sets of two to six steps with a landing in between, leading down the side of the hill, then ten steep steps and eight steps leading out to the viewing platform.

The platform encircles a large Douglas fir and hangs out over the gorge a bit, with a straight drop down that may be a little vertigo-inducing, but there is a bench to sit on.

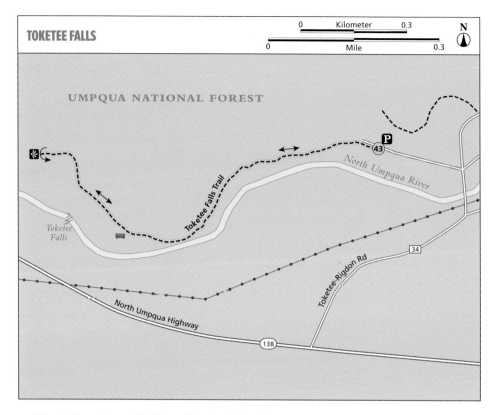

The platform is encircled by a chain-link fence, but sections are sometimes torn down, so be careful with children and pets. The falls seem to magically appear out of a tall basalt cliff, dropping 40 feet into a pool and then plunging 80 feet over the sheer rock. The view is incredible but you are a distance away, so you may want to consider binoculars or a long-range camera lens to get a really close look.

MILES AND DIRECTIONS

0.0 Start at the trailhead at the end of the parking area. Immediately cross a small footbridge.

0.2 Take two sets of stone stairs totaling forty steps.

0.3 Take two sets of wood stairs totaling fifty steps.

0.4 Take three sets of stone and wood stairs totaling fifty-six steps.

0.5 Take a set of wood stairs totaling approximately sixty steps to the viewing deck. Reach the viewing deck, then turn around and return the way you came.

1.0 Arrive back at the trailhead.

SOUTHWEST OREGON

Southwest Oregon is an incredibly unique region. Much drier and sunnier than the northwestern portion of the state, it is home to oak savannas and rare pine forests. It also contains six Wild and Scenic Rivers. The area is surrounded by mountains—the Cascades to the east, the Siskiyou Mountains to the south, and the Coast Range to the west. The Siskiyou Mountains in particular are incredibly unique in their biological diversity, rivaling only the Great Smoky Mountains in the number of species.

The Cow Creek Umpqua lived along the South Umpqua River and Cow Creek, including the entire Umpqua watershed. The Takelma lived along the Illinois and Rogue River valleys, with several villages along the Rogue River. The Tolowa Dee'ni occupied territory along the Upper Rogue River, and had large villages on the Applegate River and at Galice Creek; these bands were imprisoned on the Table Rock Reservation after the signing of the Rogue River Treaty. The Tolowa Dee'ni Nation was established in 1908 at a rancheria in California, and have actively worked towards repurchasing their ancestral homelands. The Cow Creek Umpqua Tribe never received a reservation, but is now one of nine federally recognized Tribes in the state following restoration. Located in Roseburg, they are also buying back their land and developing multiple business enterprises. The Takelma people were forced to the Siletz Reservation, and records indicate that by 1906 fewer than ten Takelma survived.

THE HIKE

Cross the road from the pullout and take a 10% decline for about 15 feet on loose gravel. There is a sign for Rainie Falls, two trash cans, and an information board with details about the hike. You may encounter possible slides, downed trees, and trail-edge erosion in addition to the rocky terrain. There is also an interpretive sign about the journey the salmon and steelhead take to the falls.

Continue past the signs across a section of sharp rocks as the trail curves left and starts descending on a 20% grade for about 30 feet. Step down onto a few sharp, uneven rocks, then the trail levels out and widens to 1½ feet with a steep cliff rising above you on the left and a sharp drop-off on the right. Take about eight steps down on rocks that offer pretty level and stable footing. The trail levels out again and the surface becomes compact gravel, then enters a much more shady area as you curve left and right following the cliff side. You will continue traveling on an approximately 2-foot-wide trail, passing underneath many madrone trees. At 0.3 mile Grave Creek Falls tumbles down the Rogue River below you. You may want to pause here and enjoy this shaded, mossy area before continuing on, as the trail gets increasingly difficult.

After Graves Creek Falls the trail curves slightly left and right and then enters a much more rocky area. You'll step up and over half a dozen rocks that rise 6 to 8 inches above the surface. During spring and summer there are many wildflowers along this section; I noticed fawn lily, false Solomon's seal, and many more. The trail then continues generally level and 2 feet wide on eroded granite and gravel, curves left on a 5% incline for 10 feet, then passes underneath a rocky ledge before curving left again. You'll have to step between several large rocks with about 6 inches of clearance. The trail then continues curving along the hillside. Take a 10% decline for about 20 feet, step down on a rock, and continue curving left around the hillside.

You then come to the first section of trail edge erosion, where the outer edge has fallen away and is now supported by a wood barrier. This section is 6 to 12 inches wide with no rocks on the outer edge, or you can step over roots and rocks closer to the hillside. Whichever way you choose, after this section you will continue on rocks and then incline at 8 to 10% for 50 feet, increasing to 12% for the last 6 feet. The trail then levels out again and declines slightly for a few feet before curving left with really nice views across the mighty Rogue River. From here, the trail becomes consistently rocky for the next 0.75 mile. You'll step over and down some large rocks and then down one large boulder that crosses the entire trail; this boulder is steep and potentially slick on an approximately 15% decline for about 2 feet. Continue on the very rocky trail, passing next to a large madrone and taking several steps up on jagged rocks.

At 0.4 mile you're now traversing a rocky cliff side with a sharp drop-off on the right; the footing is pretty stable in the dry months, but would be slick in the rain. You'll alternate a few level areas with some slightly jagged rock before needing to step down about a foot onto a dirt trail surface with a trail erosion barricade on the right; step back up about 6 inches on rocks and then take a very steep step of about 2 feet onto rocks. Pass narrowly between some rocks, still continuing on a generally rocky cliff side. Thankfully there is minimum scree, but it gets a little sketchy with very narrow footing, lots of jagged rocks, and a steep drop-off on the right that lasts for about 10 feet before the trail briefly levels and widens out. You then come to another 10-foot-long section with some sketchy footing and a foot-high step up.

At 0.5 mile the trail moves away from the cliff edge and you come to a small stream crossing as it flows down a ravine in the hillside. The outer edge of the trail is pretty eroded here so the trail is narrow, but you can cross the stream on small rocks. When I was here at the end of March, the water flow was very low. On the opposite side, step up about 6 inches onto some roots and then take a moment to appreciate the small waterfall fanning down the hillside above you. You then continue traveling narrowly along the hillside. Step up narrowly on a large rocky surface, level out slightly, then take four steps up on rocks to a very narrow section with a footpath around a boulder. Step up a few more times on rocks, traversing a steep slope with a rockslide. There is lots of scree here, but it was pretty easy to step across. The trail then rises approximately 10% for about 30 feet and gets even rockier as you curve around the peak of the exposed cliff. The trail surface becomes slightly looser gravel and rocks. You'll pass a unique rock formation on the right while stepping up gently on some rocks. Continue on a 5% incline for a couple hundred feet.

At 0.7 mile come to a large rock outcropping. Be cautious here—it is very narrow with jagged footing as the trail curves left and right for about 100 feet on a 5% incline. This is another spot to look for wildflowers during the season. Pass another trail erosion barrier and then come to a 15 to 20% incline as you approach another 50-foot-long rock outcropping. This one is a bit tricky to navigate; you can cross to the right on gravel and then step up on rocks and get a narrow foothold on the folded surface. The trail surface returns to generally gravel interspersed with large rocks to step up on before taking a 10 to 15% incline for 75 feet. You're now high above the river, with trees on the hillside above and below you.

At 0.8 mile come to another very narrow rocky crossing at a gully down the cliff side. There are decent toeholds stepping up on the rocks; it's slightly slippery, but fairly easy to navigate. This is a really cool little spot with green mossy rocks all the way down the cliff side and a huge boulder above you. The trail surface then returns to eroded granite and is 2 feet wide and level as it curves a few times. You then come to a rockier section on a decline; step down about six times on a rocky surface, curve left and right, then come to an 8% decline on rocks with slightly unstable footing. You then approach another large rocky outcropping. Step down on a boulder with a 5 to 8% decline. This area has some very narrow and unstable footing, with large angled rocks to step down on. The trail continues on an 8 to 10% decline with more rocks before leveling out again. You hug the cliff side, passing next to a large Douglas fir and taking a few more steps on rocks, then come to another small stream crossing the trail. Step over the wooden barrier and then down about 6 inches on roots with a few more rocks and curve left. The trail changes elevation a few times, first declining on a 10% grade for 20 feet, then rolling to a 10% decline for about 15 feet.

At 1.0 mile the trail continues rolling slightly as it hugs the cliff side. You travel pretty easily beneath some large madrones on a generally level surface. You then arrive at a large rocky outcropping on the right with some trees. This is a nice place to stop and take a break in the shade. Just beyond this area you can start to see a waterfall on the right as the trail inclines at 5% for 50 feet. At 1.2 miles come to another stream crossing—step down about a foot on eroded roots and then cross the stream; there was only an inch or two of water about a foot and a half wide when I was there. The trail then curves left and comes to a 20% incline for about 30 feet, passing narrowly to the left of a Douglas fir. You then have another 1-foot-wide stream crossing where you can step on an eroded log and across small rocks, then step up on a 25% incline about 3 feet long. The trail then levels out again and continues generally even to slightly rolling. You'll notice a large gravel bank on the right then curve to the right next to a large tree before taking an 8% decline.

At 1.3 miles you enter a very nice section of woods as the trail levels out. Pass underneath two very large madrones, stepping up 8 to 12 inches over their roots. Curve left and right a couple of times, take a slight incline, and then come to a large, open, flat area on the right with a nice view of the river. This is a beautiful spot to rest underneath madrones, oaks, and other large trees. Beyond this area, the trail narrows a bit and gets a little rockier for about 10 feet with rocks rising 4 to 6 inches above the surface. Still slightly rocky, it narrows to about 1½ feet in spots and curves sharply left over some large rocks. Your footing will get a little more uneven here, so be careful on the rocks. Pass underneath a large madrone on the left with a big hole in its roots and enjoy the view ahead to the opposite cliff side.

At 1.4 miles the trail leaves the woods and goes back to following the cliff side as you reconnect with views of the river. The next 0.6 mile is very difficult, with some precarious spots along the cliff. First take a very large 2-foot step down on some rock with very narrow footing before curving narrowly around a rocky outcropping as you step on rocks with unstable footing. Continuing to travel on rocks, step up on two practically vertical rocks that are a couple of feet tall.

At 1.5 miles the trail turns into barely a footpath with a wet surface. Step up very narrowly and practically vertically on some rocks that are about 3 feet tall. The trail gets very rocky again as it curves left and right and left, then passes next to the hexagonal remnant of a suspension bridge that was built in 1908 and destroyed in 1927. You are basically scrambling along the rocky cliff side with very narrow and unstable footing, continuing until you come to a small waterfall flowing down the cliff side and step easily across a stream.

From here the trail continues narrow and slightly less rocky, with clear views to the river for a couple hundred feet before mounting another rocky cliff side at 1.6 miles. Curve left, crossing the rocky outcropping, and take a 1-foot step down then come to another steep rocky area. Step up steeply along some narrow rocks to a 10% incline. Navigate a very steep, narrow, rocky section, then step up about 2 feet on more steep rocks and cross a rock slide. This slide is very steep and narrow with a steep-drop off on the right—if you are even slightly afraid of heights or experience any vertigo, I recommend not looking down. The trail continues on eroded granite at an 8 to 10% incline. Traverse another very steep 3-foot-tall rock outcropping before the trail levels out for 50 feet, then cross narrowly on more rocks.

At 1.7 miles the trail continues fairly narrow along the cliff side with more outcroppings. You'll come to another rocky section on a descent, stepping down on lots of jagged rocks, then come to another rocky outcropping at 1.8 miles as the trail curves sharply left, stepping up very steeply 2 to 3 feet on a rocky outcropping. There is a small viewpoint off to the right along the edge of the cliff. You then step up on a very steep, practically vertical boulder before the trail levels out briefly then climbs again on more rocks. The next obstacle is a very large, steep boulder that I had to scoot down. Step down narrowly between a fallen tree and then more rocks, and come to a very steep, almost 45% decline on rocks. Then take a 20% decline on more rocks to another small waterfall on the left. Cross the shallow stream and then step down very steeply on roots and rocks. You are

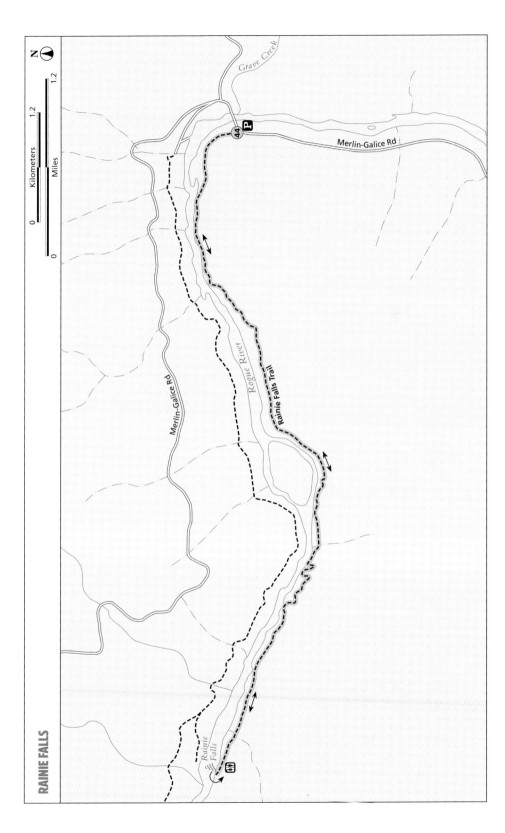

RAINIE FALLS

N

Grave Creek

44 P

Merlin-Galice Rd

Rogue River

Merlin-Galice Rd

Rainie Falls Trail

Rainie
Falls

Kilometers
0   1.2

Miles
0   1.2

now at river level. The trail surface continues to be slightly wet, very narrow and rocky, and bordered by brush.

At 1.9 miles the surface becomes covered in more scree as you step up on large boulders. The trail is basically a rock scramble for the next 0.2 mile—you're really stepping over and around and up and down rocks and boulders the entire time. But you can start to see and hear the falls up ahead in the river, telling you your destination is close. At 2.0 miles come to a rocky 15% incline as you pass narrowly next to a tree, continuing to climb up and down the rocky terrain. The trail levels out slightly then arrives at a small, fairly dry stream crossing with a 2-foot-high step down and 1-foot-high step up. Continue generally level after the stream for a couple hundred feet, then come to a pretty mossy area that slopes gently down to the river; step up over two rock outcroppings. The path is very narrow on a steep 20% decline between rocks, but the sound of the falls is growing continuously louder. Stay to the left where it looks like the trail forks along the riverbank, and continue level until a slight rise and the sound of flowing water. You've arrived at a beautiful waterfall and a large stream. The stream crossing was approximately 15 feet wide but fairly shallow when I was there, except for the very far end where it was rather narrow and 3 inches deep. It is a very narrow and steep step up onto the opposite side. The trail continues generally level as you travel nearer to the waterfall. Do you start to notice a different quality to the air here?

You then arrive just above the rushing Rogue River. There is a toilet 100 feet up a very steep and slick hill to your left. To get down to the falls, take a steep, nearly vertical decline for about 30 feet to river level. There are plenty of places to get down by the river or sit and relax on the rocks. I enjoyed sitting here for a while and watching the falls as the river rushes through the gorge. You'll definitely want to rest up for the trip back.

MILES AND DIRECTIONS

0.0   Start at the trailhead across the road from the parking area.

0.3   Pass above Grave Creek Falls.

0.4   The trail begins traversing a rocky cliff side.

0.5   Cross a narrow stream.

0.7   Cross a large, narrow, and uneven rock outcropping. The trail continues over rocky terrain.

1.2   Cross a narrow stream.

1.3   Enter a nice area in the forest with places to rest.

1.4   The trail becomes very rocky and narrow.

2.1   Cross a wide stream with a waterfall.

2.2   Reach the Rogue River. Take a steep decline to river level and Rainie Falls. Return the way you came.

4.4   Arrive back at the trailhead.

45 LIMPY CREEK BOTANICAL AREA

WHY GO?

The Limpy Creek Botanical Area supports some of the greatest bio-diversity in the Pacific Northwest, including many plants that are found nowhere else in the world. A multitude of habitats are found here. On this 1-mile loop, you'll experience serpentine areas, riparian zones, mixed forest, and rock outcropping communities, plus bonus waterfalls. Please be respectful visitors to this unique place—do not collect anything, and remain on trail as much as possible.

THE RUNDOWN

Spoon rating: 2 spoons. Not wheelchair accessible. Prolonged 2 to 5% grades, with maximum 10%. A few footbridges. Surface has rocks and roots and potentially slick areas. Several benches. Partially shaded.
Type: Loop
Distance: 1 mile
Elevation: 1,280 feet
Elevation gain: 148 feet
Max grade: 10%
Max cross-slope: 5%
Typical width: 2 feet
Typical surface: Natural
Trail users: Hikers
Season/schedule: Year-round
Water availability: None

Amenities: Vault toilet, picnic table, benches
Dog-friendly: Yes, on leash
Cell phone reception: Spotty
Nearest town: Grants Pass
Land manager: Rogue-Siskiyou National Forest, Wild Rivers Ranger District, (541) 592-4011
Pass/entry fee: Federal recreation pass
Land acknowledgment: Long before white botanists discovered the unique species of this area, the Takelma, Cow Creek Umpqua, and other Indigenous peoples cared for the land and gathered food here.

FINDING THE TRAILHEAD

Getting there: From Grants Pass, head south on US 199. In 7 miles, turn right onto OR 260E/Riverbanks Road. Continue 4.5 miles, then make a left onto Limpy Creek Road/FR 2800. Continue 2.5 miles on the paved forest road. The last half mile is a wide single-lane paved road. Parking at the trailhead is very limited; the main gravel lot has space for three cars, with room for a few more along the road. GPS: 42.42744, -123.54417
Start: At the edge of a small gravel parking lot, next to a trail information sign

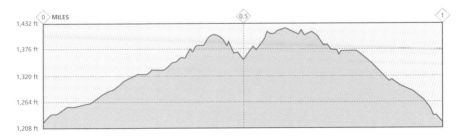

Limpy Creek

THE HIKE

The trail begins to the right of the restrooms. There is a picnic table on the right next to three large interpretive signs. The signs are all faded or damaged so may be difficult to read; they describe the various habitats found in the botanical preserve. Just past the interpretive signs, the trail forks to form the loop—go right.

The trail starts on a gentle 5% grade, 3 feet wide on compact gravel, passing through a dry mixed forest of Oregon myrtle, Pacific madrone, pine, and cedar. Step over two log barriers rising about 8 inches above the trail and then come to a very rutted area with lots of roots rising 2 to 4 inches across the trail. You then take an 8% incline, stepping up on roots and rocks. The trail levels out and passes between three incense cedars. Step over some rocks and come to an interpretive sign for the mixed forest community. Take a 10% decline for 10 feet, then level out as you approach Limpy Creek, entering a more riparian area with large mossy trees. The trail curves left on a slight incline, following the creek on the right. Pass between two trees, stepping up over large roots, then pass through a slightly wet area with a narrow, shallow stream. The trail then curves right around a Douglas fir with a root rising 8 inches above the surface. It then gets very rocky and uneven for a few feet. Step down between more Douglas firs, with roots and rocks in the trail.

At 0.18 mile a footbridge leads over the creek to a short spur trail along the opposite side of the creek that takes you to a small waterfall. The spur is very narrow, uneven, and brushy, but there is a bench just across the bridge to sit and enjoy the creek for a while. Continue to the left on the main trail, rising up a slight hill on 2 to 5% grades for 100 feet. The surface is very narrow and eroded, with several steps onto roots and rocks—the last one is almost 2 feet tall. You are following the beautiful creek with several small waterfalls.

At 0.2 mile you reach a trail intersection at a switchback. A half-mile loop goes to the left—it continues uphill on 5 to 10% grades for 0.1 mile before reconnecting to the main loop and returning to the parking area. To continue on the main loop, go right across a level 10-foot-long footbridge. The trail curves sharply left, following the creek. Take an 8 to 10% decline for 50 feet, then continue on natural surface, 3 feet wide, rolling slightly as you follow the rushing creek.

At 0.3 mile the trail switchbacks left on a 15 to 20% incline. A small footpath on the right leads to a nice spot on the creek. The switchback continues on a 10 to 15% grade for 40 feet, then continues at 5 to 8% for a couple hundred feet until it levels out at the top of the hill with the creek now on your left. There is a bench overlooking the hillside with an interpretive sign about Pacific dogwood. Continue on a generally 5% incline as the trail continues rising through lovely mixed forest. The surface is pretty eroded in places, with roots crossing the trail. The grade increases to 10% as you pass above a water-fall in the creek, levels out briefly, then comes to another 10% incline, passing narrowly along the hillside on some slippery rocks for about 100 feet. The incline then decreases to generally 5% as the trail curves left and right.

At 0.4 mile come to another footbridge over Limpy Creek. The water rushes and bubbles along mossy rocks through a shallow gully. Take three steps up, then transfer level back onto natural surface on the other side, where a bench sits overlooking the creek and a small waterfall. The trail curves left, continuing to pass through the forest. Take a short incline next to a Douglas fir. The trail levels out briefly then starts a gradual 5% decline for 200 feet as you approach a large blowdown on the right and another foot-bridge over the creek. The surface becomes very wet with lots of roots as you arrive at the footbridge; the right side is a little more even and dry. The footbridge is level, with four steps down and a 6- to 10-inch rise on the other side. Cross over an exposed culvert and then step down on some rocks.

At 0.5 mile you reach a 20-foot-tall cascade waterfall. There is a bench and a couple of small paths leading towards the waterfall, but getting close to it requires scrambling down wet rocks. You then take a 10% incline, stepping up on some rocks as the trail curves right. Pass a large boulder covered in plants and an interpretive sign about rock outcropping communities. The trail continues generally level as it curves left and right a few times and passes between incense cedar, pine, and madrone. Curve sharply right on a 10% incline, stepping up over several roots and rocks. Level out briefly, then continue on an 8 to 10% incline for 200 feet.

At 0.6 mile you enter the edge of the forest and pass through an open grassy area, traveling between wood posts. The trail is 2 feet wide and natural surface and slightly muddy, with evidence of people traveling outside the edge of the trail—please remain between the wood posts. Step up over a rock and then come to a 100-foot-long board-walk with a 6-inch step down; continue on a slightly wet and rocky natural surface. The trail then declines slightly over a wet area with exposed roots, and then curves right next to a sign about the wet serpentine community. As you may have noticed, this area holds water longer into the summer, providing an important source of water through the dry months. The boardwalks have been constructed over these wet serpentine areas to protect the natural flow of water. You then come to another wet section of trail and then another level boardwalk. Continue on a 5 to 8% incline for 20 feet, then level out and reenter the forest.

At 0.7 mile a bench sits in a really beautiful wooded area. The trail continues on a 5% decline, passing through incense cedar and madrone. Take a 10-inch step down on some roots onto a wet section of trail. The trail surface transitions to compact gravel, continuing on a gradual decline. The trail then curves sharply left and a short path on the right leads to a bench with a beautiful view across the rocky, grassy hillside to the Siskiyou Mountains. The trail curves left again then switchbacks downhill on a 5% decline for 100 feet, continuing along the open hillside. Curve right then step down over a log and then onto another boardwalk with a 6-inch step down on the other side. The trail curves left again and you step down over another log, continuing on an 8% decline on gravel surface. Step down on another log, then cross a 6-foot-long boardwalk with a 6-inch step down. The trail curves left, continuing down the hillside on a slight grade. Pass a sign about the dry serpentine community (sometimes called a Jeffrey pine savanna)—the soil contains concentrations of elements that are considered toxic to many other plant species, making it unique. Continue on a very uneven 10% decline; there may be water flowing down the center of the trail and it is very slick if so.

At 0.9 mile the trail levels out and connects with the shorter loop. Take a short 10% decline of about 5 feet and turn right. Continue down the open hillside with incredible views, on a 8 to 10% decline for 200 feet. Come to a sturdy 8-foot-long footbridge across a small stream with a 6-inch step down. Continue on a very gradual decline on compact gravel with some rocks, but the surface is drier with sturdier footing. Cross over a 3-inch-wide gully and then continue to follow the gravel path straight ahead, taking a 10 to 15% decline for about 10 feet. Cross another footbridge with an 8-inch step down, and continue straight back to the parking area.

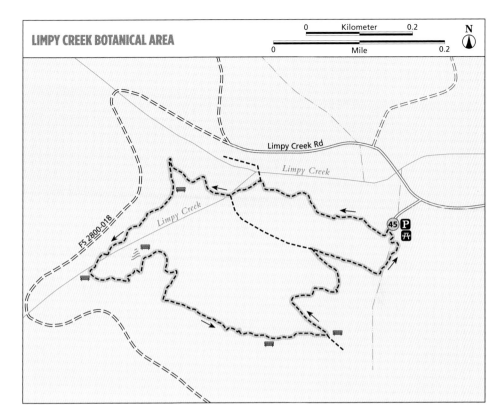

MILES AND DIRECTIONS

0.0 Start at the trailhead next to the restrooms and interpretive signs. Go right at the fork to begin the loop.

0.18 A spur trail on the right leads over the creek to a small waterfall.

0.2 Junction with the cutoff trail for the short loop. Continue to the right and cross a footbridge.

0.4 Cross a footbridge over Limpy Creek.

0.5 Pass a 20-foot-tall cascade waterfall on the left.

0.6 Enter an open wet and grassy area. Continue on a couple of boardwalks.

0.9 Junction with the end of the cutoff trail for the short loop. Turn right to return to the trailhead.

1.0 Arrive back at the trailhead.

46 EAST APPLEGATE RIDGE TRAIL

WHY GO?

Hike along a ridgeline with all of the incredible views and none of the elevation gain. This section of the East Applegate Ridge Trail (EART) averages only a 3% grade and passes through mixed forest, oak savanna, wildflower-covered hills, and open slopes with views of the Applegate Valley and Siskiyou Mountains. The entire trail is stunning, so you can decide how far you want to go. This is one of my favorite trails in this book.

THE RUNDOWN

Spoon rating: 3 spoons. Generally gentle grades. Narrow, exposed trail with some steep drop-offs and few places to sit or move off trail.
Type: Out-and-back
Distance: 5.4 miles
Elevation: 3,024 feet
Elevation gain: 440 feet
Max grade: 20%
Max cross-slope: 10%
Typical width: 1½ feet
Typical surface: Natural
Trail users: Hikers, mountain bikers
Season/schedule: Spring through fall

Water availability: None
Amenities: Picnic table at the trailhead
Dog-friendly: Allowed on leash, but not recommended due to narrow trail and mixed use
Cell phone reception: None
Nearest town: Jacksonville
Land manager: Bureau of Land Management, Medford District, (541) 618-2256
Pass/entry fee: None
Land acknowledgment: Takelma

FINDING THE TRAILHEAD

Getting there: From Jacksonville, head west on Applegate Street, which turns into Cady Road, for 1.9 miles. Turn left onto Sterling Creek Road and continue 4.1 miles. Turn right onto BLM Road 38-2-29.1. This road is hidden and very easy to miss—look for what appears to be a gravel driveway that veers to the right, with a marker set back off of the road. There may be colored marker flags tied onto the trees and a rough sign. Continue for 0.6 mile on the rough gravel road, inclining up the hill. It is generally passable for any passenger vehicle, but watch out for potholes. Park in the large gravel lot with no designated parking spots. The trailhead is on the west side as you drive in. GPS: 42.24511, -122.97811

Start: West side of the parking area as you drive in, next to an information sign and picnic table

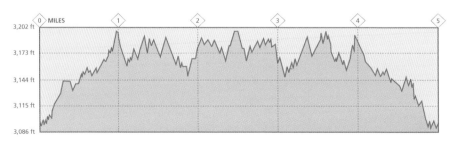

Winding along the hillside

THE HIKE

The stunning views begin at the start of the trail. Pass between two boulders at the trailhead, then stop at the trail information sign, which has a map and elevation profile. Continue on a generally 3% incline as you travel through small madrone, pine, and oak woods on a 2-foot-wide dirt trail. The mountains provide peekaboo views through the trees. Pass next to a very large pine on the left, and enter an oak savanna at the transition between forest and open slopes. Take a 5% incline, being careful around some holes along the edge of the trail. Pay attention for oak woodpeckers, which make all of the tiny holes you may notice on the oak trees.

Move out of the oak savanna, cross an open slope with the first real view at 0.1 mile, then move into an area of large madrones, taking an 8% incline for 100 feet. The trail levels out and continues to follow the hillside. Curve to the right and then continue on a 5% incline for a few feet. It levels out again for 100 feet and then rises on a 10% incline for about 30 feet before leveling out next to some large Douglas firs. Step over a root rising 3 inches above the surface.

At 0.4 mile the trail widens to 4 feet and briefly reenters madrone and oak woods. Curve left at a sign pointing left, then pass between some old fallen logs and incline at 5% for 30 feet. At 0.5 mile the trail curves left and leaves the woods, moving out onto the open slopes. You now have unobstructed views of the mountains. The trail curves right along the ridgeline, passing underneath a few oaks—be careful of some holes in the trail. Take a 15% incline for 8 feet, then the trail generally levels out again but narrows to 1½ feet and continues a bit uneven and bumpy.

At 0.7 mile you get a long view of the trail ahead as it follows the ridgeline then curves around a hill. The trail curves left at another left-pointing arrow. It then widens to 2 feet and gets a little rocky. Take a 5% incline for a few feet, skirting the tree line on your right with the open hillside on your left. Come to a 10% incline for about 50 feet as the trail starts to curve right around the ridgeline. The trail then continues generally level for the next 0.1 mile, with some rough, uneven surface.

At 0.9 mile curve left around another hill with stunning views all around you, and continue on a general 8% incline. The trail narrows to 1½ feet with a sharp drop-off on the left. Pass very narrowly around large boulders, curving towards the right. The next 0.5 mile generally follows the hillside on a narrow trail with a drop-off on the left, which varies from a rolling hillside with a narrow shoulder to a steep drop-off with rocks below. But you have stunning views across the valley to the surrounding mountains and snowcapped peaks.

At 1.0 mile you start curving left below the ridgeline, taking a few short 10 to 15% grades. Pass next to large rocks protruding out of the hill, with lots of shallow rocks in the surface of the trail. They provide a nice leaning-place if you need to rest. Pass a large solitary pine on the left, continuing on a 5 to 8% incline, then curve right around the hillside. At 1.1 miles you now have a view looking down the valley, across some open farmland surrounded by mountains. The trail continues low along the hill ahead of you. Begin a generally 5 to 10% decline for the next 0.1 mile, with a couple of short 20% grades, before leveling out along a gentle hillside dotted with oaks.

At approximately 1.4 miles curve right around a hillside again and enter a Douglas fir forest along a north-facing slope. Continue generally level but rocky through the forest, being careful of several roots and possible holes and short eroded sections on the outer edge. At 1.5 miles pass an old trail on the right. Take a 20-foot-long hill with a 10 to 15% incline and decline.

At 1.6 miles the trail rolls a few times on grades up to 10%. A dry streambed crosses the trail. Take a 15% decline for about 15 feet as you start to leave the Douglas fir forest. The trail rolls a few more times on short grades up to 8%. Take a 5% incline as you move into an oak savanna. Take another 8% incline for about 20 feet, then level out at a slightly wet area. Take another slight incline on an uneven trail surface pockmarked with shallow depressions from horseback riding in wet conditions. You then pass into a madrone woods with some pine and fir. The trail narrows briefly, with some roots and rocks pinching the edges.

At 1.7 miles come to a short, steep roll at a 15% grade, stepping over a root next to an old stump. The trail then levels out and becomes more uneven with rocks, roots, and divots, continuing about 1½ feet wide. Reenter an area of fir forest, with filtered views across the mountains. Come to a 15% incline for 5 feet, then a 5% incline for 5 feet. The trail levels out again.

At 2.0 miles move into an old madrone woods, with very large trees. There are more roots and rocks in the trail here, but it continues generally level. As you pass next to lots of manzanita on the left, the trail becomes very uneven and bumpy. Take a 5% decline for a few feet as you move back into an oak savanna. Pass next to a large boulder on the left and continue on a slight incline. Curve to the right and take a 15% incline as you round the hill at 2.1 miles, passing another old trail on the right. The trail then levels out, with some rocks in the surface. There are astounding views out to the mountains again. The trail continues on a generally 5% incline for a couple hundred feet, rolling through open savanna.

At 2.2 miles the trail widens with a shoulder on both sides. You can see snowcapped peaks in the distance. The trail surface becomes heavily pockmarked and broken with some rocks in the trail as it curves sharply right around the hill. Continue through oak savanna on a slightly rough trail. At 2.3 miles you reach a bench up on the hillside

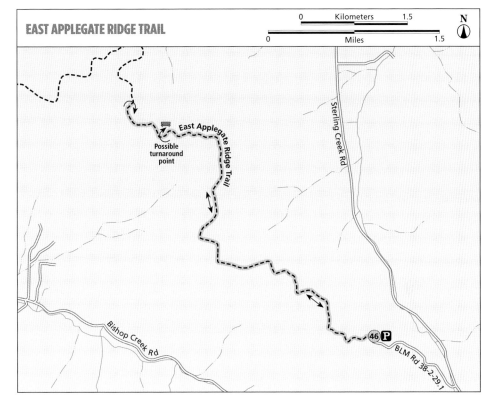

offering an incredible view of the valley and Siskiyou Mountains. This makes a good place to turn around, but you can continue another 0.3 mile through open oak savanna and past some really cool boulders, with more incredible views. The trail then reenters the forest and begins a steep decline for 2.5 miles to the other trail terminus.

MILES AND DIRECTIONS

0.0   Start at the trailhead on the west side of the parking area.

0.1   The trail moves out of the woods and opens up for the first mountain views.

0.4   Reenter the woods and curve left at a sign pointing left, past an old trail.

0.5   The trail leaves the woods and continues on an open slope with expansive views.

0.7   Curve left at another left-pointing arrow.

1.4   Enter a Douglas fir forest.

1.5   Continue straight past an old trail.

2.0   Enter a mature madrone woods.

2.1   Continue straight past an old trail on the right.

2.3   Reach a bench on the hillside in an oak savanna. This is a possible turnaround spot.

2.7   The trail reenters the forest and begins a very steep decline to the other terminus. Turn around here.

5.4   Arrive back at the trailhead.

ADDITIONAL RESOURCES

Find more trail guides, resources, and information about group hikes at
https://disabledhikers.com/.

National Park and Federal Recreational Lands Access Passes can be obtained at
https://www.nps.gov/subjects/accessibility/access-pass.htm.

Washington State Park discount passes for disabled veterans, people with disabilities, and limited income seniors can be obtained at https://parks.state.wa.us/205/
Discount-Passes.

Information on Washington State Park pass exemptions for people with a disability
placard can be found at https://discoverpass.wa.gov/131/Exemptions.

A simplified fact sheet about wheelchair and OPDMD use is provided by the Department of Justice at https://www.ada.gov/opdmd.htm.

National Park Service rules for wheelchairs and OPDMD can be found at
https://www.nps.gov/subjects/accessibility/mobility-devices.htm.
Similar rules apply at National Forests.